OYE LOCA

OYE LOCA

From the Mariel Boatlift
to Gay Cuban Miami

SUSANA PEÑA

University of Minnesota Press
Minneapolis
London

The University of Minnesota Press gratefully acknowledges financial assistance for the publication of this book from Bowling Green State University's Building Strength Program.

A different version of chapter 2 was originally published as "'Obvious Gays' and the State Gaze: Cuban Gay Visibility and U.S. Immigration Policy during the 1980 Mariel Boatlift," *Journal of the History of Sexuality* 16, no. 3 (2007): 482–514; copyright by the University of Texas Press; all rights reserved. A different version of chapter 4 was originally published as "*Pájaration* and Transculturation: Language and Meaning in Miami's Cuban American Gay Worlds," in *Speaking in Queer Tongues: Globalization and Gay Language,* ed. William L. Leap and Tom Boellstorff (Champaign: University of Illinois Press, 2004), 231–50; copyright by the Board of Trustees of the University of Illinois; reprinted with permission of the University of Illinois Press.

Published by the University of Minnesota Press
111 Third Avenue South, Suite 290
Minneapolis, MN 55401-2520
http://www.upress.umn.edu

Library of Congress Cataloging-in-Publication Data

Peña, Susana.
    Oye loca : from the Mariel boatlift to gay Cuban Miami / Susana Peña.
    Includes bibliographical references and index.
    ISBN 978-0-8166-6553-2 (hc : alk. paper) — ISBN 978-0-8166-6554-9 (pb : alk. paper)
    1. Gay men—Florida—Miami. 2. Gay men—Cuba. 3. Cuban Americans—
Cultural assimilation. 4. Immigrants—Florida—Miami. 5. Gay culture—
Florida—Miami. I. Title.
    HQ76.2.U52M5257 2013
    306.76'609759381—dc23

                                                                      2013014539

Printed in the United States of America on acid-free paper

The University of Minnesota is an equal-opportunity educator and employer.

20 19 18 17 16 15 14   10 9 8 7 6 5 4 3 2

Para Mami

CONTENTS

INTRODUCTION

THE 1980 MARIEL BOATLIFT was a turning point in Miami's Cuban American and gay histories. During just a few months, approximately 125,000 Cubans entered the United States in a massive and highly publicized migration that garnered national and international media attention. Among them were many homosexual men and women who migrated partly as a response to a particularly repressive era in Cuba in relation to homosexuality.

During a period of tense U.S.–Cuban relations and at the beginning of a U.S. presidential election year, a Cuban bus driver drove his bus full of passengers into the Peruvian embassy in Havana. As the driver and passengers sought and waited for asylum, Cubans around the island became increasingly restless. Many were hoping for an opening to leave the island—after years of very limited emigration options. Others, still supportive of the regime, sought to publicly express their disdain for those wanting to leave. This started a series of events that culminated with Cuban leader Fidel Castro announcing that all Cubans wishing to leave the island would be allowed to depart—but only through the port of Mariel. He invited Cuban Americans to come to Mariel with boats to pick up any relatives wanting to leave Cuba. When Cuban Americans arrived in the port of Mariel, they found that they were expected not only to transport the relatives they came for but also to take other Cubans who wanted to leave the island and had been given permission by the Cuban government. The day after Castro's invitation, the first 55 Cubans disembarked in Key West via what would eventually become a massive flotilla. The images of boats of all sizes, in various conditions, filled with Cubans of all colors and ages became media fodder. By October, 124,776 Cubans had arrived in the United States as part of Mariel.

The Mariel boatlift was an immigration crisis and a public relations nightmare for both the United States and Cuba. As images of thousands of Cubans wanting to leave Cuba circulated in the international media, Castro began a disparagement campaign in which he labeled the migrants *escoria* (scum), lumpen proletariat, *antisociales,* prostitutes, and homosexuals.[1] Castro argued that those who wanted to leave Cuba were simply the dregs of society who did not want to work. For U.S. president Jimmy Carter, this apparently uncontrollable migration of undesirables (during an election year) was far from ideal. To make matters worse, the Cuban government's insults were echoed among Miami's existing Cuban American population as they began noticing that the Mariel migrants were more likely to be black, poor, and less educated than previous Cuban immigrants.[2]

Cubans who had immigrated to the United States since the 1960s had been depicted in fairly positive terms. According to dominant representations, they were well-educated, hardworking families and victims of communism who had become successes. Media images of white, upper- and middle-class families leaving Cuba in orderly air flights while wearing business suits and fashionable attire during the 1960s and 1970s contrasted vividly with the images of Mariel migrants overcrowded on ships, entering the United States on an apparently unstoppable flotilla. As a highly stigmatized and disparaged migration, Mariel challenged the image of Cuban American success in the U.S. national imaginary. The threat posed by "Marielitos" was likely evident first to Cuban Americans already living in Miami.[3] After the euphoria of being reunited with relatives had passed, many Cuban Americans began noting the differences between themselves and these new migrants who, according to them, looked different, spoke Spanish differently, and suffered from having been raised under the values of a communist government. As consensus grew about the undesirability of this migrant generation, flamboyant gender-transgressive male homosexuals, or *locas,* were identified as one of the group's undesirable elements.

I was a young girl when the Mariel boatlift happened. Just as this dramatic series of events transformed broader Miami and its Cuban American community, my own neighborhood, the southern part of Miami Beach, was equally transformed. Before Mariel, the neighbor-

hood was known as a retirement community for mostly Jewish elderly
residents who lived in low-rent and increasingly dilapidated apartment
units. Although Latino families like mine were becoming a more common part of the neighborhood, Miami Beach was far from a Cuban
enclave.[4] After 1980 the Cuban population of Miami Beach expanded
as many Mariel migrants moved to the area, attracted to the lower-
priced rental apartments. During this time, the area was also known
for a surge in crime rate, and it was largely considered a dangerous and
unsavory place to live.

Among the Mariel migrants who settled in this neighborhood were
many gender-transgressive Cubans—many of whom understood themselves to be homosexual men—who had developed a distinctly effeminate and flamboyant style and who had come to the United States
searching for the freedom to be the way they wanted to be, a freedom
that continued to elude them. These visibly identifiable gay men became part of my surrounding world. They were my neighbors, students at the adult education program that shared a building with my
elementary school, and fellow shoppers, pedestrians, and community
members. With a distinct style that was both undeniably Cuban and
unabashedly gay, this generation of Mariel gay men provided my first
glimpse at gay *cubanidad*. The *locas* of this generation, or the most
gender transgressive of the gay men, quickly transformed the neighborhood's street culture. Shortly after Mariel, it was not uncommon to see
men wearing women's clothes during the day, something I had never
before seen. I remember how "obviously gay" men became a regular
fixture at department stores, both as clients and as employees, their
mannerisms and talk marking them as other even if they did not wear
women's attire. My grandmother, who worked at a women's clothing
store, would regularly report that yet another man had insisted on trying on a dress in the fitting room.

I use the term *loca* in the title and throughout the book to emphasize
the role gender transgression played as mode of expression for Cuban
and Cuban American gay men. *Loca* is a feminine-gendered noun and
vernacular expression that literally translates to "crazy woman" and
is used to denote an effeminate homosexual man. In his discussion
of Dominican immigrant gay men's use of the term, Carlos Ulises
Decena clarifies that performances of *la loca* do not reflect "the *desire
to be a woman* . . . but rather [the desire to be in] a male body that
stages femininity through the deployment of stereotypes associated

with women. . . . la loca operates as the symbolic other through which informants detour to inaugurate and sustain themselves."[5] In other words, many homosexual men in the Spanish-speaking Caribbean understood gender transgression as a socially recognizable way to mark themselves as homosexual.[6] In the Cuban context, Carlos Paz Pérez defines *loca* as a "homosexual masculino muy amanerado que ostenta su condición" (a very affected male homosexual who flaunts his condition).[7] Throughout this book, I highlight precisely how ostentation, flaunting, and visibility were perceived as threats to the state. As Pérez also explains, the term can be offensive to masculine gay men because it describes the stereotype of an effeminate man.[8] While I recognize that many Cuban American gay men do not identify as *locas,* I still center the term in order to recognize how the gender-transgressive practices and their shameless deployment by some Cuban American gay men were a central component of homosexual expression. While *loca* can be used pejoratively, I hope to invoke (starting with the title of this book) the way the term is sometimes used within Cuban and Cuban American gay circles as a term of validation and identification. The *locas* who arrived as part of the Mariel boatlift were the original inspiration of this project: The men who crowded into small apartments together so they could afford the rent, who bleached their hair with peroxide and wore housedresses in the street because that was the drag they could afford, who endured the insults hurled at them because they were both Marielitos and *maricones,* presented a challenge to homogeneous images of Cubans in the United States. They challenged a young *cubanita* to rethink what it meant to be Cuban in Miami.

Drawing on historical sources and ethnographic data, *Oye Loca* tells the story of the development of a Cuban American gay male culture in Miami, Florida. It examines the discourses about Mariel that both sensationalized and silenced the gay presence, the challenges faced by homosexual men who entered as part of the boatlift, and the emergent Cuban American gay culture that transformed Miami's ethnic and sexual landscapes. My theoretical framework critically analyzes the politics of visibility related to sexual, national, and racial/ethnic cultures. I juxtapose different kinds of visibility mediated by diverse social actors in various sociohistorical contexts: U.S. immigration officials, Cuban state authorities, gay rights activists, recently arrived immigrants, and second-generation Cuban Americans. The book's first part explores those events occurring before, during, and immediately after the Mariel boatlift in both Cuba and the United States that created the foundation for the demographic, political, economic, racial, and sexual changes that followed. Specifically, I examine how the Cuban and U.S. states stigmatized, identified, and tracked the movement of sexually transgressive bodies within and across their national borders and how visibility was key to both repressive and liberatory projects in Cuba and the United States. I use Mariel as way to discuss the intersection of hegemonic nationalist discourses and heterosexual masculinity, and examine the state practices that both identified homosexual men and made them disappear. In chapter 1, I juxtapose a discussion of the ways the Cuban state targeted gender-transgressive gay men in the 1960s and 1970s with an analysis of the 1977 antigay rights struggle led by Anita Bryant in South Florida, highlighting the tension between gay visibility and the silencing strategies. In chapter 2, I focus on the migration experiences of homosexual men who arrived as part of the Mariel boatlift, focusing on how the gaze of the Cuban state and U.S. state identified this population and the ways in which these identification systems intersected with state interests and desires. Chapter 3 focuses on how the Mariel migration was remembered and renarrated in subsequent decades. I analyze the intense visibility of one of the most marginal Mariel subpopulations—gender-transgressive *locas* whose relationships with sponsors failed ("broken sponsorship" cases)—tracking how public responses to their representation shifted from the 1980s to the present.

This historical analysis frames the book's second half, an ethnographic study of contemporary Cuban American gay male culture since the 1990s. I examine the complex culture that developed among Cuban-born immigrant men and U.S.-born Cuban Americans who shared a city with other gay men from throughout Latin America, the Caribbean, and the United States. These chapters focus on the linguistic practices of Cuban American gay men (chapter 4); how gay men constructed narratives of Cuba (chapter 5); gay men's relationships with families of origin (chapter 6); the racialized discourses of masculinity that Cuban American gay men negotiate (chapter 7); and an analysis of Cuban American drag performances (chapter 8). By juxtaposing Cuban American gay cultures in 1980 with those in the 1990s and into the new millennium, I hope to track both the continuities and discontinuities in these gendered and racialized cultures. Central to both the continuities and discontinuities are the politics of visibility that can be linked to systematic state repression, politics of liberation, shame, and disidentification.[9]

Methods

When I started this project, my intention was to draw primarily on interviews with Cuban American gay men and participant observation of gay social centers in Miami. To that end, I lived in Miami and conducted intense participant observation between 1998–99 and 2004–5.[10] During these periods, I attended events throughout the city, observing gay clubs at least twice a week on average. I also collected written and promotional documents to evaluate how these events were marketed. I observed political rallies for gay rights, gay film festivals, everyday interactions in various neighborhoods, and drag performances in gay club venues, Cuban American theaters and cabaret venues, and competitive drag events.[11]

As part of my research, I had informal conversations and formal interviews with Cuban American gay men. I conducted eighteen formal, in-depth, confidential interviews with Cuban American gay men ages twenty-two to fifty-one. During these semistructured interviews, which lasted between one and three and half hours, I spoke with men about a range of subjects including their current lives (work, social, and romantic); their relationship to Cuba and to Cuban Miami; their relationship to their families of origin; their relationship to gay life and politics; coming out; and their migration experiences, if they were not born in the United States. Interviews were conducted in Spanish, English, or a mixture of both, depending on the interviewee's preference. I conducted interviews at a location chosen by the respondents. Some interviews were conducted at my home; others at respondent's homes; some at their workplace; and some at a neutral location such as a restaurant. One was conducted over the phone. Interviews were conducted between 1995 and 1999. Although I initially planned to use snowball sampling to recruit respondents for this study, I eventually pursued a more aggressive campaign in order to interview a wider variety of men in a limited amount of time. I produced a club-card description of my research calling for interview participants and distributed this card informally through research contacts and formally through an organizational distribution list of identified Latino gay men.[12] I also provided token compensation ($20) to men who agreed to be interviewed.[13]

The men I interviewed represent a range of class, occupational, and generational perspectives. Two of the men identified their class background as upper middle class, six identified as middle class, three

¿CUBANO? ¿GAY?

Estoy conduciendo entrevistas como parte
de un estudio sobre la cultura
gay cubano-américana. Pase 2-3 horas
hablando de su historia personal.
Será compensado por su tiempo ($20).

Para más información:

Susana Peña, M.A.

This club card was distributed by the author in her recruitment of respondents. Design by author and Pedro Porbén.

identified as lower middle class or working lower class. The remaining seven men identified as working class or used descriptors to refer to the difficulty of their economic situation. For example, one respondent identified his class background as "miserable"; another used the Cuban expression "me estoy comiendo un cable" in response to this question.[14] In terms of highest level of education achieved, two men interviewed had graduate or professional degrees, three had some graduate training, one had a B.A., eleven had some college, and one had a high school diploma (or equivalent). The men's occupations ranged from attorney, psychotherapist, and business owner to retail clerk, student, and part-time employee. Eight of the men were in their twenties at the time of the interview, four were in their thirties, and six were in their forties or early fifties. Eight of the men were born in Cuba, nine were born in the United States, and one was born in Puerto Rico.

As part of my research, I also spent time informally with a small circle of Cuban American gay men with whom I attended clubs, shared meals, and chatted regularly. All of the men were aware of my research project. One of these men played the more formal role of my research assistant. In this capacity, he reviewed my field notes of events we observed, added commentary, and discussed research implications with me. His observations were a necessary backdrop for my study, but I do not represent his observations of events as my own in what follows.

Conversations with Cuban American gay men—in the form of interviews and more casual conversations—serve as both the foundation and the heart of this project. However, as my writing progressed, I realized that I could not fully do justice to the complexity of these men's lives without putting them in a larger historical and structural context and that I could not fully contextualize my analysis by drawing on interviews alone. I did not find the kind of historical analysis I was searching for in the existing literature on Cuba, Miami, and the Mariel boatlift. Therefore, I reluctantly set out to conduct some historical research myself, intending only to fill some gaps in my work. The result of that archival research can be found in the next two chapters. I was surprised at the richness and complexity of the materials I was able to find at archives and even more surprised by how seduced I became by the practice of archival research itself. In my research, I focused on the files of the Cuban–Haitian Task Force, a federal government task force that analyzed the post-Mariel migration crisis, at the Jimmy Carter Presidential Library. At the Human Sexuality Collection at Cornell University, the Kinsey Institute at Indiana University, the Gay and Lesbian Historical Society of Northern California, and the Florida Moving Images Archives, I focused on Anita Bryant's antigay campaign in the late 1970s as well as the role of national and local gay and lesbian organizations resisting Bryant and aiding gay immigrants from Mariel. I also collected and analyzed magazines and zines produced during my research period including two that catered specifically to Latino gay men, *Perra!* and *Nosotros*. As part of my analysis of *Perra!* I interviewed the founder and editor of the magazine, Eduardo Aparicio, on several occasions.[15]

This project is therefore an interdisciplinary study that draws on qualitative sociological methods of interviewing and ethnography and historical methods of archival research. My goal is to provide a historically situated analysis of Cuban American gay culture that acknowledges the intersection of social hierarchies of race, gender, and sexuality.

Where Is Gay Miami?

As I set out to study Cuban American gay Miami, what was I studying exactly? While I am interested in Cuban American gay male *identity*, I realized early in my academic career that a focus on identity in isolation would not allow me fully to address the inequalities and geopolitical structures that limit the identities we can conjure. The concept of gay *community,* on the other hand, seemed to make connections between identities and historical/economic forces in productive ways. Scholars have identified several features of the gay community including institutional elaboration in the form of gay bars, clubs, bookstores, and so on; residential concentration; the creation and primacy of "families we choose"; the presence of collective political action; and a system of social support for group members.[16] John D'Emilio and Allan Bérubé discuss the importance of internal migration in the development of gay communities, especially as facilitated by World War II mobilizations.[17] D'Emilio argues that World War II "uprooted tens of millions of American men and women, many of them young, and deposited them in a variety of nonfamilial, often sex-segregated environments," many of which were in "impersonal metropolitan areas."[18] This displacement produced radical shifts in American family and housing configurations and helped foster the kind of homosexual communities and cultures that now exist in San Francisco and New York City.

Fifteen years after Mariel, South Beach most closely resembled this model of gay community. Although, by the 1990s, the generation of *locas* who inspired this project were less commonly seen on the streets of South Beach—many had passed away while others had moved to more affordable neighborhoods because South Beach had morphed into one of the most desirable and increasingly expensive places to live. South Beach had become a nationally and internationally recognized destination for gay tourists and residents alike. The new gay mecca boasted an emerging arts scene and was becoming a popular location for modeling, television, and film shoots.[19] Exciting dance clubs with amazing sound systems filled with "exotic" men, miles of beaches, and rediscovered and renovated Art Deco architecture (the aforementioned dilapidated housing of the 1980s) made the area even more attractive. Identified most strongly with gay males and commercial club locations, South Beach was labeled a decadent party town in most journalistic accounts. Throughout the 1990s South Beach was home to new gay businesses, a concentration of gay residents, and a proliferation of gay events that attracted gay men from throughout the United States.

Although South Beach of the 1990s most closely fit this definition of a gay community, I did not focus exclusively on this neighborhood in this study. As the home of many Mariel gay men in the 1980s and the neighborhood most identified with gay male culture in the 1990s, South Beach rightfully appears often in this book. However, this is not the study of one clearly geographically delimited gay neighborhood or community. In my research I found that South Beach catered to particular sectors of the gay population more than others. Anglo gay men were more likely to be concentrated in South Beach than in any other Miami neighborhood in the 1990s. Cuban Americans who lived and/or socialized primarily in South Beach were also more likely to be young and U.S.-born than Cuban American gay men who lived and socialized elsewhere. Because South Beach is increasingly gentrified, gay men who are poorer and more transgressive find it more and more difficult to afford rents. Also, in my study I interviewed many gay men who either lived with or near their biological families. These men were more likely to live in predominantly Latino areas of the city such as Southwest Miami and Hialeah. I also found that Latino gay venues outside South Beach differed markedly from those in or near South Beach. For example, South Beach venues that regularly catered to Latino gay men and several venues hosting weekly Latino parties were located in areas of gay business and residential concentration, and Latinos who attended these events tended to be young and conformed to the dominant model of gay masculinity. In contrast, gay social centers catering to Latino gay men in mainland Miami were attended by men of more diverse ages and body types and were not part of a geographically based community but instead were situated in isolated locations (e.g., a warehouse district in a commercial area by the Miami River) or simply not near a concentration of businesses catering to gay men.

To be clear, a study of South Beach's gay community would not have excluded Cuban Americans entirely. Many Cuban American gay men lived, shopped, or socialized in the area, and Latino gay men are often cited as part of the attraction of South Beach as a gay mecca. However, a study of South Beach's gay community would have provided a highly selective view of Cuban American gay life, at best. A focus on Miami's gay community, narrowly defined, would therefore emphasize the experience of Anglo gay men and a particular subgroup of Cuban American gay men—the most economically privileged, the young and attractive.

For these reasons, this is not a study of gay *community* as defined above but rather a study of Cuban American gay *culture*. I define culture as the complex interrelationships among lived practices, self-

ффф the

identifications, social institutions, produced texts, and a more ephemeral form of cohesion Raymond Williams called a structure of feeling.[20] By this definition that is deeply inspired by the Birmingham School of cultural studies, culture includes consciously produced actions and words as well as less-articulated ways of being. By focusing on culture, I am able to target particular ethnic/racial groups (in this case, Cuban Americans) whose formations around sexuality may or may not take the cohesive, institutional, and territorial forms of gay community that sociologists have identified. This definition of culture points to the contradictory strands, the heterogeneity, and the shifting and contextual nature of what I am calling Cuban American gay male culture. By this definition, culture is not singular, homogeneous, or self-contained. Under this rubric, I address complex interrelationships within an individual's life (e.g., tensions between self-identification and lived practices) as well as the dense network formed by people who were born in or trace their descent to Cuba, who understand themselves as men, who understand their desire for men as part of their identity, and who live in South Florida, but who might be quite different in other ways. I understand culture to be structurally constrained but not structurally determined. This approach insists on an analysis that is sociohistorically specific in order to analyze what Antonio Gramsci would call "conjuncture." It highlights both structural forces that constrain our actions and identities, and people's creative work to make meaning of their own lives and their social context within these constraints. As my work demonstrates, this creative work is not necessarily resistant or regressive. For example, sometimes this meaning-making leads to the reinforcement of racial privilege; other times it can challenge existing racist assumptions; and sometimes it can do both simultaneously. I contrast this definition of culture with culturalist analyses of Latino lives that see "Latino culture" as ahistorically static, traditional, and homogeneous.[21] I purposefully center the heterogeneity of Cuban American gay male culture. Therefore, this study includes U.S.-born and foreign-born men; men of different social classes and occupational groups; gay men who see themselves as very masculine and are proud of how they can pass as straight and gay men who believe their gayness is utterly obvious; men who are upwardly mobile professionals and men who are unemployed; men who speak only Spanish, men who speak only English, and bilingual (and multilingual) men; those who understand themselves as unquestionably white and racially unmarked and those who understand themselves to be racialized in particular ways; those who lived in Miami's quintessential gay neighborhood of South Beach, those who lived in its quintessential Cuban neighborhood of *la sagüesera* (of Southwest Miami), and those who lived in the very Latinized suburb of Kendall.

The participants of this Cuban American gay culture lead quite different day-to-day lives that may cross occasionally, often, or not at all. In this diverse culture, similar lived practices can occur under radically different conditions to produce different effects. For example, among my interview participants, it was fairly common for Cuban American gay men to have extensive relationships with biological family, and it was not uncommon for men to live with biological family (a topic I explore in chapter 6). However, this cohabitation is experienced quite differently by an economically independent U.S.-born man who might temporarily live with a family member in need of caretaking than it is by a recent Cuban immigrant who is unemployed, does not speak English, and out of necessity lives with a homophobic relative.

Migrations

As mentioned previously, some sociological and historical accounts of gay community did center the importance of migrations—mostly domestic or internal migrations of Anglo men to urban centers. Tomás Almaguer has argued that white, middle-class gay men had more access to these gay communities than other groups:

> It is very apparent . . . that the gay identity and communities that emerged [in the United States] were overwhelmingly white, middle class, and male-centered. . . . Moreover, the new communities founded in the postwar period were largely populated by white men who had the resources and talents needed to create "gilded" gay ghettoes. This fact has given the contemporary gay community—despite its undeniable diversity—a largely white, middle-class, and male form. . . . [White men's] collective position in the social structure empowered them with the skills and talents needed to create new gay institutions, communities, and a unique sexual subculture.[22]

Almaguer raises an important point: not everyone could afford *that kind* of migration. On the other hand, international migration, between Latin America and the United States, structures many (but not all) Latino gay men's lives. Recent scholarship by Lionel Cantú Jr., Eithne Luibhéid, Carlos Decena, Martin Manalansan IV, Arnaldo Cruz-Malavé, Gloria

González-López, and Héctor Carrillo has helped us theorize the relationship between sexuality and international migration.[23] In his work on Mexican immigrant men who have sex with men, Cantú analyzes the "queer political economy of migration." Like Cantú, I hope not only to shed light on a particular gay population but to examine sexuality as an "axis of power relations," in order to make "'regimes of normalization' visible."[24] Cantú's critique of culturalist paradigms and focus on political economy provides a useful guide for my study of Cuban American gay male culture.

The migration that has affected my respondents most directly is the migration from Cuba to the United States—either their own or that of their parents and/or grandparents. The dynamics of this migration, especially in that it has tended to keep biological families together, as opposed to separating young men and women from the strictures of family control, has direct effects on the configurations of gay life. Thus the particular case of Miami helps us distinguish what characteristics are common to gay communities and what characteristics are more specific to particular race and class communities.

Miami's Racial Landscape

Miami is undeniably a Latino and Caribbean city. Labeled as the gateway to the Americas, it is an entry point of Latin American and Caribbean capital, immigrants, tourists, and media into the United States. In 1990, 49.2 percent of Miami–Dade County's population identified as Hispanic; by 2000, a majority (57 percent) identified as Hispanic, and by 2010, 65 percent identified as Hispanic.[25] White non-Hispanics (20.7 percent in 2000, 15.9 percent in 2010) and black non-Hispanics (19 percent in 2000, 17.6 percent in 2010) made up the declining portions of the area's population.[26] In the new millennium, Miami–Dade County was also home to an increasingly diverse Latino population including Cubans (50.4 percent of all Hispanics in 2000 and 52.7 percent in 2010), Puerto Ricans (6.2 percent in 2000, 5.7 percent in 2010), Nicaraguans (5.4 percent in 2000, 6.5 percent in 2010), Colombians (5.4 percent in 2000, 7 percent in 2010), Dominicans (2.8 percent in 2000, 3.6 percent in 2010), and Mexicans (2.9 percent in 2000, 3.2 percent in 2010).[27] Although Miami's Latino population is far from homogeneous, Cuban Americans form Miami's largest Hispanic national origin group, and they exert political, social, and economic influence in most realms of urban life.

Although Cubans had been living in South Florida before 1959, they began arriving in large numbers after Castro's entry to power at the end of that year. During the first years of Cuban mass migration to the United States (1959–65), close to 300,000 Cubans entered the United States. After the Cuban missile crisis in 1962, the migration slowed substantially as flights between Cuba and the United States were canceled; however, Cubans continued to enter the United States through third countries. In 1965 large-scale migration from Cuba to the United States resumed. In what would become a preview of the Mariel boatlift, in 1965 Castro invited Cuban Americans to come in boats to pick up their relatives from Camarioca harbor. As five thousand Cubans entered the United States in the boatlift, the two countries signed an agreement permitting commercial flights between Havana and Miami. In the United States, the migration of Cubans through this air bridge became known as the Freedom Flights. Between 1965 and 1973 (when Castro terminated the flights), more than 340,000 Cubans entered the United States. The period between 1973 and 1980 constituted another slow period of Cuban migration: only 24,000 Cubans entered the United States either by leaving Cuba clandestinely or by entering the United States through a third country.[28]

During the 1960s and 1970s Cuban immigrants were generally portrayed as desirable immigrants fleeing Castro's regime for political reasons. The Cubans who came to the United States in the year or two after the revolution have been called the "golden exiles" and characterized as the elites of Cuban society. Generally, they were professionals, business owners, and landowners with ties to U.S. business and/or the previous Cuban regime of Fulgencio Batista who were alienated from the revolution during the first phases of the nationalization process. Between 1960 and 1962, middle-class entrepreneurs became part of the migrant flow when rental property began to be confiscated in Cuba. Some scholars have argued that the elite nature of these immigrants has been overstated. Thomas D. Boswell and James R. Curtis argue that although early (1959–62) Cuban immigrants were not representative of the Cuban population, they were not homogeneously elite either. According to Boswell and Curtis, only 40 percent of this migration might be considered elite. The other 60 percent consisted mostly of clerical and sales workers (31 percent) and skilled, semiskilled, and unskilled workers (20 percent).[29] The immigrants who arrived in the United States via the Freedom Flights consisted of different segments of Cuban society: close to half the immigrants were blue-collar (skilled and unskilled) workers, while some 10 percent were agricultural workers and fishermen.[30] Sheila L. Croucher comments:

> Much of the public discourse on Cuban immigration, whether it emanates from the immigrants themselves or from the society at large, paints a portrait of Cubans in the United States as an economically powerful, politically united, and culturally homogenous ethnic group. Neither this image nor many of the assumptions upon which it is based is well grounded in empirical reality.[31]

Although the demographic profiles of these waves of migration are diverse and indicate that the elite nature of migrants declined greatly in more recent migrations, throughout the 1960s and 1970s the portrait of the white, well-educated, elite, hardworking, model minority Cuban family became increasingly popular in the U.S. media and among Cubans themselves.

Unlike other Hispanic groups in the United States who have been identified as nonwhite in the regions of their settlement, Cuban Americans who arrived between 1959 and 1980 were generally racialized as white in the context of South Florida. Benigno Aguirre outlines a set of reasons explaining the disproportionate racial distribution of Cuban migration. The early mass migration was attractive to the elites of Cuban society. Because Cuba was a racially stratified society where blacks were less likely to be elites than whites, the majority of early migrants (post-1959) were white by Cuban standards. The ensuing chain migrations along with the U.S. family reunification policy that privileged migrants who already had relatives in the United States further excluded black Cubans. In addition, the Cuban Revolution targeted racism and promised a society free of racial discrimination. This ideology, along with real improvements in the position of blacks in some areas of Cuban society, made staying in Cuba more attractive to black Cubans, especially prior to 1980.[32] Therefore, there are a series of reasons why those considered white in Cuba were more likely to migrate to the United States. However, as the history of Latino immigration to the United States teaches us, white racial status in Latin America does not necessarily translate to white racial status in the United States after immigration. Nevertheless, Cuban Americans in South Florida in many ways achieved white racial status. This significant difference with other U.S. Latino/a groups can be attributed to a range of factors including class, racial, and phenotypical characteristics of the first massive wave of Cuban immigrants; the ties to U.S. businesses many immigrants had before migration; the fairly welcoming stance of the U.S. government; the economic support provided by the Cuban Refugee Program; and the subsequent socioeconomic position of many Cuban Americans.[33]

Cuban American definitions of whiteness are greatly influenced by Cuban racial categories. After the virtual elimination of Cuba's indigenous population through violence, displacement, illness, and suicide, African slaves became the primary source of labor on the island.[34] The history of black–white relations on the island are complex. On the one hand, Cuba "received African slaves into the 1860s and was the last Spanish colony to abolish slavery (1886)." On the other hand, in the 1800s a sizable population of free blacks lived on the island, universal male suffrage was granted by the 1901 constitutional convention (women gained the right to vote in 1934), and the first "racially defined national political party" was organized by blacks in 1912.[35]

Especially after the success of the Haitian Revolution, Cuban elites developed an ostensibly inclusive discourse of the nation that at least symbolically incorporated blacks with the hopes of avoiding a black uprising. As Alejandro de la Fuente explains,

> the nationalist ideology envisioned a new republic that would be not only politically independent but egalitarian and inclusive as well—a republic "with all and for all," as José Martí had called it. The existence of "races" was seen as a social reality, but within an encompassing notion of Cubanness that was supposed to subsume, and eventually erase, racial identities.[36]

Since then, ideologies of a racially inclusive Cuba have coexisted with racial discrimination and chronic (if not unchanging) patterns of racial inequality in radically different state contexts. Fuente has argued that a discourse of mixed-race origins of the Cuban nation actually served to silence issues of race:

> The very governments that have pledged allegiance to the ideal of a racially integrated nation, as they all have done since the early republic, also have implemented policies that resulted in the survival and reproduction of socially constructed perceptions of race.[37]

In Cuba an ideology of racial inclusiveness, a reluctance to discuss contemporary racism, and a persistence of racial inequality have coexisted before and after the Cuban Revolution.

The definitions of racial categories themselves also responded to the demographic changes in Cuba and the specter of the Haitian Revolution. As Mirta de la Torre Mulhare explains, when faced with a disproportionate increase in the black population, Cuban elites increased "the ranks of the whites through the gradual acceptance of part-whites as whites."[38] In contrast, faced with a similar demographic shift, elites in the U.S. South defined anyone with "one drop" of black blood as black.[39] Silvia Pedraza-Bailey highlights the extent to which definitions of racial categories in Cuba were related to class: "Social class and race overlapped in the extreme. So that Cubans valued whiteness as tantamount to beauty, status, and honor. Contrary to American practice, color gradations had meaning particularly when buttressed by income and authority."[40] Mulhare also comments on the "defensiveness" of Cubans about their own racial composition. A doctor she interviewed shed further light on this phenomenon:

> If they were not so afraid of having black blood themselves, they would not talk so much of their whiteness. It is nothing but hypocrisy. They pretend as if they do not see color if it is light enough or if the black relatives are hidden, and they see it only when it is very dark or very poor.[41]

The mass migration of elite Cubans to Miami, a city dominated by the black–white U.S. binary, did not allow for the acknowledgment of racial gradations, but it did foster the strategic employment and further redefinition of Cuban whiteness. Miami bears the scars of being a Southern city. These scars mark a clear racial segregation that separates dark-skinned Miamians from light-skinned Miamians. Miami's African Americans, Haitian Americans, and Bahamian Americans, as well as dark-skinned Latinos, are defined as black.[42] Both Anglos and light-skinned Latinos are defined as white. In addition, the vast majority of Latinos in Miami do not self-identify as black. For example, in 1990, 2000, and 2010, only 2 to 3 percent of Miami–Dade Hispanics identified as black.[43]

The 1980 Mariel migration challenged the image of Cuban success and Cuban whiteness. Various stigmas were associated with the boatlift. According to popular representations, Marielitos were criminals, prostitutes, mental patients, and homosexuals. The Marielitos also were more likely to be dark skinned, which posed a challenge to Cuban American claims to whiteness.[44] In other words, the same migration that was stigmatized in terms of sexuality was also stigmatized because of its racial composition. Given this racial context, this study examines the racialization of Cuban American gay men. In chapter 5, I describe how narratives of Cuba are central to understanding Cuban American gay men's ethnic identities. I explore how Cuban American gay men negotiate racial boundaries of exclusion through these narratives. In chapters 7 and 8, I explore the racialized meanings of masculinity that Cuban American gay men contend with in the development of their gender and sexual identities. I argue that although the Cuban American gay men I interviewed reject the notion of themselves as nonwhite, they nonetheless describe a distance between themselves and those masculinities identified with white gay men. Throughout the book I counterpose men's apparently transparent white self-identifications with evidence of a different racialization that is not necessarily articulated in the language of race.

A Focus on Men

One central concern of this book is the apparent contradiction between the visibility of gay men in Cuban culture and their simultaneous invisibility. I trace the tension between visibility and silence, beginning with an analysis of events surrounding the Mariel boatlift. This dialectic between visibility and silence is particular to Cuban American gay men and quite different from the ways in which Cuban and Cuban American lesbians are interpellated (or not) by the state and in popular culture. For example, as I discuss in chapter 1, the Cuban state explicitly targeted homosexual men and articulated a discourse that identified male homosexuality as a product of bourgeois capitalist decadence. Although Cuban lesbians, masculine women, and women who had sex with women were not free from persecution, they were not visible to or identified by the state in the same way as gay men. The intense focus of the state gaze on gender-transgressive male homosexuals, in particular, and the public discourse against effeminacy and male homosexuality were explicitly tied to an emerging national discourse about a virile new Cuban nation and society. In other cultural realms, there are similar differences between gay men and lesbians. Whereas Cuban American gay men are often vilified in Cuban jokes, mocked in Spanish-language soap operas, and identified with visible gender transgressors (effeminate gay men), Cuban American lesbians are hardly represented at all. In addition, whereas Cuban American gay men participate in public and commercial gay male cultures, Cuban American lesbians are more likely to congregate in private settings like house parties. Gay commercial venues in Miami cater predominantly to men and are highly gender segregated. Lesbians of all races have only begun to claim these commercial spaces as their own, usually through new theme nights specifically geared toward lesbians. Although there are exceptions, I did not find that Cuban American gay men and lesbians interacted extensively with one another as groups.

In short, I would argue that whereas homosexual men in both Cuban and Cuban American contexts have to contend with a stigmatizing hypervisibility, lesbians in these same contexts have had to face cultural unintelligibility. Given these differences, a study of Cuban American lesbians would require a different kind of ethnography centered on a different set of questions. This is, therefore, a study of Cuban American gay male culture and not lesbian culture.[45] That being said, my research on the race, sexuality, and gender of a group of men has been guided by the transformative work of queer Latina feminists. In her call to bring Chicano gay men into a discussion of Queer Aztlán, Cherríe Moraga provides a model for a feminist engagement with queer masculinity— one that embraces gay men of color's marginality while never justifying patriarchy.[46] As I have argued elsewhere, empirical social science research on Latina lesbians is quite limited, but I hope my study will inspire future researchers to explore Latina lesbian sexuality and culture on their own terms.[47] In particular, my study questions how masculine privilege intersects with gay sexuality. Regarding women who are not raised with the freedom of movement, respect, and authority given to Cuban American men, I would ask, how do they negotiate relationships with biological family? Given that Latina lesbians (at least in Miami) do not inhabit commercial venues organized around sexuality to the same extent men do, what kinds of social spaces are central to their lives, identities, and cultures? How have interventions by medical institutions affected Cuban and Cuban American lesbians? What are the challenges and possibilities posed by lesbian invisibility in regard to the state and popular culture?

Rastros

During one of my interviews with Eduardo Aparicio, editor of *Perra!*, I asked him if he saw the publication as a way to create or develop a Latino gay community. He responded:

> Mi postura siempre es que esa comunidad existe, solamente que no hay evidencia de esa comunidad. Entonce era más bien para evidenciar esa comunidad. Ver lo que están haciendo Juan y Pedro en su casa y cuando limpian, [simplemente] lo mas ordinario, lo que hacen para cocinar, o que hicieron hoy, o cómo se conocieron, ¿no? Esa comunidad existe. Lo que no existía era algún tipo de evidencia escrita, palpable, que podías tener en tus manos.

> My position has always been that this community already exists. There simply isn't any evidence of that community. Therefore, the point of *[Perra!]* was to provide evidence of that community. To see what Juan and Pedro were doing in their house, when they're cleaning, [simply] the most ordinary things, how they cook, or what they did today, or how they met. That community exists, what didn't exist was any type of written, palpable evidence of it that you could hold in your hands.[48]

Aparicio begins his answer with a claim—a claim of the existence of gay Latino community. He knows this community exists because he is a member of it, because he has participated in it, because he has seen it. If the gay Latino community is so visible and so present, then how can it also be true that there is no material evidence of it? Why would the evidence be so fleeting as to lead Aparicio to remark that it is not "palpable"?

In contrast to nonpalpable evidence, Aparicio wanted to produce something that would be palpable and that would leave "un rastro" (a trace), as he told me. He wanted to produce something that would exist in the physical world after its moment of production (something "you could hold in your hands"). The importance of the lasting physicality of the "rastro" became clear when we talked about drag shows. I mentioned that drag shows were another site where I saw evidence of a Latino gay community. Although he agreed with this, he did not believe a drag show left any lasting evidence of its existence: "¿El show que se hizo en septiembre del 96, dónde está ese show, dónde quedó?" (The show that was performed in September of 96, where is it? Where did it end up?). On the other hand, a magazine produced in September 1996 could be right here, in my hands, providing physical, undeniable proof of its existence, leaving *un rastro*.[49]

As a social analyst, I was very appreciative of having the material evidence produced by Aparicio, evidence that I could hold in my hand (and photocopy, code, and manipulate in other sociological ways). However, not all *rastros* of Cuban American gay culture were this material in their form. From my incipient interest in gay Mariel, I knew I would have to develop ways to investigate what was made invisible, what undeniably existed but was evidenced only by a fleeting visibility.

In *Ghostly Matters,* Avery Gordon discusses the sociology of haunting as a theoretical framework for grasping the effects of the unseen, invisible, and hidden in our social world.[50] She draws on Raymond Williams's concept of structures of feeling. Williams argues that these less-articulated ways of being are a central part of any culture under study, yet they are not usually the object of social analysis. They are often misclassified as whimsical, personal, unimportant, or mystical. Williams insists that structures of feelings "do not have to await definition, classification, or rationalization before they exert *palpable* pressures and set effective limits on experience and on action."[51] Therefore, he challenges social analysts to expand our methodological tools as well as to expand our definition of the social in order to understand the determinants of our social world. Williams argues that nonmaterial *rastros* also have palpable effects. Gordon puts it another way: the "ghosts are real . . . [and] they produce material effects."[52]

Why should we study, analyze, write about structures of feelings that are not clear or fully visible? Why not stick to what we can see clearly? The answer is that, as social analysts, what we see and how we see are deeply embedded in power hierarchies. There are those who have been systematically excluded from scholarly texts. The ostentatious Mariel *locas* who everybody saw but no one was willing to recognize as legitimate subjects form the most obvious example of this paradox. As we try to write "histories of the present" that confront the structures that silence, we challenge ourselves to articulate what is on the "edge of semantic availability."[53]

> Perceiving the lost subjects of history—the missing and the lost ones and the blind fields they inhabit—makes all the difference to any project trying to find the address of the present. . . . To write the history of the present requires stretching toward the horizon of what cannot be seen with ordinary clarity yet. And to stretch toward and beyond a horizon requires a particular kind of perception where the transparent and the shadowy confront each other. As an ethnographic project to write the history of the present

requires grappling with the form ideological interpellation takes—"we have
already understood"—and with the difficulty of imagining beyond the limits of what is already *understandable.*[54]

In this ethnography of Cuban American gay culture, I have tried to be
cognizant of the "lost subjects of history" that "haunt" the clubs I attended, the stories I heard, and the newspaper articles I read. By juxtaposing a transnational historical context and men's self-articulations,
lived practices, and social context, I hope to track not only what is
said but also what is not said (or silenced) and to be able to analyze not
only what is hypervisible but also fleeting visibilities. I hope that my
presentation of the *rastros* of Cuban American gay male culture does
justice to the challenges, joys, and complexities of these men's lives.

1 FROM Umaps TO SAVE OUR CHILDREN

Policing Homosexuality in Cuba
and Miami before 1980

BY THE TIME THE MARIEL BOATLIFT BEGAN in 1980, male homosexuality was already political center stage in both Cuba and Miami. In Cuba during the late 1960s and early 1970s, male homosexuality and the gender-transgressive practices associated with it became the target of a state seeking to define itself and its citizenry. Male homosexuality was seen as a threat to the new communist nation, a vestige of American capitalism, and an entity truly foreign to the Cuban national project. An oppressive set of state policies, enforcement practices, and political discourses about masculinity, homosexuality, and the nation elevated male homosexuality into public, official visibility and played a formative role in the lives of the gay men who came to the United States during the Mariel migration.

In Miami during the late 1970s gay men and lesbians also invoked a politics of visibility, although for very different purposes. During this period of redefinition for gay men and lesbians, the visibility of their community (achieved partly through coming out) became the foundation for claims to equal rights. While some successes were achieved both locally and nationally, these newfound rights and the visibility on which they were based became the target of conservatives who equated gay rights and gay visibility with a threat to American families and children. This organized, conservative backlash against gay rights led by the Christian entertainer Anita Bryant gained prominence precisely in Dade County, Florida, where the majority of Cuban immigrants had settled and where most Mariel immigrants would eventually arrive.

The homosexual men who arrived as part of the Mariel boatlift were marked in profound ways by their experiences with an emerging Cuban state that wrestled with homosexuality as part of its project of national redefinition. Ironically, although these men were leaving Cuba to enter what many believed was a land of gay freedom, their point of entry into the United States was an urban center that had just become the birthplace of a conservative movement which sought to limit gay rights. In both Cuban and U.S. contexts, gay visibility was at the heart of both the repression of gay culture and of the struggle for gay rights.

In this chapter, I argue that forms of homosexual political persecution in the United States and Cuba prior to the 1980 Mariel boatlift helped define the parameters of gay identification and political mobilization for the gay Mariel generation. On the one hand, what was understood to be visible homosexuality was targeted by the state in Cuba and by conservative political forces in the United States. On the other hand, homosexuals in Cuba and the United States were increasingly engaged in a politics of visibility that challenged these repressive forces. Although the form and cadence of these gay politics of visibility differed on either side of the Florida Straits, they would eventually come together on the tumultuous South Florida streets of the early 1980s.

This chapter is divided in two parts. First, I discuss the Cuban state's repression of homosexuals between 1959 and 1980 and its focus on gender-transgressive male homosexuality. Second, I analyze ethnic and sexual politics in South Florida immediately preceding the boatlift, specifically the growing influence of Cuban Americans, the rise of a public gay culture, and the conservative backlash organized against the perceived threats represented by that culture. In relation to the campaign against gay rights, I am especially interested in how conservatives targeted gay visibility and in the visibility of Latinos on both sides of the gay rights struggle.

Homosexuality in Cuba, 1965–80

After the 1959 Cuban Revolution, the homophobia and heterosexism that already existed in Cuba became more systematized and institutionalized.[1] Gender and sexuality explicitly entered political discourse, and vaguely worded laws were increasingly used to target gender-transgressive men believed to be homosexual. Fidel Castro clearly argued that the revolution was incompatible with homosexuality:

> We would never come to believe that a homosexual could embody the con-
> ditions and requirements of conduct that would enable us to consider him
> a true Revolutionary, a true Communist militant. A deviation of nature
> clashes with the concept we have of what a militant communist must be.[2]

From the mid-1960s to the late 1970s, the Cuban government defined
homosexuality as a capitalist construct imported from America and a
"product of bourgeois decadence" antithetical to the revolution.[3] Following this logic, the new revolutionary state targeted male homosexuals
as part of its effort to "recuperate the national dignity."[4]

The creation of a dignified society, revolutionaries believed, required
the emergence of a "New Socialist Man." As articulated by Ernesto
Che Guevara, the concept of *el Hombre Nuevo* became a powerful,
foundational revolutionary discourse that proposed productivity and
socialist morality as essential to the formation of new Cuban identities and a new communist/socialist society.[5] The New Man and the
homosexual became mutually constitutive categories, with the New
Man representing the positive goal of revolutionary efforts and the homosexual embodying the vestiges of capitalist domination. The New
Man needed to be masculine, virile, strong, healthy, hardworking,
generous, motivated by a commitment to helping his fellow man, and
willing to contribute economically, socially, and morally to the new
Cuba. The New Man was most likely to emerge from rural areas of
Cuba, which were believed to be less affected by capitalist intervention
and free of urban vices such as homosexuality. In contrast, the homosexual was effeminate, nonproductive (and nonreproductive), weak,
selfish, counterrevolutionary, and decadently urban.[6] As the following statement by the Cuban revolutionary intellectual Samuel Feijóo
indicates, this opposition between the New Man and the homosexual
was not just implied but clearly articulated and circulated in political
discourse. Identifying the vice of homosexuality as "one of the most
nefarious and regrettable legacies of capitalism," Feijóo laments that
by 1965 the revolution had yet to eliminate it. His polemical article
graphically characterizes how the revolution imagined the New Cuba
and its Homosexual antagonist:

> We fight and will continue to fight against [homosexuality] until it is
> eradicated from a virile country, caught up in a life-and-death struggle
> against Yankee imperialism. And this extremely virile country, with its
> army of men, should not and cannot be represented by homosexual and

pseudohomosexual writers and "artists." Because no homosexual represents the revolution, which is a matter of men, of fists not feathers, of cour-
age not trembling, of certainty not intrigue, of creative valor not syrupy
surprises [*sorpresas merengosas*].[7]

Trapped in this binary, the homosexual became the antithesis of the
true revolutionary.

This discourse was made operational in a series of laws and enforcement practices. The most extreme and well-known example was
the establishment of reeducation camps known as Unidades Militares
para el Aumento de Producción (UMAPs) (Military Units for Increased
Production). Beginning in 1965 (the same year Feijóo published his
article on vices and the revolution), homosexual men—along with
Jehovah's Witnesses, Seventh-Day Adventists, and others defined as
social deviants—were sent to army special unit camps to be isolated
from the general population and rehabilitated through military disci-
pline and productive labor conducted in the purifying environment of
rural Cuba.[8] It was thought that homosexuality, in particular, would
be cured "through performance of manly activities."[9]

The camps crystallized the Cuban state's position on homosexuality
and its discourse about the relationship between productivity, gender,
and homosexuality. Likewise, the camps provided a vivid and fright-
ening example to homosexuals on and outside the island, an example
that highlighted their marginal place in communist Cuba. Even though
the camps themselves were short-lived, their example was not easily
forgotten.[10] Although this experiment in social control still lurked in
Cuban popular memory, many more Cuban homosexuals were person-
ally affected by the routine persecutions of the 1960s and 1970s. These
included informal exclusion from the Communist Party, individual arrests, *recogidas* or street sweeps of ostentatious homosexuals, and the
exclusion of homosexuals from certain professions.[11]

Rafael, who left Cuba during the Mariel migration, characterized
life in Cuba prior to 1980 in the following way:

Allá nos divertíamos; éramos muy perseguidos, pero ya convivíamos con
la persecución. Ya era muy normal que te arrestaran, te metieran en un
calabozo, te soltaran a la semana o los 28 días, y salir a la calle. Era como
una rutina, una cosa muy normal.

[In Cuba] we had fun; we were very persecuted, but we lived with the persecution. It was very normal for them to arrest you, stick you in a cell, and

let you out in a week or twenty-eight days, and then back to the street. It
was like a routine, a very normal thing.[12]

Several laws in the Cuban penal code justified the generalized persecution of homosexuals. In the early years of the revolution, the Cuban
state continued to use the 1936 penal code. After extensive study and
consideration, the code was revised in 1979, one year before the Mariel
boatlift. During this massive revision, existing laws targeting homosexuals were updated, and some new sanctions were added.[13] These
revisions give us some sense of how earlier laws aimed at homosexuals
were already being interpreted by the new state. For example, laws
concerning "Escándalo Público" ("Public Scandal") included both revisions and additions concerning homosexuality. First, the law was
updated to replace older terminology like "active or passive pederasty"
with modern equivalents like "homosexual condition." The revised
portion sanctioned anyone who "would make a public display of their
homosexual condition or importune or solicit another for [homosexual]
purposes."[14] In addition, the 1979 version of the public scandal law included new sanctions against homosexual public sex—penalizing public
homosexual acts and private homosexual sex that could be involuntarily seen by others.[15] As the title of the relevant sections of both the
1936 and 1979 penal codes suggests, this law was centrally concerned
with visibility: the updates of the law clarified the association between
Escándalo Público and homosexuals specifically to expand sanctions
against visible homosexuality.

Another law commonly used to target homosexuals as a deviant
group did not explicitly mention homosexuality in either earlier or later
versions of the penal code. In fact, the ambiguously worded Ley de
Peligrosidad, or Law of Social Dangerousness, invoked a concept of precriminality; that is, it did not identify people who had committed an
illegal act but rather those believed to have a high potential to violate
laws.[16] Only slightly changed in 1979, the revised law defined social
dangerousness as habitual behavior that demonstrated a "special pro-
clivity . . . to commit criminal acts, as demonstrated by observed conduct which is manifestly against the norms of socialist morality."[17] The
1979 code identified seven indices of social dangerousness including
the "exercise of socially repugnant vices"—changed from "morally repugnant vices" in the 1936 penal code.[18] Also, the revised code added a
new index, "antisocial conduct." As Ian Lumsden points out, "In Cuba,

antisocial has been a code word for allegedly ostentatious homosexuality, amongst other forms of 'deviant' behavior."[19] Therefore, although the law against social dangerousness did not explicitly identify homosexuals, numerous reports indicate that prior to Mariel, visibly gay men were often arrested and charged under this law.[20]

Although homosexuality in general might have theoretically been the focus of this legal persecution, blatant gender transgression and effeminacy were the principal objects of the Cuban state gaze. Luis Salas argues that this was partly a response to the challenge of enforcing laws related to homosexuality:

> In the absence of actual proof as to the acts being performed, the police assume a wide array of suppositions in order to apprehend the homosexual. Thus, it is presumed in many instances that those persons that frequent certain places, dress in a set manner, and act in an effeminate way, or engage in specific professions are homosexuals.[21]

Long hair, tight pants, colorful shirts, effeminate mannerisms, "inappropriate clothing," and "extravagant hairstyles" were seen as visible markers of male homosexuality.[22] These visible markers were not just a way to facilitate the enforcement of homosexual repression. Rather, visibility and gender transgressions themselves were a central part of the problem identified by the revolution. Even in the severest period of enforcement, Marvin Leiner reminds us, private homosexual expression was never the main target. Rather, "during this period of the camps and public arrests, the major concern, as it had always been, was with the public display of homosexuality."[23] The gravest crime was not engaging in same-sex sexual acts per se but transgressing gender norms in ways associated with male homosexuality or, in other words, being visibly or obviously gay.

In addition to criminal and police persecution, homosexuals were also excluded from certain forms of employment. Attempts to systematize these job restrictions emerged in 1971 out of the National Congress on Education and Culture. Although the congress declared that homosexuality was not a central or fundamental problem in Cuban society, its attention to and recommendations about homosexuality suggested otherwise. It defined homosexuality as a social pathology and "resolved that all manifestations of homosexual deviations are to be firmly rejected and prevented from spreading."[24] Concerned about the influence of homosexuals on youth, the congress recommended that homosexuals be barred from educational positions where they could directly affect young people.[25] In the same spirit, it recommended that a study be made of how best to approach the "presence of homosexuals in the different parts of our cultural sector" because it was not "permissible that because of their 'artistic merit,' known homosexuals gain influence on the formation of our youth."[26]

The congress not only commented on the impact of cultural workers (writers, artists, etc.) on Cuban youth but also recommended that homosexuals be banned from artistically representing Cuba abroad. This additional recommendation revealed the revolution's concern with its own international image. Moreover, the language of the recommendations echoed Feijóo, who advocated eliminating homosexuals from cultural positions as a project of "revolutionary social hygiene."[27] Cuba needed real revolutionaries both domestically (to influence a new generation) and internationally (to represent the "virile" nation of "men"). As Feijóo clarified, "Real revolutionary literature is not and never will be written by sodomites."[28]

The emphasis on visibility is clear in the labor restrictions passed in 1974 upon the congress's recommendation. The labor (not penal) code indicated that people could be dismissed from their jobs and reassigned to another field for practicing

> homosexualism, publicly known, and other reproachable forms of conduct, which projected publicly, may have a negative influence on the education, conscience or public feelings of children and young persons, by those persons employed in cultural activities or artistic recreative functions and presenting themselves through public means of diffusion.[29]

As written, the law repeatedly targets homosexuals who are "publicly known" and who project themselves "publicly."

Homosexuals in revolutionary Cuba were subjected to frequent repression by police, restrictions in terms of employment, and distaste in popular sentiment, but the state gaze fixated on gender-transgressive male homosexuals—or obvious gays. For all practical purposes, these political discourses, laws, forms of enforcement, and labor restrictions penalized looking gay.[30] The appearance of homosexuality was key. As Carlos Alberto Montaner explains in his decidedly anti-Castro account:

> The government wasn't concerned with—it's never concerned with—realities, but with appearances. It wants masculine men, with shortly trimmed

hair, loose fitting pants, perfect guayaberas, even if that outfit was hiding an effeminate creature *[una criatura feminoide]*. What was important was the damn image of the revolution.[31]

The state's concern with appearances and public display were accompanied by formal antihomosexual state actions directed specifically at male homosexuals who were visible to the public.

Visible homosexuals were also subjected to more informal forms of social control. For example, one of my respondents, Armando, who left Cuba as part of the Mariel boatlift, described how he was blocked from pursuing a career as a teacher. He begins his story by drawing attention to the visibility of his homosexuality: "I wanted to be a teacher, and I don't consider myself very butch. I know I'm obvious, like you talk to me for a while, [and] you know I'm gay." Although he saw his own homosexuality as obvious and visible to others, he was hopeful about getting a job as a teacher because his father had connections in the Ministry of Education. Although his father's connection was "muy amable" (very nice/kind/helpful), his efforts to find employment were continually blocked:

Hasta al fin una señora un día me dijo, "¿Tú crees que,"—Y fue muy amable, al decírmelo, fue muy nice. Eso lo tengo que decir. Pero ella me dijo—"que cuando tú te pares delante de una aula de muchachos de quince y dieciséis, diecisiete años, tú tengas el carácter para, para que esos muchachos te respeten, siendo tú como eres?" Me dijo así mismo, y yo dije bueno, that's true. So I went for accounting.

Until finally one day a lady told me, "Do you think that,"—And she was very nice when she told me. I have to admit that. But she said to me—"when you get up in front of a classroom filled with fifteen-, sixteen-, and seventeen-year-old kids, do you think you are going to have the character [strength of personality] to get those kids to respect you, being the way you are?" She said it just like that, and I said, well, that's true. So I went for accounting.

Armando's account illustrates one of many, often unofficial ways in which homosexuals were dissuaded from seeking certain lines of employment. Specifically, he was steered away from a field where his visibility or obvious homosexuality was seen as a problem because of its potential impact on youth; thus, he resigned himself to a profession where visibility mattered less, accounting. While the logic of this restriction was clearly strengthened by the Congress's declarations and the labor law that followed, in Armando's case—perhaps because of his father's connections—he was not formally restricted and thus avoided a more public outing and humiliation. By his account, he was treated "nicely," a benefit not extended to everyone.

The Cuban state's efforts might have been geared toward making homosexuality invisible by eradicating homosexuals from the public sphere, but state labeling and control strategies actually increased the visibility of male homosexuality as it promoted its constitutive other, the revolutionary, virile, masculine New Man.[32] José Quiroga captures the irony of the Cuban state's focus on the visibility of male homosexuality:

> The revolution itself rendered the issue of homosexuality *visible* in the first place—visible in the sense of its being transparent to the society as a whole. As early as 1962 . . . the Cuban Revolution already indexed homosexuality as a condition that needed to be extirpated in order to fulfill an economic and political program that in turn became affixed to the nationalist ideology.[33]

Specifically, the Cuban state designated an already stigmatized form of male homosexuality as outside revolutionary culture. The revolutionary state identified specific manifestations of homosexuality as problematic: visible manifestations of effeminacy and transgressions of accepted masculinity. For homosexual Cuban men who experienced this period of the revolution, visibility was political, whether they liked it or not. And, as Reinaldo Arenas explains, Cuban homosexuals countered state repression with defiant acts of homosexual visibility:

> There was another powerful homosexual scene in Havana, underground but very visible. . . . I think that in Cuba there was never more fucking going on than in those years, the decade of the sixties, which was precisely when all the new laws against homosexuals came into being, when the persecutions started and concentration camps were opened, when the sexual act became taboo while the "new man" was being proclaimed and masculinity exalted. . . . I think that the sexual revolution in Cuba actually came about as a result of the existing sexual repression. Perhaps as a protest against the regime, homosexuality began to flourish with ever-increasing defiance. . . . I honestly believe that the concentration camps for homosexuals, and the police officers disguised as willing young men to entrap and arrest homosexuals, actually resulted in the promotion of homosexual activities.[34]

As Arenas describes, the identification of male gender transgression as a threat to the communist state and the heightened persecution of those thought to transgress the boundaries of acceptable gender behavior were accompanied by defiant homosexual cultures. These defiant acts of visibility were pesky reminders to the state that its attempts to remove homosexuals from the public sphere (by sending them to UMAPs, incarcerating them, and discriminating against them) were ultimately unsuccessful. The Mariel boatlift would provide yet another opportunity for the Cuban state to eliminate the gender-transgressive homosexuality that continued to exist despite clearly articulated policies against it. By encouraging and/or permitting gender-transgressive homosexuals to leave the country during the boatlift, the Cuban state would try to export the defiant cultures of gay visibility that continued to trouble its virile self-image.[35]

Cuban Americans and Gay Rights: The Anita Bryant Campaign and Its Aftermath

It is ironic that while homosexuals in Cuba were targeted because of their presumed association with capitalism, homosexuals in postwar America had been targeted because of their presumed association with communism. The post–World War II period in the United States brought with it a chilling conservative climate in which anticommunism became increasingly linked with homophobia.[36] During the McCarthy era, as homosexuals became targets of the House Un-American Activities Committee, gay and lesbian activists responded with a "plea for tolerance" from mainstream society.[37] By the 1970s, however, young lesbian and gay activists had broken with their predecessors, whom they saw as accommodationists, and had begun to promote a more militant and defiant political strategy.

A central component of this new political strategy was the belief that group visibility was the foundation for political struggle. Dennis Altman argues that "between 1969 and 1980 the basic strategy of the movement [was] one of coming out, asserting homosexual visibility as a basis for demanding certain basic rights."[38] John D'Emilio explains further that this generation of activists understood coming out as "the first essential step toward freedom": he indicates, "they acted on their beliefs by being as visible as they could in every sphere of life."[39] Thus, during the same period that the Cuban state was repressing visible expressions of male homosexuality, homosexual men and women in the United States were making themselves increasingly visible in order to assert political claims about their rights.

With the increased visibility of gay men and lesbians during the 1970s, gay political goals, especially the passage of antidiscrimination legislation and ordinances, were slowly becoming reality.[40] Although cities like New York and San Francisco were at the center of gay and lesbian activism, South Florida gays and lesbians could also claim some political victories, including successful legal challenges of local and state laws used to persecute homosexuals.[41] In January 1977, local gay activists achieved their most significant political achievement to date. Under the leadership of Jack Campbell, Bob Kunst, and Robert Basker (who had recently been expelled from Cuba after trying to organize Cuban gays and lesbians during a trip to visit his children), the Dade County Coalition for the Humanistic Rights of Gays convinced the Dade County Commission to amend the county's existing human rights statute to include "affectional and sexual preference."[42] After its introduction by Commissioner Ruth Shack, the commission voted 5–3 to pass the amendment to ban discrimination against gay men and lesbians "in the areas of housing, public accommodations, and employment."[43]

One of Commissioner Shack's former supporters, Anita Bryant, attended the public hearing on the proposed amendment. Bryant, a South Florida resident, was a popular Christian entertainer who served as the national spokesperson for the Florida Citrus Commission and was represented by Shack's husband, a booking agent. At the hearing of what they considered an appalling amendment, Bryant and her husband, the former disc jockey Bob Green, reportedly met Bob Brake, another conservative moral reformer who had previously tried to ban local theaters from screening *Woodstock*.[44] After sharing their outrage about the proposed amendment, they founded the organization, Save Our Children Inc. (SOC), which mounted an emotional campaign to collect signatures in support of their efforts to repeal the gay antidiscrimination ordinance.[45] SOC's successful petition drive forced the commission to choose between repealing the amendment they had just passed or letting the issue be decided by referendum. On March 14, 1977, the commission voted to allow a referendum on the amendment. This meant that the issue of gay rights would be decided by a countywide public vote.

In the widely publicized media debate that followed, SOC appealed to public sentiment in order to challenge the gay rights amendment. SOC argued that "homosexuals who keep their sexual activity in the privacy of their homes face NO discrimination or recrimination from society"; consequently, they did not need legal protection.[46] Rather than being victims of discrimination, SOC argued, homosexuals posed a threat to society. While gay activists asserted their civil rights to equal opportunity, SOC interpreted this public assertion of homosexuals' rights as a threat to American families and children. An SOC-sponsored advertisement labeled the antidiscrimination ordinance an "INVITATION TO RECRUIT OUR CHILDREN." They argued that "the recruitment of our children is absolutely necessary for the survival and growth of homosexuality—for since homosexuals cannot reproduce, they must recruit, must refreshen their ranks."[47] The association of homosexuality with child molestation, "recruitment," and other threats was repeated time and again in SOC newspaper advertisements and reiterated in newspaper articles on the SOC campaign. This scare tactic proved highly effective in mobilizing voters.

SOC also distinguished between overt and covert homosexuals, identifying the most visible as the biggest threat. Altman argues that the "effectiveness of [the visibility/coming-out] strategy was demonstrated by the fact that it was precisely the open declaration of homosexuality that was most opposed by homophobes . . . who sought to link it with a threat to children."[48] Indeed, when Bryant discussed SOC's antigay campaign, she associated the threat of homosexuality with identifiable out-homosexuals. Questioned on the issue, she explained: "Well, if the person's in the closet, and they're not flaunting their homosexuality in front of my children, then there's no threat that I can see."[49] Asked further about a case of a veteran lesbian teacher who lived in fear of being discovered, Bryant responded with ostensible sympathy:

> A lot of people like myself might not have been aware of these nice, intelligent, warm, articulate individuals who didn't want to tell me their sexual preference or flaunt it on my children. They were happy to live their own lives and I was happy to let them.
>
> But with this ordinance, you are dealing with a totally different kind of individual. They're militant, they have used their sexual preference to become a political bloc, and they're not satisfied with staying in their own backyard.[50]

Presenting a unified message, Bryant and SOC claimed a sympathetic tolerance of homosexuals who were discreetly in the closet while identifying gay visibility or "flaunting" as the gravest threat to American children and families.

In contrast to SOC's apparently unified front, gay rights activists ended up fighting for the antidiscrimination ordinance (and against repeal) under a divided umbrella. The organization that originally lobbied for the amendment, the Dade County Coalition for the Humanistic Rights of Gays, had emerged out of a July 1976 coalition-building meeting of representatives from different local gay organizations held at Campbell's house on Basker's recommendation.[51] The nondiscrimination ordinance was the first major goal of this "loose coalition" of eleven South Florida groups.[52]

Attempting to broaden its appeal, the organization that spearheaded the amendment changed its name to the Dade County Coalition for Human Rights (DCCHR) "in a move designed to enlist more support for the gay community."[53] As the campaign took on national significance, the coalition's insufficient funding became apparent. In response, wealthy national gay leader David Goodstein stepped in, providing financial support, bringing in professional political consultants (like Ethan Geto), and helping set the tone of the campaign.[54] Leonard Matlovich, who had recently become a Miami resident and whose well-publicized challenge to the military ban on homosexuals led to his dismissal from the air force in 1975, was named campaign spokesperson. In contrast to Basker's background in community organizing and gay liberation, Goodstein and Geto hoped to be part of a "gay rights era" that favored a professional political strategy and distanced itself from direct action and grassroots political organizing.[55]

In South Florida, Geto produced a "professionally directed media campaign" that emphasized human rights issues by drawing on images of the "endangered American constitution" and arguing that the erosion of rights for gay men and lesbians would lead to the erosion of rights for other minority groups, especially Jews and blacks.[56] The DCCHR's "high-toned" appeal to human rights backfired, as local newspapers took to referring to its professional consultants as "imported talent."[57] As a consequence, the DCCHR's efforts were not nearly as effective as the emotionally charged campaign waged by SOC, portrayed in the media as a community-based organization despite its extensive national network.

In addition to accusations that the coalition was run by outsiders, dissent also predominated among local gays and lesbians. For one thing, the coalition was primarily male and primarily Anglo. As the gendered attacks on Bryant became more intense—she was referred to as a "bitch," "whore," and so on—feminists and lesbians became increasingly uncomfortable with the campaign's misogynistic tone.[58] Discussing the group's gender and racial composition at the weekly coalition meetings held at the upscale Candlelight Club (owned by coalition member Bob Stickney), Jesse Monteagudo added that "most of the participants were men—a state of affairs that would continue to hold true throughout the organization's history; there were no blacks, and only a handful of Latinos."[59] As I show, these racial/ethnic tensions would continue to plague the coalition and the battle for gay rights in Miami.

Perhaps sensing defeat, perhaps seeking the media limelight, Kunst, the most controversial and provocative of the gay rights leaders, left the coalition to found the Miami Victory Campaign along with the bisexual psychologist Alan Rockway.[60] The coalition announced the split in a letter to supporters, "Unfortunately, Mr. Kunst cannot agree to operate under the banner of the coalition and is not a representative of our organization. Also, he does not represent the overwhelming majority of the gay community here in Miami."[61] Described in a *Miami Herald* article as "the most visible of Miami homosexuals," Kunst deliberately courted both local and national media. Although other gay rights supporters saw him as a "loudmouth maverick, a headline grabber, 'an embarrassment,'" Kunst and the Miami Victory Campaign engaged in fund-raising activities and campaigned hard for the antidiscrimination ordinance.[62]

While the Coalition and Miami Victory Campaign pursued their divergent strategies, a lesser-known organization, Latinos pro Derechos Humanos or Latins for Human Rights, emerged in the fight against Bryant and SOC.[63] Allied with the coalition, this group of gay and lesbian Latino activists struggled for their place within the gay rights struggle. As I discuss below, the work of this organization and the challenges it faced complicate the conventional wisdom about Cuban American participation in the gay rights issue.

Despite the effort of these diverse gay rights groups, on June 7, 1977, the Human Rights Ordinance was repealed by referendum. The vote was not close: 70 percent, or 202,319 voters, favored the repeal of the antidiscrimination measure.[64] The high voter turnout for a special election (45 percent of registered voters participated) suggests the effectiveness of SOC rhetoric.[65] Moreover, with extensive media coverage, a national audience watched as Dade County became the first major metropolitan area in the United States to overturn an antidiscrimination gay rights statute, but where did Miami Cubans stand on this very public debate about visibility, sexuality, and family values?

Conventional Wisdom: Cuban Support for Bryant

In the late 1970s Cubans were becoming a major presence in South Florida. Not yet the dominant economic and political force they would soon become, their increasing numbers and their growing awareness that their migration to the United States was not temporary contributed to their importance. In recognition of that fact, Bryant and the SOC actively courted the Latino/Cuban American vote. The SOC produced pamphlets in Spanish quoting José Martí, the hero of the Cuban war for independence from Spain ("Children are the hope of the future"), and they put together a "Latin delegation" who could speak with Spanish-language media. Moreover, Bryant held a rally with Cuban Americans in the Little Havana Community Center, during which she made introductory remarks in Spanish and geared her comments toward the Cuban audience.[66]

Diverse reports from the late 1970s suggest that this lobbying was successful and Cuban Americans strongly supported Bryant. The scholar–activist Martin Duberman, for example, claimed that she was "heavily supported" by "the Cuban community."[67] In a televised news report, Walter Cronkite asserted that the strongest support for repeal came from Cuban voters.[68] In her own political/religious testimonial, Bryant acknowledged the "overwhelming support we received from the Latin community" and stated that the gay rights "issue became a unifying force for Latin and Anglo church groups in Miami."[69] Thus gay rights activists, the mainstream media, and Bryant herself seemed to agree on one thing: Cuban Americans were pro-Bryant.

Most scholars have reiterated this assessment. For example, writing in the mid-1980s, B. Ruby Rich and Lourdes Argüelles argued that the Bryant initiative inspired Cuban Americans to participate more actively in the U.S. political process than they had in the past.

> During the 1960s and early 1970s, Cubans had shown little interest in social issues that originated outside the enclave; this time, however, Cubans responded feverishly in favor of the Bryant initiative. Community leaders organized demonstrations and registered new Cuban voters. C., a social worker, suggests reasons for the massive Cuban mobilization: "They were seeing their kids getting lost in all the 'depravity.' They felt this was a way to stop it, to stop change."[70]

Although Rich and Argüelles's article is about gay and lesbian Cuban Americans, they characterized Cuban Americans in general as "feverishly" supporting Bryant and opposing gay rights.[71]

Newspaper reports also seem to indicate that Cubans supported repeal. Coverage in the *Miami Herald* mostly confirms the predicted pattern: Jewish voters were more likely to vote for the amendment; black voters were least likely to come out to vote either way; and Cuban voters were more likely to vote for repeal. On the day after the election, the *Herald* reported that the "greatest repeal margins appeared to come from heavily Cuban and single-family home, middle-class neighborhoods."[72] An analysis of selected precincts published the same day further confirms this analysis. Of selected precincts, Little Havana, the emerging center of the Cuban American enclave, had the largest percentage of voters (85.8 percent) supporting repeal. The *Herald* also added that 887 of the total 1,460 registered voters in the precinct were "Latins."[73] In a more detailed analysis a few days later, the *Herald* added that "in a few spots in Hialeah the percentage soared past 90 as 'rednecks' and Cubans found an issue on which they could join forces."[74]

Although *Herald* polls generally support the consensus that Cubans were homophobic and supported Bryant, there is also more ambivalent evidence. Whereas Rich and Argüelles argue that Cubans were inspired to vote by this domestic issue, reporters at the time commented on the low level of voter participation at the Little Havana precinct.[75] Only 43 percent of registered voters participated in the special election compared with the 73.5 percent who voted in the November general election: "Election officials attributed lower turnout to low interest among Latins in local, as opposed to national, elections."[76] Also interesting is the apparent ethnic identity of interviewed voters who self-identified as gay/homosexual. In the extensive coverage of the election in the *Miami Herald,* many voters were asked why they voted for or against repeal. Only three people are quoted as stating that they supported the ordinance because they themselves were gay/homosexual. Of these all are men, and the two identified by name both have Spanish surnames and were interviewed at precincts with substantial Hispanic populations. For example, Jose Espino of North Hialeah stated that he was a homosexual and added: "I don't think that any minority group should be singled out for any sort of discrimination."[77]

Whereas evidence that Cubans supported Bryant is reinforced by conventional wisdom about the conservativeness of Cubans in Miami, these attitudes about the Cuban community actually predate the election (as I show below). There is also some evidence, even in superficial newspaper coverage, that Latinos/Hispanics were part of an out-homosexual voting public that openly supported the ordinance.

Challenging Conventional Wisdom: Latino Gay Activists

While it is clear that SOC did get significant support from many Cuban Americans in Miami, Cubans were also an important component of the emerging gay community in South Florida and were among the activists who struggled for gay rights before, during, and after the 1977 battle. The struggles of these Latino pioneers and the short life of Latins for Human Rights (LHR) points to the difficulties Latino gay men and lesbians faced with regard to both the mainstream Cuban American community and the gay community.

Latinos were active participants in the growing South Florida gay scene. Lamenting the absence of a politically active Cuban gay community, the chairperson of LHR, Monteagudo, nevertheless described immersing himself in a "Cuban gay male scene" in the early 1970s with frequent visits to "bars, beaches, and *posadas* (pay-by-the-hour motels)."[78] Already gay clubs catered to a Latino clientele, including Club Miami, described by Monteagudo as "particularly popular among youthful Latinos and their Anglo admirers."[79] The centrality of gender transgressions in the Cuban American neighborhood of Little Havana in Southwest Miami was clear even to an ambivalent Monteagudo:

> I was able to enjoy many of the pleasures Little Habana's gay demimonde had to offer. From other gay Cubans I learned how to dress (bell bottom pants and platform shoes were then the rage—I almost fell off one of those shoes!), to stay up late, to hold my liquor, to cruise, and deal with rejection (nonchalantly). I even "learned" to camp it up, adopt an effeminate pose, and to refer to myself and others as "she"—though this was something I never cared for. There were probably more drag queens per square foot in Little Habana than anywhere in South Florida![80]

As described by Monteagudo, this scene had the shared fashions, values, and languages of an easily identifiable gay community (even if that community was not necessarily out by U.S. standards). While Monteagudo's account reveals the presence of an elaborate Cuban gay male culture in Miami, his point is to highlight its political apathy. As he wrote for the gay newspaper *TWN,* "Latin involvement in the gay scene is limited to bars."[81] For Monteagudo, the Little Havana *locas* who camped it up and referred to themselves as "she" were not the face of a political future.

While frustration with the lack of political response by Cuban homosexuals and lesbians during the Bryant campaign is certainly understandable, the activities of both drag queens and men who embraced an effeminate swagger in daily life can also be analyzed within the broader racial dynamic of the gay South. James T. Sears argues that during the mid-1970s, in the South as opposed to the North, the heroes "were not gay liberationists with queer placards and clenched fists but heroines adorned with rouge and rhinestones. Southern drag queens did more than imitate Vivien Leigh; they stood resolute against the ravaging of their homosexual Taras."[82] The place of gender transgression for men of color was even more important. "Although a few gay men of color . . . were involved in political activities during this era," Sears argues that "nonwhites were generally absent from southern corridors of gay power. In the South the only gay province for the 'talented tenth' of men of color was female impersonation."[83]

Among the few men of color who did walk through the corridors of gay power were Monteagudo and his mentor, Alexias Ramón Muni.[84] Described by Sears as a "dark, husky, bearded Cuban émigré," Muni attended the first meeting at Campbell's house where the coalition was formed.[85] As the battle between gay rights activists and Bryant's SOC campaign began to heat up, Muni also participated in forming LHR, along with Monteagudo, Manolo Gómez, Victor López, Lidia Martínez, and Ovidio Heriberto "Herbie" Ramos.[86] Robert Roth, publisher of a gay rights newsletter, commented that the formation of this group was "one of the most important and far-reaching developments of the whole Florida campaign."[87]

During the short life of this organization, members were hard-hit by a series of tragedies whose ultimate causes still remain unclear. Ramos's suicide was the first in a string of incidents. Soon after LHR formed, representatives from the group, including Ramos, Monteagudo, Muni, and Gómez, appeared on Spanish-language radio to discuss the gay rights amendment.[88] According to Perry Deane Young, SOC's "Latin delegation" had agreed to appear only if the "homosexuals repented their 'sins' and agreed to seek treatment."[89] When LHR members refused these conditions, SOC sent a recording to be used on the show. Because both sides of the debate were not represented in the studio, the moderator did not allow LHR to respond to calls. Monteagudo said LHR members were "shocked by the hatred spewed by callers, which was extreme even by Miami Spanish talk show standards."[90] Ramos, who was described as "very effeminate" and "campy," was struggling with his own family's rejection of his homosexuality and seemed especially troubled by the calls from Cuban Americans attacking them.[91] He reportedly told his best friend, "I didn't know they hated us so much."[92] The day after the radio show, Ramos unsuccessfully attempted suicide. The following day, March 16, 1977, he succeeded by shooting himself in the head.

Ramos's suicide became a symbol of the costs of hateful homophobia in the gay community. Writing at the time, Monteagudo explained:

> On the 16th our Brother Ovidio Ramos (also my best friend) committed suicide, as a result of many causes, including the problem of coping with his homosexuality. The Coalition and the Latinos used this as a campaign issue (all's fair in love and war).[93]

Ramos's tragic suicide became an opportunity to increase the visibility of gay Latinos, to highlight the types of oppression faced by gay men and lesbians, and to provide a vivid example of the consequences of oppression. In the hands of LHR spokesperson Gómez, an "openly gay journalist working on *Cosmopolitan*'s Spanish edition and a 'public relations whiz,'" Ramos became a "gay legend."[94] Monteagudo explained:

> Manolo [Gómez] saw [Ramos's] death as an opportunity to launch a public relations campaign that would help our cause. Before the end of the week, "Ovidio" Ramos became a symbol of gay oppression. We told the world he was a budding activist who was hounded to his death by uncaring parents and by bigots who called the radio station to heap abuse on this sensitive young victim.[95]

The image of Ovidio Ramos took on a life of its own. Expressing apparent discomfort with the public relations use of his friend's death, Monteagudo later stated that the strategy was "unfair to the elder Ramoses, a kindly old couple who did the best to get along with their unruly son. . . . We made him out into a martyr for the gay cause, but he was always suicidal."[96]

Gómez, the "'most visible' spokesman for gay rights in the Latin community," ironically became the subject of a media debate that he was unable to spin.[97] His gay rights visibility and activism cost him his job: he was fired for circulating a gay rights petition.[98] He also became the object of attacks. After he held a press conference on March 22,

1977, on a local Spanish-language television station (Channel 23) to discuss the Human Rights Ordinance, his car was firebombed and completely destroyed.[99] In April, Gómez reported to police that he had been attacked in the hotel where he lived and had told friends that he was being followed.[100] In early May, Gómez was found unresponsive in his room. Gómez subsequently died, but the circumstances of his death remained mysterious. Members of the coalition described the incident as a fatal beating and called for an impartial investigation. Miami Beach police and the consulting medical examiner, however, found that Gómez's injuries were a result of convulsions caused by an overdose of barbiturates and tranquilizers.[101] Gómez, spokesperson for LHR and media whiz, was reduced to being described unceremoniously by the leading local newspaper as "Gomez, unemployed, lived in a second-floor room at the Collins Hotel."[102] By the end of the campaign, Gómez himself had become a symbol of the sensationalistic tactics it generated. When then *Herald* columnist Carl Hiaasen made reference to the incident in a summary article published on the eve of the election, Gómez's name, the name of the organization, and his ethnicity/nationality appeared nowhere in the story. Instead, Hiaasen used the story as an example of the gay coalition's media tactics, noting that "gay rights activists grimly told a network television audience that a fellow homosexual was 'savagely' beaten into a coma by anti-gay vigilantes when, according to the police and hospital reports, the victim took an overdose of drugs and fell down."[103]

Such negative attention, if short-lived, during the campaign, however, did compel the coalition to recognize gay Latinos. Discussing Ramos's suicide and the firebombing of Gómez's car, Monteagudo wrote that although the "Gay Coalition [was] giving us only half-hearted support . . . with the Latinos getting the headlines, the Coalition could no longer treat us as poor relations."[104] Therefore, although LHR initially faced a tepid reception from the mainstream gay group, the coalition did eventually agree to Latino representation within the organization.

This representation came with a price—an agreement to stop lobbying in Latino communities. Among the coalition, there was disagreement about this strategy. A founding member and an original backer of the antidiscrimination amendment, Basker argued that African Americans and Latinos should be lobbied. By this time, however, Basker had been demoted by Geto and held only a token position within the coalition's hierarchy. Geto and Campbell did not agree with Basker. Geto was so convinced that Cubans opposed gay rights that on the day of the election he was quoted in the *Miami Herald* predicting, "a majority of Cubans will be against us."[105] In exchange for its agreement to cease lobbying Cuban Americans, the coalition offered LHR a seat on the executive committee for Muni and agreed to include Monteagudo in strategy meetings.[106] Monteagudo explained the logic behind this decision to Sears:

> All these politicos, like Ethan Getto, decided that they would write off the Latin community because it was too conservative. "They are going to vote against us anyway, so we better let sleeping dogs lie."
>
>   Getto suggested that we would do a good service to the cause by *not* holding meetings or getting volunteers to work with the Coalition. . . . Of course, while we ignored the Latin community, the other side was encouraging Latins to come out and vote—and they did! While most Latinos would have voted against us in any case, we wouldn't have cost the Coalition any votes had we been in there fighting. We might have gotten more people to come out.[107]

Barry Adam confirms that the gay rights coalition did not make an effort to win the Cuban vote. They "eschew[ed] door-to-door canvassing and ignor[ed] Miami's large Cuban and black communities."[108] Edmund White's conversations with Miami gays also corroborate this stance:

> One Cuban who worked for the gay coalition told me that he felt gay leaders had made a mistake to ignore the Spanish-speaking population. "Out of state consultants from New York and San Francisco had decided in advance that Cubans don't vote and are best forgotten. . . . We were not permitted to phone people with Spanish surnames. The result was that gays lost 93 percent of the Cuban vote."[109]

In a letter to Roth written during the campaign, Monteagudo also expressed his apprehension about this arrangement, but explained LHR's inability to challenge the decision.

> They are treating us lightly—either ignoring us or taking us for granted (Blacks and Lesbians are accorded the same treatment). In my opinion there is discrimination involved, although they deny it. They mention the fact that our group is listed on their new letterhead, as if symbolic courtesies could take the place of more substantial concessions. Then last night (at our weekly meeting) we met with our Campaign Director, Ethan Gaeto . . . who told us that, considering the Homophobia prevalent in the

> Latin Community, the Coalition would not campaign there, fearing a re-
> action. Not wishing to show disunity, and having no money, we agreed.[110]

Muni and Monteagudo continued to work with the coalition, but LHR's "activities [were] restricted to the Latin gay population, running rap sessions, offering services, and sponsoring a group trip."[111] These low-visibility activities were designed so as not to provoke heterosexual Cuban Americans who were assumed to be irrevocably homophobic.

The Anita Effect

By the end of June 1977, Bryant and SOC had successfully won re-peal of the referendum, while local gay rights activists had suffered a staggering loss. However, the loss of this battle was not the end of the gay rights struggle. Rather, it marked the beginning of a new phase that led to increased visibility and politicization of gay men and les-bians around the country. Tina Fetner has argued that the Save Our Children campaign had some positive effects on national gay social movements: namely, increasing national visibility of gay rights issues, providing a concrete example of discrimination faced by gay people (in terms of SOC's homophobic rhetoric), and "personify[ing] the homo-phobic sentiment of the nation."[112] This assessment reflected feelings in South Florida. During the campaign, local gay rights activists had insisted that "Anita Bryant was the best thing that ever happened to the gay rights movement."[113] One coalition participant agreed that "it was a loss that did us a lot of good. . . . We got united, and since then we've advanced a lot."[114]

Despite these unintended positive effects, on a local level the Bryant campaign painfully revealed the vulnerability of gay Latinos in South Florida. By June, LHR had disbanded, as members left the area or joined other local groups. By March 1978, a discouraged Monteagudo pronounced that "Latins for Human Rights are, to all intents and pur-poses, dead and buried. Cuban-American Gays and Lesbians are para-lyzed by apathy, by fear, and by the right-wing reactionary thinking that permeates Cuban-American culture."[115]

In the end, Monteagudo's pessimistic assessment reinforced conven-tional wisdom about Cuban Americans, the assumption that Cuban American culture is homogeneously homophobic and socially conserva-tive. The account presented here, however, illustrates the varied ways in which this homophobia was contested by Cuban American gays and lesbians, including by Monteagudo himself. Cuban Americans and Latinos may have been voting and demonstrating in support of Bryant, but they were also organizing in support of gay rights and suffering the consequences of those brave actions. The story of Latino participation in the 1977 campaign indicates the double bind faced by Latinos who actively chose to identify as gay. Gay Latino activists not only endured a range of abuse from verbal attacks to physical attacks: they also weathered a tepid response from their gay and lesbian brothers and sisters in the coalition. As second-class coalition members, they were treated as tokens and denied a voice in strategic planning even when it came to issues of special importance to them like the decision to campaign in predominantly Cuban neighborhoods.

If it is true that Bryant and Save Our Children owed their success to Cuban American support, it is also true that there was a flourishing Cuban gay scene in South Florida. Even allowing for hyperbole, Monteagudo's comment that Little Havana had the highest drag-queen-per-square-foot ratio suggests that gender transgressions were a visible part of everyday life in the emerging Cuban American enclave. While many—including Monteagudo himself—did not understand this visibility as political, I argue in the pages that follow that those who participated in everyday gender-transgressive practices were engaging in their own kind of politics.

Gay Visibility: A Transnational Analysis

During the 1960s and 1970s, in Cuba and the United States, gay male visibility was at the center of debates about sexual politics. These debates were not just about gender and sexuality but also about community and national identity. While homophobic campaigns against visible gayness were mounted in defense of both the Cuban Revolution and ostensibly threatened U.S. children, homosexual men also engaged in politics of visibility. In Cuba, in defiance of harsh policing and explicit discrimination, *locas* continued to wear their hair a bit too long, risk imprisonment for choosing a too-brightly colored shirt, and test the waters by slipping into gay vernacular with a stranger. In the United States, Latino gays and lesbians who participated in more formal politics achieved another kind of visibility, one based on being out and struggling for group rights in the formal political sphere.

These emerging activists were marginalized both by mainstream Cuban Americans and by predominantly Anglo gay activists. Like their Cuban *loca* counterparts, Cuban American queens also staked out their territory in Cuban American neighborhoods and participated in emerging gay scenes in and outside the enclave.

In 1980, these visibility politics collided, as homosexual men who had lived through the severest period of Cuban antigay enforcement migrated en masse to South Florida. Precisely because gender transgressions had been the object of state surveillance and control, some gay Cubans departed their homeland in search of freedom and a place to be visibly gay without political repercussions. Unknown to many of these homosexual migrants, they were entering a community that only a few years prior had witnessed a media frenzy over gay rights that culminated in a major political defeat and political backlash against gay visibility. The South Florida gay rights struggle had several consequences. Some have argued that the defeat encouraged many in the gay community to come out in order to challenge bigotry and repression. However, the blow of the defeat was swift and powerful for Latins for Human Rights, the budding Latino gay group of political activists. As the potential organizational basis for Latino gay politics disintegrated, the association between Cuban Americans and conservative homophobia was further reinforced—an association that many heterosexual Cuban Americans were proud to embrace.

2 OBVIOUS GAYS AND THE STATE GAZE

Gay Visibility and Immigration Policy
during the Mariel Boatlift

Armando's Story

On the day Armando went to the police station to ask for permission
to leave Cuba, he wore the gayest outfit he could find. Having been
dissuaded from being a teacher because he was so "obvious," Armando
had experienced firsthand how a visible gay man's life might be limited
in Cuba. Although spared the more intense forms of repression faced
by others of his generation, Armando was determined to see if the
tumultuous events in Cuba during the summer of 1980—events that
would come to be known as the Mariel boatlift—would really culmi-
nate in the promise of exile.

   During our interview almost twenty years later, he explained how
he had purposely picked out a flowery shirt and a little chain that fit
snugly around his neck ("una cadenita bien pegadita al cuello") for his
interview with the Cuban police officials who would decide whether
he should receive an exit permit. In the Cuba of 1980, such fashion
choices were seen as gender transgressive, so Armando hoped they
would confirm that he was a counterrevolutionary homosexual who
would, therefore, be permitted to leave the country. Before this day,
he had thought his homosexuality was obvious, but for this important interview with Cuban officials he did not rely on the everyday
visibility of his homosexuality: instead, he made sure to perform the
loca, the gender-transgressive effeminate homosexual man. Armando
successfully passed the test. The Cuban state identified him as socially
undesirable, *escoria* (scum), and homosexual, designations that facilitated his exit from the country. At age twenty-six, Armando crossed
the Florida Straits on a ship named the *Spirit of Ecstasy.*

Unfortunately, his ecstasy soon gave way to confusion and instability. Armando describes a chaotic scene in Florida. Mariel entrants were required to have a sponsor (either a family member or a volunteer) in order to be released from state custody. Although Armando did have an uncle who was willing to sponsor him, a miscommunication after Armando arrived in Florida prevented him from making contact with that uncle. Thus, like many Mariel entrants, Armando was taken to Fort Chaffee, Arkansas, one of several resettlement camps around the country. He spent two months there, but he tells me it felt like two centuries. He does not remember if camp officials asked him about his sexuality. On July 4, 1980, after successfully contacting his uncle, Armando left Fort Chaffee.

Armando's convincing performance of the ostentatious homosexual facilitated his exit from Cuba, but it was unclear how a similar performance might affect his entry into the United States. The clarity with which he recalls his exit interview with Cuban police contrasts sharply with his recollection of how or whether sexuality was considered during his processing by U.S. authorities. While the U.S. Immigration and Naturalization Service (INS) might have evidenced a certain lack of interest in this particular immigrant's sexuality, the historical record suggests that the agency was, in fact, quite concerned with matters of sex and sexuality in its broader handling of the boatlift. As this chapter demonstrates, the U.S. government—from national, state, and local politicians to INS officials to local law enforcement—demonstrated a strong but troubled interest in the sexuality of Cuban Mariel immigrants.

In this chapter I examine the state gaze in relation to male homosexuals on both sides of the Florida Straits. I use the term *gaze* to describe both the methods used by the state to identify sexual populations and to highlight how these identification systems intersected with state interests and desires.[1] The state's gaze relied on an assumption of readily identifiable gayness. In practical terms, the state's interest in homosexuality necessitated a mechanism by which the state could identify the gay population. As Armando's case makes clear, in Cuba this mechanism involved openly evaluating visible markers of homosexuality. In contrast, his vague account of his experience in the United States suggests that the state's long-standing interest in sexuality conflicted with the special treatment previously accorded Cuban refugees under Cold War immigration policies. This conflict required that U.S.

authorities develop a more selective gaze, sometimes seeing and sometimes refusing to see homosexual Mariel Cubans.

As I trace the migration process of homosexual Cuban men like Armando, I put the state gaze in national context. I analyze how both states defined homosexuals, the identification procedures used by both, and both states' vested interests in their own identificatory practices. In Cuba, the state facilitated the exit of visible homosexuals, a group already stigmatized by official discourses and state policies. In this case, state interests were served by clearly identifying homosexuals in order to expedite their departure. The U.S. federal government's role in processing and identifying homosexuals was much more complicated.

During the Cold War, relations between the United States and Cuba were tense, at best. Because of this political acrimony, Cubans seeking to enter the United States had been accorded preferential treatment for their symbolic value as a people fleeing communism. However, homosexuals had been formally and categorically excluded by U.S. immigration policy. Even as Armando and other gay-identified Mariel Cubans were traveling by boat to Florida, the United States was recodifying a long-standing immigration policy that explicitly excluded homosexuals.[2] Because of its massive scale, the Mariel migration also posed procedural challenges to any systematic identification of immigrant characteristics. Finally, given the national media attention focused on the boatlift, the identification of homosexuals posed a public relations dilemma for the U.S. government. I examine these complications by focusing on how homosexual Cuban men entering the United States were seen and not seen by the U.S. state gaze. During the boatlift, conflicting immigration policies and procedures clashed, as men who were both Cuban and visibly gay entered the country under the glare of the media spotlight.

Leaving Cuba

A week after a bus driver drove his busload of asylum seekers into the Peruvian embassy in Havana on March 28, 1980, Fidel Castro announced that anyone seeking asylum would be allowed to leave Cuba and withdrew the troops guarding the embassy. Two days after the announcement, over ten thousand Cubans had crowded into the embassy hoping to hold Castro to his word.

The first wave of emigrations from the Peruvian embassy consisted of air flights to Costa Rica followed by eventual resettlement in countries that had agreed to accept a predetermined number of immigrants, including Costa Rica, Peru, Spain, and the United States.³ After the international news media began to circulate images of the celebratory arrival of Cuban migrants to Costa Rica, Castro announced that Cubans could leave the country only by flying directly to their final destination, thereby lessening the spectacle of fleeing Cubans disembarking en masse. In 1980, a total of seventy-five hundred Cubans emigrated through these flights.⁴

This more orderly phase of emigration ended on April 20, when Castro announced that all Cubans wishing to leave the island would be allowed to depart—but only through the port of Mariel—and invited their Cuban American relatives to pick them up. What followed was a massive flotilla, and by October, 124,776 Cubans had arrived in the United States.

Tensions in Cuba escalated as more Cubans sought an opening to leave the country while others demonstrated against them. Under the circumstances, Castro needed to explain why so many Cubans wanted to emigrate. He responded with a discourse that disparaged hopeful emigrants and characterized those who wanted to leave as undesirables, antisocial elements, lumpen proletariat, and *escoria,* and he added that the United States was "performing a tremendous sanitary service" by accepting them.⁵ Cubans on the island who had not declared their desire to leave were encouraged to demonstrate against those who had by participating in *actos de repudio* (acts of repudiation) against the *escoria.* In the United States, the media picked up on this characterization of the migrants, and news reports repeatedly affirmed that Castro had emptied his prisons by sending criminals to the United States and that the migrants included members of other undesirable groups such as mental patients, prostitutes, and homosexuals. In addition, both the U.S. media and the South Florida Cuban American community began commenting on the demographic and cultural differences between the Mariel immigrants and previous groups of Cuban immigrants. The perceived racial and class difference of the so-called Marielitos added to their stigmatization and contrasted sharply with the historically preferential treatment of light-skinned immigrants to the United States, a special treatment accorded previous generations of anticommunist Cuban refugees. Racialization, class stigma, and sexual deviance were thus embedded in coverage of the Mariel migration, reinforcing the notion that these migrants were no loss to Cuba and posed a potential problem for the United States.[6]

As the Cuban government began sorting out those who wanted to leave on the boatlift, it developed a selective process to facilitate the exit of those already identified as undesirable. By prioritizing undesirables, Cuban officials hoped to eliminate problem populations. When Cuban Americans arrived in Cuba with empty boats hopeful that they would be reunited with family members, they were required to transport not only their relatives but also other people the Cuban government had approved for departure, among them homosexuals, criminals, and the mentally ill.

Once the bureaucratic process for requesting permission to leave Cuba began to develop, word spread that homosexuals would be allowed to leave the country. As discussed in chapter 1, prior to 1980, the Cuban state had targeted homosexual men, most of whom had suffered a range of consequences from limited career options to detention in reeducation camps. The state had especially targeted gender-transgressive, ostentatious, or obvious homosexuals. Once the boatlift phase of Mariel began, this state identification facilitated exit from the country: some Cuban homosexuals were even given the choice of serving jail time or leaving the country to encourage their departure.[7] Others, like Armando, were able to request permission to leave.[8] Drawing on interviews with 180 Mariel entrants, Margarita Garcia concluded that anyone "who went to the police station and declared him or herself to be a homosexual could get an exit permit."[9] She added that documentation of their antisocial status, such as proof of previous detention under the Law of Dangerousness, could further facilitate the process.[10] In a speech in May 1980, Castro denied that anyone was being forced to leave the country, but added that "we have the right to authorize the exit of the antisocial elements, and that is what we're doing."[11]

Accounts of gay men who went through this declaration process reveal the ways in which authorities evaluated and confirmed homosexuality to facilitate hasty exits. For example, in memoirs written shortly after the Mariel boatlift, Antonio L. Conchez describes how he and a childhood friend declared themselves homosexuals to Cuban police after he found out that homosexuals were being given permission to leave. After taking their statements, the police asked them to return the following day to pick up "official letters confirming that we were homosexuals, thieves, marijuana users, antisocials and counterrevolutionaries."[12] Conchez did not initially receive the letter because he was identified by the local Committee for the Defense of the Revolution (CDR) as being a good student and coming from a decent family. According to his account, he was ready for the challenge presented by his good social standing:

> I had gone prepared with an eye-catching outfit, my hair messed up and a little bit of make-up on my eyes and face. I also spoke in a fake voice, exaggerating my mannerisms so that they would be convinced that I was a homosexual, and then I talked to them and I pleaded with them to give me that letter. And God let it be so, and they gave me the letter where it said I was the scum of society, that I did not work or study, that I had been imprisoned, that I was not in favor of the revolutionary process and other additional horrors and slanders.[13]

Similarly, in *Antes que anochezca (Before Night Falls),* the author Reinaldo Arenas describes his exit interview. In his case, homosexuality marked him as undesirable and, therefore, a good candidate for an exit visa; however, because he had published his work outside Cuba he was banned from leaving the country. He therefore presented himself to authorities as a *loca* and made no reference to his literary contributions. He brought along his *carné de identidad* (identification card) where his previous charge for having caused a "public scandal" was reported. He explains the processing at a local police station:

> At the police station they asked me if I was a homosexual and I said yes; then they asked me if I was active or passive and I took the precaution of saying that I was passive. . . . The Cuban government did not look upon those who took the active male role as real homosexuals. There were also some women psychologists there. They made me walk in front of them to see if I was queer *(si era loca o no)*. I passed the test, and a lieutenant yelled to another officer, "Send this one directly." This meant that I did not have to go through any further police investigation.[14]

With his public scandal arrest and his *loca* strut for the psychologists, Arenas was certified as a visible homosexual and allowed to leave the country "como una loca más."[15]

Evidence indicates that many who did not consider themselves homosexuals claimed to be in order to leave the country. Arenas himself says that "people who were not even homosexual pretended to be gay in order to leave the country."[16] It is important to remember, however, that even those who had previously identified as homosexual also performed gayness in these exit interviews. When Armando picked out his flowery shirt, Conchez exaggerated his mannerisms, and Arenas strutted for the psychologists, they were deliberately performing the category of flamboyant, effeminate homosexual for state officials.

The category of homosexual was reinforced, constructed, and redefined in these interactions. All these accounts confirm that the officially recognized (and stigmatized) homosexual was a gender-transgressive male who took the passive sexual role and whose public behavior was ostentatious. As men who understood themselves to be homosexual performed this *loca* character, they reflected the official caricature of the homosexual back at the state that had heightened its stigmatization. There is a bit of condescension here, for the men exaggerated a stereotype that they knew did not encompass who they were or who homosexuals were in general. This consciously constructed performance was not a cheap joke, however, because the test had real consequences. If the men were convincing, authorities expedited their exit from the country. If they were not convincing, not only would they be refused an exit permit but would be marked as wanting to leave—a uncomfortably counterrevolutionary position given the acts of repudiation directed at the *escoria*. Their detailed accounts also suggest a bit of liberation in the performances, for these men exaggerated effeminate or ostentatious mannerisms precisely in front of those government officials from whom they would most likely have hidden under normal circumstances.

At this moment in Cuban history, state policy toward homosexuals, while still oppressive, was quite unambiguous. Homosexuals continued to be stigmatized and defined as alien to the Cuban national project. The most socially dangerous homosexual type was further crystallized as the effeminate, gender-transgressive, ostentatious, passive homosexual man. As these accounts illustrate, homosexual men understood the state's categorization scheme and aptly performed the expected role. In other words, because the state had persecuted visible homosexuals and because passive homosexuals were the most despised subgroup, men seeking permission to leave Cuba deliberately claimed the passive role and displayed the outward gender markers that proved ostentatious homosexuality to the police.

Thus the interests of the Cuban state and homosexuals wishing to leave Cuba coincided in unexpected ways. Between 1959 and 1980, emigration from Cuba was increasingly controlled, and expressing a desire to leave the country was viewed as a political betrayal. By 1980 though, the Cuban state embraced the opportunity to remove homosexuals from the island in order to enhance the virile image of the revolutionary nation and prevent possible future resistance from this stigmatized group. Cuba's neat binary between the masculine socialist man and the effeminate capitalist homosexual (and the state policies legitimated by this binary) had been troubled by the overlap between leftist supporters and gay/lesbian political activists outside the island. Cuban persecution of homosexuals, as witnessed by visiting U.S. leftists on the Venceremos Brigade, for example, was insulting to some gays, lesbians, and their allies.[17] The international Left split on this issue, and this split had weakened the support base of the revolution. Eliminating homosexuals from the population (through voluntary or semivoluntary departure) was an easy way to sidestep this dilemma.

The migration of a large number of homosexuals, a minority group also stigmatized in the United States, also helped explain the mass exodus in a way that was favorable to the revolution. According to the official Cuban discourse, the mass exodus did not prove the failure of the revolution. Rather, the hopeful emigrants were all undesirables, the lazy lumpen dregs of society consumed by the vices of capitalism (homosexuality, crime, prostitution, etc.). By including and drawing attention to groups widely stigmatized in the United States, the Cuban state was able to discredit the emigrants, support its own revolutionary image, and create future challenges for the immigrants.

In general, those factors that may have motivated emigration are not easy to disentangle.[18] Some Cuban homosexuals might have wanted to leave the island because of repression, while others might have been more motivated by economic concerns. Regardless of motivation, Mariel provided a brief opening for those who wished to emigrate. In contrast to previous Cuban state policies toward homosexuals, the identification of homosexuals during Mariel in effect provided a desired outcome (at least for those homosexuals who *wanted* to leave) as opposed to a repressive consequence.

Entering the United States

In the United States, the interests of the state and of homosexuals did not line up so neatly. Homosexual Cuban immigrants, ostentatious ones at that, presented three major complications for this receiving nation. The first complication was that homosexual Cuban Marielitos embodied many of the existing contradictions and ambiguities of U.S. immigration policies. On the one hand, since the rise of the Cold War, the United States had warmly received Cuban immigrants, using their desire to leave Cuba as proof of the failure of communism. On the other hand, the United States had a long-standing, albeit selectively enforced, ban against homosexual entrants. These two policies clashed on the bodies of gay Cubans.

Whereas in Cuba the state actively sought to identify homosexuals in order to expel them and homosexuals actively identified themselves to the state in order to facilitate their own expulsion, in the United States the purpose and the process of identification was inconsistent and often contradictory. The U.S. state had competing imperatives: to see and not to see the homosexual Cubans. How these conflicting policies would be put into practice posed the second complication. The identification of Cuban homosexuals was complicated by the fact that not all Mariel Cubans were processed in the same way. Rather, they were processed by federal, state, local, and voluntary agencies in different locations throughout the United States. These bureaucratic and jurisdictional differences inevitably led to disparate identification procedures.

A final complication resulted from the flood of national media attention that surrounded Mariel. The U.S. government was no less interested than Cuba in the public relations impact of the boatlift. For an international audience, the boatlift could confirm the failure of Cuban communism and the supremacy of U.S. capitalism: why else would so many desperate Cubans want to come to the United States? At home, the reinforcement of U.S. superiority also served to quiet growing uneasiness about a weak national economy. Given the economic situation and the upcoming presidential election, domestic perception of the Mariel immigrants was especially important. Would voters perceive them as valued immigrants who would contribute to the U.S. economy (as they had perceived the "golden exiles" who preceded Mariel), or would they perceive them as undesirable immigrants who threatened national well-being?

Immigration Policy Conflict: To Exclude or to Welcome?

Few Mariel Cubans were defined as either political refugees or asylees.[19] Instead, they were issued paroles, and a new category was created for them, namely, "Cuban–Haitian entrant (status pending)." This ambiguous status allowed them physical but not legal entrance into the country, and it became the foundation for the systematic denial of rights to Mariel Cubans.[20] Unlike previous Cuban immigrants who had been processed by the Cuban Refugee Program, this new wave became "the first sizeable group of Cuban immigrants to experience the Immigration and Naturalization Service's personnel and operations."[21] Therefore most Mariel Cubans encountered more difficult immigration procedures and policy hurdles than the post-1959 Cuban immigrants who preceded them.

Homosexual Mariel immigrants faced an additional hurdle because just as they were entering the United States, the INS was redefining its homosexual exclusion policy. As Eithne Luibhéid explains in *Entry Denied: Controlling Sexuality at the Border,* homosexuals had been formally excluded from entering the United States since the early 1950s. Beginning in 1952, people identified as homosexual had been issued Class A medical exclusions because they were classified as having "psychopathic personality."[22] Between 1965 and 1979, homosexuals were reclassified as "sexual deviates" and still subjected to Class A medical exclusions.[23] However, in 1979—six years after the American Psychological Association's 1973 decision to drop homosexuality as a mental illness—the surgeon general ordered the Public Health Service to stop issuing automatic Class A medical exclusions to homosexuals. This order denied the INS the bureaucratic identification mechanism that had facilitated homosexual exclusion.[24]

The INS had yet to resolve the situation when, between April and late September 1980, a sizable population of gay men and women—Armando among them—entered the United States from Cuba. It was not until September 1980, with the boatlift almost over, that the INS responded with a new policy on homosexual exclusion designed specifically to bypass the surgeon general's order. Given the timing of the decision, we can deduce that the INS felt the need to clarify its policy in order to deal with the sudden mass influx of immigrants and the increasing media questions about homosexual Cuban migrants. On September 8, acting INS commissioner David Crosland sent an agency memo announcing the new procedures, which no longer required medical certification from the Public Health Service. According to the new policy, "aliens" were not to be asked about their sexual preference during "primary inspection." However, if "an alien [made] an unsolicited, unambiguous oral or written admission of homosexuality" or if "a third party who presents himself or herself for inspection voluntarily states, without prompting or prior questioning, that an alien who arrived in the United States at the same time and is then being processed for admission is a homosexual," then a private, professionally administered "secondary inspection" of the alien would follow. Crosland's memo directed that, during this secondary inspection, the alien "shall be asked *only* whether he or she is homosexual. If the answer is 'no,' the alien shall not be detained for further examination as to homosexuality. If the answer is 'yes,' the alien shall be asked to sign a statement to that effect . . . [and] he or she shall be referred to an immigration judge for an exclusion proceeding."[25]

Gay rights activists, who had been struggling against the INS's broadly construed gay and lesbian exclusion policies, perceived this new policy as a partial victory. In fact, in a press release, the National Gay Task Force called this an "immigration victory for gays" because with the new policy, "gay aliens [would] no longer be subject to probing interrogation on their private sexual life by immigration authorities."[26] Under the new policy, people entering the United States were no longer to be singled out because of gay pride paraphernalia such as books and T-shirts, and it would be easier for gay men and lesbians to avoid identification by the state. Moreover, even if individuals did make a declaration of their homosexuality during primary inspection, they could simply answer that they were not gay in the secondary inspection and the INS would not detain them.

For Cuban men whose identification as homosexual had just facilitated their exit from Cuba, avoiding state identification in the United States might not have been an obvious strategy. Although national gay rights activists viewed the new INS procedures as an improvement over previous methods, the new policy did continue to exclude homosexuals who made an "unsolicited, unambiguous" statement to INS inspectors; thus these inspectors became the official new front line in homosexual identification. Nevertheless, while this new policy continued to allow the federal government to exclude homosexuals, it also provided room for plausible deniability that could be used to allow entrance of obvious homosexuals arriving from Cuba.

Even after the INS's ostensible clarification of its policy toward homosexual immigrants, the U.S. state confronted conflicting imperatives. On the one hand, identifying homosexuals would allow their exclusion—still a desired outcome from the department's point of view, as its new policy made clear. On the other hand, the possibility of excluding a large number of Cuban immigrants because of their sexuality posed a practical problem: What would the U.S. government do with a large group of excludable homosexuals who could not be returned to their home country?

Inconsistent Identification: The State Gaze in Practice

In addition to this policy dilemma, practical issues on the ground made the Mariel boatlift a logistical nightmare for the agencies charged with processing immigrants. As the scale of the migration became clear, entry procedures shifted to accommodate the challenges posed by the sudden entrance of tens of thousands of immigrants. In general, upon entry into the United States Mariel Cubans went through a few intense days of processing by federal agencies, local officials, and voluntary agencies. Although the location and intensity of procedures varied according to when a Mariel Cuban entered the country and whether she or he was sent to a resettlement camp, certain elements of processing were applied to the entire population. A description of the typical process for a Mariel entrant arriving in July 1980 (after one hundred thousand Cubans had already entered the United States) provides a sense of what these common procedures were like and reveals the intensity of the bureaucratic gaze to which all entrants were subjected regardless of their status.

Processing began when Mariel entrants arrived in Key West and were issued provisional I-94 cards. From there, they were sent to Krome North, an INS facility located on the southern outskirts of Dade County. At Krome North, they were welcomed by the facility's Cuban American director, Siro del Castillo, who conveyed "to the new arrivals that they [had] left a repressive country and entered a free one."[27] Mariel Cubans turned in their Cuban passports and I-94s to camp officials and received clothing and other provisions donated by the Red Cross. They were then divided into groups and assigned a tent. Families, single men, and unaccompanied minors were all housed separately.

The next day, they were bussed to the INS District Office where they filled out a DS 103 form and were fingerprinted, photographed, and interviewed by INS and FBI officials. INS officials conducted a biographical history using the G-325A form and administered an I-589 application for asylum for those who expressed a "well-founded fear of persecution if returned to Cuba."[28] After a separate interview, the FBI decided whether to issue a security clearance. If a Mariel Cuban received the FBI security clearance, she or he was issued a provisional parole with employment authorization valid for sixty days. (Extension of parole required another interview.) They were then interviewed by the voluntary agencies (VOLAGs) charged with facilitating their placement with family or volunteer sponsors and issued a VOLAG registration card. Finally, they were bussed back to Krome North.

The next day Mariel immigrants were bussed to the Public Health Service (PHS) where their medical histories were taken. In addition they were checked for venereal disease, x-rayed for tuberculosis, and given any necessary vaccinations. Information about active and inactive cases of venereal disease and tuberculosis was sent to the Centers for Disease Control in Atlanta, Georgia. After health screenings, they were returned to Krome North where VOLAGs assisted in reunifying families, finding volunteer sponsors, or relocating Cubans outside Dade County. All Mariel Cubans needed a sponsor in order to be released from state custody. During the height of the boatlift, the South Florida VOLAGs had only seventy-two hours in which to identify local sponsors. If a sponsor was found within seventy-two hours, the Mariel entrant would be released after the sponsor signed a release form. However, if family sponsors had not been located after seventy-two hours (as was the case with Armando), the entrants were sent to resettlement camps outside Dade County where other VOLAGs would help them find sponsors.[29]

Most Mariel Cubans went through a basic process similar to the one described above during which authorities consistently identified personal characteristics of interest to the state. These included specific aspects of their medical condition, their fingerprints, their self-reporting of criminal history, and so on. In these first days of processing, the state gaze was refracted through several federal agencies including those concerned with immigration status (INS), law enforcement and security (FBI), and public health as well as several voluntary agencies charged with resettlement. While this initial processing was fairly consistent across the Mariel entrant population, processing from this point on varied dramatically, and the route a Mariel entrant followed to sponsorship had a significant impact on the subsequent intensity of the state's fractured gaze. After this initial common processing, Mariel Cubans followed one of three routes: (1) direct resettlement in South Florida for those with available sponsors; (2) review at Federal

Correctional Institutions (FCIs) for those suspected of having a criminal background; and (3) confinement at a resettlement camp for those without available sponsors. Those Mariel Cubans whose family sponsors were found within the seventy-two-hour window were held in custody for only a few days and never left South Florida. Others were held in state custody for months in processing camps scattered throughout the country, including Fort Chaffee, Arkansas; Fort Indiantown Gap, Pennsylvania; Fort McCoy, Wisconsin; and Fort Walton Beach, Florida. Homosexuals and nonhomosexuals followed all three routes. However, the precision and intensity of the U.S. state gaze in relation to homosexuality varied considerably depending on the route.

Route 1: South Florida Resettlements

The easiest route for entrants was to locate a family or unrelated volunteer sponsor quickly while they were still in the South Florida area. About half of the Mariel entrants were directly placed with such sponsors.[30] Those with family members willing to sponsor them and those who were attractive, nonthreatening candidates for volunteer sponsors were placed more quickly. Less attractive candidates (single men, black men, obvious homosexuals) were more likely to be sent to resettlement camps outside South Florida.

Given that about half of entering Mariel Cubans were resettled directly out of South Florida, it is likely that many Cuban gays and lesbians were resettled in this way. However, because this group was in state custody for the least amount of time, we have the least information about them. It appears that certain demographic characteristics influenced how quickly VOLAGs found a sponsor for Mariel Cubans. For example, race had a major impact on the likelihood of an entrant finding a sponsor. Only 8 to 10 percent of the Mariel immigrants processed in Miami were black, while approximately 50 percent of those processed through resettlement camps were black or mulatto.[31] Blacks made up 75 percent of those Cubans still awaiting sponsorship in Fort Chaffee after the consolidation of all resettlement camps in October 1980.[32] Gender and marital status also played a major role, with single males encountering more difficulties finding a sponsor than families and single females.[33] Although records are lacking, we can hypothesize that the highly gender-transgressive homosexual men within this group had an even harder time finding sponsors. Certainly, this was the case in the resettlement camps where voluntary agencies acknowledged their poor placement record for this population. Judging from the records of the Cuban–Haitian Task Force (CHTF), however, the sexuality of successful South Florida resettlement cases did not seem to have concerned the state. There is no evidence that U.S. officials formally identified, enumerated, or differently processed the homosexuals among this population.

Route 2: Federal Correctional Institutions

Mariel Cubans suspected of having a criminal background were sent to FCIs for further review. Homosexuals who had been arrested in Cuba for crimes related to their homosexuality and who verified as much during INS or FBI questioning would have been processed in this way. Because U.S. authorities were invested in identifying criminals in the Mariel entrant population and because certain expressions of homosexuality were criminalized in Cuba, this portion of the homosexual Mariel population did fall directly under the state's gaze.

Mariel Cubans who admitted to serving jail time in Cuba were issued a 2-C classification and were sent to an FCI for further investigation. Given the fact that admission of homosexuality to state officials had very recently facilitated exit from Cuba and the belief among some that the United States was less repressive of homosexuals, it is probable that many homosexual Mariel Cubans would not have hidden any previous homosexuality-related incarceration from INS officials. According to Krome North director del Castillo, a distinction was supposed to be made between Cubans who had committed a "blood crime" and those who had been incarcerated for acts not criminalized in the United States. Only those having committed serious crimes were to be held in the FCIs. However, del Castillo lamented that

> in practice, political prisoners, those who declared themselves to be prostitutes, deviants, or criminals to obtain permission to leave Cuba, and those who were "criminals" only by Cuba's standards, as well as others merely suspected of having a criminal background have been given 2-C classification and detained in the FCI.[34]

A review of information about the Mariel Cubans released from the FCI in Talladega, Alabama, suggests that homosexuals were a significant portion of the 2-C population.[35] A "fact sheet" explained the procedures that led to the August 1980 "release" of Mariel Cubans either directly to sponsors or to a resettlement camp. Before recommending release, INS deportation officers extensively interviewed detainees and prepared case files on them that were, in turn, reviewed by an INS attorney who also interviewed each detainee. This file was then reviewed by the INS Commissioner's Office in Washington and finally by Attorney General Benjamin Civiletti. Based on this review process, a total of 215 detainees were released because they had not committed a serious crime, had not committed a crime recently, had already served a sentence for their crime, or were not considered a threat to society.

To justify their decision to release the detainees, the fact sheet included a "sample profile of offenses committed in Cuba." Interestingly, two of the ten sample profiles involve arrests related to homosexuality.[36] While we do not know if this is a "representative sample"—in which case we could deduce that 20 percent of those sent to FCIs had been arrested in Cuba for some crime related to same-sex behavior or identity—this memo at least suggests that a significant number of homosexuals were identified as part of the "criminal element" and segregated upon initial screening.

The sample profiles include brief descriptions of the detainee to be released including age, date, and description of criminal offense. Although brief, the descriptions provide considerable insight into the state's concerns about homosexuality. First, authorities were clearly interested in identifying and not releasing pedophiles. Both references to the homosexual detainees attempt to clarify that they are not pedophiles. The first is identified as a thirty-four-year-old who had "1971 and 1978 convictions for homosexual acts, never with boys." The other was described as a thirty-one-year-old "practicing homosexual" with a 1975 "conviction for corrupting a minor": "police said it involved a 16 year old boy, he says no."[37] Second, all profiles include a brief reference to possible sponsors upon release. The thirty-four-year-old "has aunts and uncles in the U.S., who may support him" and the thirty-one-year-old "has a sister in New Jersey, who will help and support him." The presence of willing family sponsors reinforces the assessment that these Cubans would be accepted into society and would not become part of the population stranded in resettlement centers. Finally, the sample profiles and the description of the evaluation procedure confirm one way in which information related to the homosexuality of Mariel Cubans was recorded by the state. These three-line profiles include not only references to particular crimes but also to sexual identity ("practicing homosexual"), references that demonstrate that the state gaze, at various levels of evaluation, did identify homosexuals and was concerned with how homosexuality would affect their incorporation into U.S. society. This identification, however, was not criteria for attempting to exclude them.

Route 3: Resettlement Camps

Although information about the homosexuality of Cubans detained in FCIs was collected, this information was not necessarily public and did not capture the media's attention as did, for instance, criminals convicted of rape and murder. Homosexual Mariel Cubans who were sent to resettlement camps, on the other hand, did attract media attention. The CHTF was aware of media interest and carefully monitored newspaper articles in both national and local publications covering homosexual Mariel Cubans.[38] In the CHTF's final report, they reflected on the impact of this media attention:

> During the summer months, there was media coverage of the presence of homosexuals among the Cuban entrants. The self-segregation of these homosexuals in the resettlement centers gave them a high visibility which facilitated the media coverage.[39]

According to the CHTF, "widespread publicity" increased the difficulty of finding sponsors for the homosexual Mariel Cubans.[40] Federal officials also felt that the visibility of homosexuals contributed to the overall negative perception of the migration. By August 1980, a Harris poll found that 70 to 80 percent of American opinion on Cubans and Haitians was negative, and a Gallup poll reported that 75 percent of Americans believed the Cuban refugee situation was "bad for our country." Responding to these polls in a Department of State memo, CHTF director of public affairs Arthur P. Brill identified "reasons for negative public opinion," including "negative performances by Cubans":

> Last, but certainly not least, is the wide media attention given to the bad performers. The hijackers, rioters, criminals, malcontents, homosexuals, and prostitutes have received the limelight. . . . As a result, the malperformers are giving the impression to the American people that the entrants are not grateful.[41]

To challenge this negative impression, the federal government denied any systematic knowledge or identification of homosexual immigrants in the camps. However, because obvious homosexuality and gender transgression did impede resettlement, homosexuality had to be taken into account to facilitate the processing of homosexual Cubans. Therefore authorities simultaneously claimed to not see homosexuals in order to deny their presence to the media and actively sought to identify this population in order to move them out of the media spotlight.

The resettlement camp population became the primary focus of media debates about homosexual Mariel Cubans for several reasons. First, they were held in state custody for longer than those resettled directly from South Florida. Second, obvious gays or gender-transgressive male homosexuals were generally segregated or self-segregated within the camps and were therefore more visible to visitors and the press. Finally, obvious gays were more likely to be confined in the resettlement camps for longer periods of time than less visible homosexuals—and, in turn, more likely to be included in the categories difficult-to-place Cubans or "special cases."

That homosexuals were a recognized category within the resettlement population was not a secret to camp residents, camp officers, or the media. For example, a newsletter produced by camp residents and staff at Fort Chaffee contained two sections on health advice related to venereal disease and addressed to homosexual men ("compañero gay") and women ("amiga homosexual") at the camp.[42] Despite official denials, camp officials were clearly aware of the homosexual population. In a State Department memo in response to direct questions about the homosexual population, Senior Civilian Coordinator Donald Whitteaker described the presence of "two different types of homosexuals at Fort Chaffee, admitted and closet." According to Whitteaker, the homosexuals were "consenting adults and segregated by their design. Lifestyle is casual and open." Whitteaker also responded to concerns about unaccompanied minors by acknowledging that "there may be some young males or females 18 to 20 years of age that are victims of male and female homosexuals and prostitutes. However, as these are identified, action is taken to protect them by segregating them or moving them to a new area."[43] This detailed response indicates a high level of attention to the homosexual population on the part of government authorities despite official denials.

Before the gay Mariel story broke in the national media, local newspapers were asking camp workers about the presence of homosexuals as a distinct group within the camps. For example, one article from a newspaper from an area outside Fort Indiantown Gap camp published

an article on Cuban gays. The photograph illustrating this article featured four gender-transgressive men identified in the caption as "admitted Cuban homosexuals." Quoted officials openly discussed male
homosexuals at the camp, consistently referring to them as "the faggots." Justifying the need to segregate homosexuals in a separate area,
camp workers also discussed violence between homosexuals and nonhomosexuals. In reference to an incident in which a gay man defended
himself by knocking out another man with the lid of a garbage can, a
soldier explained: "They are faggots but they have man muscles."[44] In
addition to local newspapers, the gay press (including the *Sentinel*, the
Blade, and the *Advocate*) reported on the gay Mariel story.[45]

Editors and reporters from the national mainstream press also knew
about the gay population early on. In a *Columbia Journalism Review*
article, Michael Massing quotes editors and reporters from *Newsday*,

This photograph accompanied an article in *Lebanon Daily News/Sunday
Pennsylvanian* on July 6, 1980, on Cuban homosexuals at Fort Indiantown
Gap resettlement camp. I first came across this photograph in the Cuban
Haitian Task Force files in the Carter Presidential Library. Photograph cour-
tesy of *Lebanon Daily News.*

the *New York Times,* and the *Boston Globe* who were clearly aware of the gay presence among Mariel migrants, including the presence of segregated homosexual barracks in resettlement camps; some had observed same-sex couples walking hand in hand at the camps. Until July 7, 1980, however, the national mainstream media avoided the topic of gay men among the Mariel entrants, citing the "unavailability of reliable data" as the reason for this omission.[46] The theme of unreliable data would emerge again and again as state officials attempted to silence the gay Mariel story.

Homosexuality and Gender Transgression in Resettlement Camps: What Happens When José Is Wearing a Dress?

Although an overall demographic picture identifying the sexuality of Mariel Cubans was not available, public health, mental health, and medical professionals working with and for the state constructed their own version of reliable scientific data. These medical professionals identified the presence of homosexuals as a topic of interest and responded to state concerns about the population. Medical professionals were less concerned with the public relations implications of identifying particular populations. As they identified homosexuality as a potential social problem related to issues of public health, they turned their well-honed gaze on this captive population.[47]

For example, medical adviser Dr. Harold Ginzburg provided an assessment of Mariel Cubans that was subsequently summarized in a memo from Bill Schroeder to Nick Nichols. The physician, working with mental health services, constructed three categories of homosexuals. The first category included Cubans who claimed to be homosexual in order to leave Cuba and did not engage in homosexual activity in the camps. The second category, "situational homosexuals," were "heterosexuals, who, while imprisoned, practiced homosexuality, but once released, reverted once again to heterosexuality." The third category he labeled "gays." Gays were "naturally inclined to homosexuality," tended to "keep to themselves," and posed "no threat to society." Although not posing an active threat themselves, Ginzburg expressed concern that "gays" were often victims of violence. He was especially concerned with homosexual rape and explained that "in some instances this occurs because some of the men are 'teasers' and, in the eyes of the aggressor, warranted the attack. Some rapes occur between two gays in circumstances where they are fighting due to a separation."[48]

A controversial report cowritten by a physician and a public health specialist emphasized the disruptive presence of homosexuals in one resettlement camp. The August 1980 "Report on Status of Cuban Refugees at Fort McCoy, Wisconsin" by Rachel M. Schwartz and Peter D. Kramer painted a grim picture of camp life that highlighted violence and the prevalence of criminals who were not readily identifiable as such. Schwartz and Kramer repeatedly asserted that homosexuals were an "excludable category, by act of Congress" even though they were not being moved to exclusion hearings.[49] Like Ginzburg, they expressed concern for violence against homosexuals, stating that "sexual abuse of homosexuals by heterosexuals is not uncommon, and apparently accounts for a fair amount of violence."[50] According to them, "jealousy over the homosexual love affairs" led to stabbings, and "apparently frequent" homosexual rape: "at least it [was] commented on frequently in conversation and [was] a constant fear of weaker homosexual youths."[51] They also describe homosexual prostitution in the camps, identifying a "male whorehouse" and a "homosexual whorehouse."[52]

In a review of the Kramer Report, Ginzburg refuted some of their allegations. For example, while he acknowledged the occurrence of homosexual rape, Ginzburg stated that he was unaware of the "statistics" Schwartz and Kramer had used to indicate that minors were unaccounted for and that led them to suggest that "these children (teenagers) are hidden in the men's barracks, where they are used sexually by or otherwise paired with adults." Ginzburg did agree that homosexual men were "safer" in the family compound and that sexual activity was occurring "between consenting men." As a rejoinder to the Kramer Report's sensationalist language, Ginzburg added, "homosexual activities are not criminal offenses in many states in which they involve consenting adults."[53] The tension between Schwartz and Kramer and Ginzburg reminds us that the medical gaze itself was fractured and provided, at best, overlapping and often contradictory representations of Mariel homosexuals.

In addition to identifying the homosexual population, the medical gaze also offered a glimpse of the cultural practices that developed in the camps—a culture that federal bureaucrats preferred to ignore or downplay. For example, Schwartz and Kramer gesture toward the role of gender transgression and cross-dressing in the camps:

> Walking around the camp one is likely to encounter attractive young women made-up and dressed in colorful clothing. On careful inspection, however, these women are men. Many of the homosexuals have migrated to the family compound because they feel it is safer. They have created their own subculture.[54]

For homosexual men who had long suffered the consequences of being visibly gay in Castro's Cuba, the Mariel boatlift provided an opening in which the gender transgression performed in the face of state oppression became a ticket out of the country. They had strategically flaunted. Many believed they were coming to a country of gay freedom. Inside and outside the camps, many embraced the notion that they were going to hide no longer. Gender transgression was one culturally resonant way in which a subpopulation of men who had sex with men and identified as homosexual expressed that identity.

Viewed in this way, the gender transgression of the gay Marielitos enacted both political resistance and community formation. However, this visible behavior posed an obstacle to traditional resettlement. For example, David Lewis, a representative of the United States Catholic Conference, explained on *The MacNeil/Lehrer Report* on September 19, 1980:

> We have a number of individuals at Chaffee whose lifestyles is obviously something that we must be very honest [about] with our sponsors. . . . And if we pick up some facets of their personality which are possibly going to be a surprise to the sponsor, if José, as it turns out, is in fact wearing a dress, it's obviously very important that we discuss this issue with the sponsor.[55]

As Lewis's comment suggests, the voluntary agencies traditionally involved with resettling refugees, many of them religious organizations, were not necessarily well-suited to finding sponsors for a dress-wearing José. Thus the situation continued to intensify. As the resettlement camp VOLAGs found sponsors for more and more Mariel Cubans, the concentration of "problem cases" or "hard-to-place" populations increased in the camps, as did their media visibility.

As the deviance of the Mariel Cuban population increasingly became the subject of sensationalist media stories, the state had an interest in dispersing the spectacle of visible, gender-transgressive homosexuals concentrated in state custody. To move the *locas* out of the media spotlight and facilitate their sponsorship, state and federal agencies needed to identify the gay population. In other words, the state gaze needed to see the gender-transgressive homosexuals in the resettlement camps to get them away from the media gaze. However, if the state formally recognized their homosexuality, they could be subject to exclusion hearings based on INS homosexual exclusion policies. To navigate these contradictions, the authorities needed to process gender-transgressive homosexuals without officially identifying them as homosexuals.

Managing Public Relations:
The U.S. Media and the Gay Mariel Story

On July 7, 1980, the *Washington Post* reporter Warren Brown published a story about gay Mariel Cubans after an anonymous government source leaked that twenty thousand homosexuals remained in the camps.[56] In addition to reporting that half of the Cubans awaiting resettlement were gay, Brown also asserted that the federal government was working with national gay and lesbian organizations to assist in resettling the remaining gay Cubans. The story was picked up by the newswire and reprinted as the *Miami Herald*'s lead front-page story under the headline "20,000 Gay Refugees Await Sponsors."[57] Brown's story focused on the resettlement camp population, and so did the debates that ensued.

The U.S. government was already aware of the homosexual population in part because of the visibility of the practices of gay male Marielitos. However, once Brown broke the "gay Mariel story," the federal government was forced to address the issue officially. The CHTF responded by taking a series of official positions in response to Brown's article. These were as follows: (1) they did not identify homosexuals in the Mariel population; (2) they did not know how many homosexuals there were; (3) they did not involuntarily segregate homosexuals in resettlement camps; and (4) they did not work with gay organizations to resettle gay Marielitos.[58]

The first position was articulated in a July 7, 1980, FEMA memo issued in direct response to the *Washington Post* article. In the memo, FEMA director John W. Macy asserted: "We have made no attempt to identify or classify these individuals at the reception and processing centers."[59] Two press guidance sheets issued in September reinforced this position, clarifying that "sexual preference in individual Cubans was not asked during INS processing."[60] The CHTF's final report also reiterates that the "INS [did] not ask" Mariel Cubans if they were homosexual.[61]

While there is no evidence that a definitive, systematic count of homosexuals in the entire Mariel population was ever made, sources suggest that at least some subgroups of the population were officially asked about their sexuality. At the same time, there seem to have been different processes for identifying gay populations at each resettlement camp and processing center. Within the camps, too, not all men who self-identified as gay identified themselves as such to government officials.

In point of fact, evidence suggests that much of the information about the homosexuality of Mariel Cubans was gathered by mental health professionals or voluntary agencies rather than by the INS. For example, del Castillo acknowledged that Mariel Cubans at the camps were asked about their sexuality by camp psychiatrists and psychologists assisting in their relocation.[62] Since del Castillo's statement focuses on mental health professionals working with VOLAGs, his assertion does not directly contradict the CHTF's public position.

Other sources, however, indicate that the INS was identifying homosexual as possibly excludable aliens. For example, in a discussion of the population being held at Fort McCoy, Schwartz and Kramer explained that "early on" in the migration, "homosexuals (an excludable category, by act of Congress)" were being identified as "disturbed" by "lay interviewers" and referred for mental health interviews. However, "it was soon decided not to move for exclusion hearings for homosexuality alone. (Hearings are 'deferred')."[63] Schwartz and Kramer further suggested that the identification of homosexuals happened during INS interviews. Seamlessly conflating "criminals" with "homosexuals," they criticize the federal government's inability to "sort" Mariel Cubans properly:

> In reality much of the information learned about the population did not result in adequate sorting of people. For example despite the rigorous nature of the INS interview numerous criminal types were admitted to the general population of single men. Homosexuality, while initially an excludable category, has been placed in abeyance, but known homosexuals were placed with single male heterosexuals.[64]

Schwartz and Kramer's assertion that the INS asked Mariel Cubans about their sexuality is substantiated by other sources. As mentioned previously, Ginzburg's report had noted that some Cubans claimed to be homosexual in order to leave Cuba and that "when they arrived in the US they informed INS as such. In nearly all of these instances, their behaviour verified their claim."[65] An *Advocate* writer quoted by Allen Young reported that at Fort Indiantown Gap, the "INS [had] been asking gay Cubans pointed questions about their sex lives and relationships."[66] In regard to processing at Fort Walton Beach, one of Young's respondents recalled that

> while being processed by American authorities, the more obvious gays in the camp were questioned as to whether they were homosexual. Some men went to these interviews wearing makeup or female clothing. Their being gay was not an obstacle to the processing, and in fact they were told that if they had any problems (from straight Cubans) the authorities would intervene.[67]

In addition to reports showing that the INS had asked some Cubans about their sexuality, federal documents also indicate that the agency had identified "homosexuals" or "gays" as a significant subgroup within the Mariel population that required special attention. Sometimes the discussion of homosexual migrants was subsumed under umbrella categories such as "undesirables," "problem populations," or "hard to place" populations. Sometimes these umbrella categories did not explicitly include homosexuals; other times they did. For example, in a July 22, 1980, State Department memo, CHTF director Thorne discussed the "problem" of "aliens with troubled backgrounds," a category that included those with a "high probability that they could not adjust to our society immediately and could cause serious problems for their sponsors and for their sponsors' local communities." To clarify which groups were included in this category he specified:

> Examples of those troubled backgrounds are homosexuals, rebellious minors, people who have spent considerable time in prison but who would not be judged as felons in our society, borderline mentally disturbed persons, prostitutes.[68]

A CHTF report written toward the end of the boatlift specifically identifies "Gays" as one of four "problem populations" and devotes an entire section to discussion of this group.[69]

A range of evidence, therefore, refutes the assertion that the federal government, including the INS, did not question Mariel entrants about homosexuality or identify homosexuals. While a systematic account of the sexuality of all entering Mariel Cubans was probably never taken, the INS and others working in conjunction with federal agencies did ask some questions about their sexuality. In addition, homosexuals as a group were identified as a subpopulation that presented particular challenges. Although some documents subsume homosexuals under nonspecific umbrella categories like "problem populations," other documents clearly include "gays," homosexuals, and/or gender-transgressive males in these broadly construed categories.

In response to Brown's estimate that twenty thousand gay Cubans awaited resettlement, the federal government made a second assertion: it did not know how many homosexuals there were among the camp population, and when forced to estimate it could only guess. A September press guidance sheet, for example, simply asserts that there was "no exact count" of the number of homosexuals in the camps.[70] The federal government asked officials to come up with a more realistic estimate of the number of homosexuals awaiting resettlement. In an internal memo, FEMA director Macy replied: "We have surveyed the camps and obtained for the coordinators their 'out of the sky' estimate that the number ranges from *200* to *500* at each camp and certainly will not exceed more than *1,750* for all four facilities."[71] Official estimates cited in media retractions were usually quite low, ranging from "only a few" to Macy's 1,750 to the comparatively high figure of 6,800.[72] From this point on, government figures referred to both the number of homosexuals among the population awaiting resettlement and the number of homosexuals among the entire Mariel entrant population. Federal officials estimated that between 1,000 and 2,500 homosexual Cubans had entered as part of the entire Mariel population.[73] In other words, some officials believed that fewer homosexuals had entered as part of the whole migration (1,000) than were awaiting resettlement (1,750), clearly a mathematical impossibility. Other government sources, however, indicate a larger population. In a draft of a document analyzing the role of the Department of Health and Human Services in the consolidation of unsettled Mariel Cubans into one resettlement camp, it is noted that "5000–8000 (probably 10,000) un-sponsored adults" remained at the camps, adding that of these, "a large share are homosexual; thus, sponsors are difficult to find."[74]

Regardless of the size of the homosexual population, it is clear that the federal government kept track of homosexual Mariel Cubans. Although some of the counts were taken in response to Brown's article, internal documents also included estimates of homosexuals awaiting resettlement as solicited by the federal government for other purposes. For example, a document titled "Questions on Consolidation: Asked by the Cuban Haitian Task Force, Washington" requested a count of people with "sexual preference (different)" by August 2, 1980.[75] Spreadsheets enumerating different classes of Mariel Cubans were compiled by different entities involved in resettlement, including the Department of State. A handwritten document found in the CHTF director's files on consolidation to Fort Chaffee (marked "not for release, for internal use only") provided estimates of different groups remaining at each of the resettlement camps, including 260 homosexuals.[76] Another spreadsheet, this time attached to a Department of State memo, outlined "resettlement coordination" and included preliminary estimates of "classes" of detainees, including male and female homosexuals.[77] These estimates were produced by and for administrators who needed data to solve the problem posed by hard-to-place populations because they were managing the resettlement process.

These figures are not presented here as accurate counts of the homosexual population. However, they do reveal the state's intent to identify certain homosexuals, usually to facilitate their sponsorship. Federal documents also suggest who the state gaze saw as homosexual. One report, written after consolidation of the population awaiting sponsorship at Fort Chaffee, explained that the homosexuals "remaining in the camp are more difficult to place due to personal characteristics."[78] A September 1980 press guidance sheet hinted at what these personal characteristics might be. After clarifying that the INS did not ask about "sexual preference," the press guidance went on to provide an estimate of homosexuals at the camps:

> Based on the number of males affecting female grooming and dressing standards in the camp, it's safe to say that the gay community within the Cuban entrant population reflects the same percentage found in any American community of similar size.[79]

The conflation of homosexuality with gender transgression is telling. First, it reflects an assumption that all male homosexuals "affect[ed] female grooming." Second, it reflects the prevalence of gender transgression among homosexuals in the camp and the identification of this style with a subculture. Finally, it reflects the selectivity of the state gaze that saw only gender-transgressive homosexual men as gay. This is most likely the case because it was gender-transgressive males— José wearing a dress—who posed the most significant challenges to VOLAGs facilitating resettlement, and it was this population that the state really needed to see, if only in order to make it disappear.

The third assertion made by the federal government in response to Brown's article was that it did not segregate homosexuals in resettlement camps: the homosexuals segregated themselves. The September press guidance sheet stated: "We do not segregate homosexuals statistically or physically within the reception centers. In the latter, we do know that homosexuals have managed to segregate themselves within some centers. But that is of their choosing, not our design."[80] At least in some of the camps, homosexual men and lesbians were kept in separate sections. In Fort Chaffee, for example, there were two barracks (one hundred men each) "given over to the homosexuals."[81] Ernie Acosta reports that at Fort Indiantown Gap the "openly gay refugees" whom he also describes as "campy, flamboyant types who bore the brunt of Castro's persecution" were placed in barracks "in the middle of the camp's single men's area . . . surrounded by heterosexual refugees who view[ed] the gays with open hostility."[82]

In most camps, the segregation appears to have been voluntarily designed by gay Cubans themselves for protection, as the press guidance sheet asserts. However, imposed segregation was recommended at Fort Chaffee by several government sources.[83] Also, the Fort Indiantown Gap After Action Report indicates that as early as May 1980, authorities "began to isolate the homosexuals in Area 3."[84] A July 6, 1980, article in the *Lebanon Sunday Pennsylvanian* confirms that this segregation was imposed because the residents of areas three and four were "considered special by base officials. Special enough to separate them from the rest of the Cuban males and keep them together. They are the homosexuals." Camp officials added that segregation was necessary because of the frequent eruption of violence between homosexuals and single heterosexual men.[85] Therefore, although homosexuals themselves did orchestrate their segregation in many cases, camps officials followed their lead and imposed segregation in other cases.

The final assertion made by the federal government's CHTF was that it was not working with gay organizations to resettle gay Cubans. A press guidance sheet dated July 7, 1980 (the very day the *Washington*

Post story ran), states that the U.S. government had not formally requested the assistance of the Metropolitan Community Church or other
gay organizations in resettling the refugees and that the resettlement
process was being handled by VOLAGs.[86] The official position, therefore, was that the federal government did not work with gay agencies,
but that the VOLAGs who handled the resettlement sometimes, in
effect, subcontracted such agencies. In a Department of State memo,
Shepard C. Lowman informed Victor Palmieri, ambassador-at-large
and U.S. coordinator for refugee affairs, as early as July 7, 1980, of the
need for special attention regarding the resettlement of homosexual
migrants. Lowman recommended "Premium R&P grants for hardcore
resettlement cases." To facilitate the grants and clarify who would be
eligible, "various categories of special cases would have to be defined
with some precision, including aged, drug cases, alcoholism, severe
physical handicapped, mental retardation, homosexuality." Next to
this recommendation is a handwritten "No." Because the memo was
dated the same day as the *Post* article, it is possible that the denial of
this request was related to Brown's claims, for this type of targeted
funding would only have drawn more media attention to the homosexual Cubans.

By July 1980, gay organizations had already been working diligently
to resettle gay Cubans. Most prominent among these was the Universal
Fellowship of Metropolitan Community Churches (MCC), which by
July had established a Lesbian/Gay Cuban Task Force to aid Cuban
refugees who were not being placed by existing resettlement agencies
because of their homosexuality.[87] During the resettlement period, MCC
churches raised $40,000 to assist gay Mariel Cubans.[88] According to
their estimates, they found housing for over ten thousand people.

The MCC did work through Church World Services, in coopera-
tion with American Baptist Churches; therefore, the CHTF could claim
that they were not directly working with gay organizations.[89] However,
the federal government was clearly aware that gay organizations were
helping in the resettlement effort. July CHTF staff meeting minutes indicate that one of the VOLAGs, Church World Services, had "agreed to
prioritize homosexuals out of Eglin and then out of other camps."[90] In
a September 26, 1980, State Department memo, Barbara Lawson also
indicated that the federal government and the CHTF were directly
involved in resettling gay immigrants. In a memo to CHTF director
Christian Holmes, Lawson referred to the tensions in the camps:

> The general Cuban population [in the camps] wanted their quick removal, but resented any effort to generate sponsorship to make this possible. In any event, the Metropolitan Gay Church, through Church World Service, has been working with the Task Force to identify sponsors and resettle the homosexuals.[91]

A Department of Health and Human Services memo on consolidating the Mariel migrants at Fort Chaffee further elaborated the government's collaboration with MCC in resettlement:

> MCC has already resettled close to 2000 gay entrants working through the VOLAGS, and has submitted a proposal to the CHTF to resettle the remaining gay entrants at Fort Chaffee. MCC provides the gamut of services including counseling, orientation, job referral, housing assistance, etc., primarily in gay communities in the US.[92]

By February 1981, a Department of Health and Human Services spreadsheet indicated that the federal government was negotiating not only with the MCC but also with BACAR, the National Gay Rights Coalition, and "Gays" to facilitate the "special placements" of Mariel Cubans awaiting resettlement.[93] An April 1981 Department of Health and Human Services memo confirmed that the MCC had received a resettlement grant to place 150 gay people in transitional environments (halfway houses) in San Francisco, Illinois, and Baltimore. The *Christian Century* reported that the grant was for $307,500.[94] According to Frank Zerilli, "Many [Mariel gays] did not last long with our membership, but quickly found jobs, went to Miami or did other things."[95]

A close examination of both the state's official press positions on gay Mariel Cubans and evidence found in internal records of federal agencies reveals (perhaps expected) contradictions. While the CHTF claimed that it did not identify, count, or segregate homosexuals and that it was not working with gay organizations, federal authorities did, albeit inconsistently, identify, count, and segregate homosexuals, and they did end up working with and partly funding gay agencies to resettle the Mariel Cubans. Clearly, the CHTF was maintaining a false front in the face of considerable contradictory evidence.

In the midst of the smoke-and-mirrors effect produced by the state's refracted gaze, it was still unclear whether homosexual Cubans who had been identified by the state in informal and formal ways were going to be allowed to stabilize their status (shifting from parolees to permanent residents) or whether they were going to be excluded formally as a group. As homosexual exclusion policy stood after its 1980 clarification, anyone who made two consecutive "unsolicited and unambiguous" declarations of homosexuality could be excluded. Because of this, gay and lesbian organizations working with the Cuban entrants demanded policy clarification from the INS and began to counsel gay men to be careful what they said to immigration authorities.

Partly in response to this pressure from gay and lesbian organizations, the INS clarified its position on gay Mariel Cubans five years later. In 1985, the INS explained that gay or lesbian refugees who entered as part of Mariel and were identified as gay or lesbian would "not be excluded from the U.S. based on that information alone."[96] In a letter to representatives of two gay and lesbian organizations, INS deputy assistant commissioner R. Michael Miller clarifies:

> This service realizes that due to a variety of reasons, some "Marielitos" were erroneously identified as being homosexual during initial interviews that occurred shortly after their arrival in the United States.
>
> Information contained in Service records, although given consideration, will not be the sole basis to deny an alien's application for adjustment of status, nor will extraneous documents or statements made by other persons. No alien will be considered ineligible for adjustment of status on the basis of sexual preference unless he/she makes or has made for the record an unequivocable, unambiguous declaration that he/she is a homosexual.[97]

This letter reasserts the September 1980 policy that only an "unequivocable and unambiguous declaration" of homosexuality would be grounds for possible exclusion. The letter also seems to suggest that a statement such as "I am a homosexual" made upon entering the United States was not to be interpreted as an "unequivocable, and unambiguous declaration" because "some 'Mariclitos' were erroneously identified as being homosexual."

Conclusion

When Armando presented himself to Cuban police officials, he wanted to be sure that the state gaze would see him as an obvious, flamboyant, effeminate homosexual. To be identified as *escoria* during that brief moment was a way out of the country and, to his young eyes, a ticket to a land of freedom and opportunity.

In Cuba, the state gaze was relatively consistent during this moment. Cuban authorities had a vested interest in identifying an already
stigmatized group, obvious homosexuals, to facilitate their expulsion
from the country. The state gaze saw men who were gender transgressive, ostentatious, and ostensibly passive. Homosexual men also understood objectionable manifestations of their sexuality and exaggerated
these characteristics for the police. To say that the Cuban state gaze
was consistent is not to say that it was necessarily precise, for during Mariel, people who had not previously identified as homosexual
claimed to be homosexual in order to leave the country. Others who
did understand themselves to be homosexual were not allowed to leave
the country because they were not identified by police as homosexual
(or as homosexual enough) or because other factors restricted their departure, as they nearly did in the case of Arenas.

In the United States, the state gaze was neither consistent nor precise. Facing competing imperatives to welcome victims of communism
while excluding homosexuals, the U.S. state carefully crafted policy
clarifications that allowed it to welcome Mariel Cubans (although not
with the same enthusiasm as previous cohorts) and to maintain a
homosexual exclusion policy (while allowing for plausible deniability).
The state thus had an interest in not seeing or identifying homosexual
entrants, since, given the tenor of the relationship between Cuba and
United States, returning Cubans to Cuba was an unlikely scenario.
Detaining Mariel homosexuals indefinitely, as the United States tried
to do with Mariel entrants unequivocally identified as criminals, was
also an expensive and unattractive option. Despite these disincen-
tives, even authorities who pretended not to see the homosexuals were
actively engaged in the politics of homosexual visibility precisely because administrative needs required the identification of those homosexuals who disrupted camp life or posed a challenge to traditional
resettlement.

In addition to these inconsistent policies, state identification of
homosexual entrants was imprecise. Not all men who thought of themselves as homosexuals were visibly identifiable as gay, nor did they
all verbally declare their homosexuality to state officials. When the
state recognized the need to identify homosexuals (to facilitate their resettlement), it acknowledged primarily gender-transgressive, obvious
gays. As various federal officials attempted to count this population,
the imprecision of the gaze was further revealed. It is impossible to

make the different government estimates add up because contradictory figures block any attempt at a coherent summation. We simply do not know how many gay men and lesbians arrived as part of the Mariel boatlift. Moreover, U.S. government estimates focused on the Mariel migrants who remained in camps, in effect ignoring the existence of other gay men and women who had already joined family members. While there might have been some data about the number of people who admitted being homosexuals to the INS or the number who were segregated in the camps, these figures represented only a portion of gay Marielitos because they excluded those who preferred to lie about their sexuality or who would not have been classified as gay based solely on their appearance. The practical impossibility of quantifying the gay Mariel migration made it easier to mute this issue in the mainstream media. By drawing attention to quantitative failures, federal authorities helped keep the potentially explosive story of gay Mariel shrouded in uncertainty.

Although inconsistent and imprecise, the federal government did at some levels identify individual homosexual entrants as well as the size of the homosexual subpopulation. And the power of state identification practices lies not in their precision. Rather, as Luibhéid has convincingly argued, identification and processing by the U.S. immigration service constructed "the very sexual categories and identities" it sought to regulate.[98] Discussing the mid-twentieth century, Margot Canaday argues that the state did not simply respond to a visible and preconstituted homosexual, but rather the federal state "also *constituted* homosexuality."[99] Canaday further elaborates: "Homosexuality was never something like tuberculosis: a problem to be discovered by the state and then simply reacted to. Homosexuality was much more like a race: a certain set of rules produced out of the state's own murky encounter with difference."[100] In the case of Mariel entrants, the state situated immigrants "within larger relations of power to which they remained subjected after entry."[101] The identification process thus constructs subject categories to facilitate the control of populations. The processing of immigrants with regard to sexuality provided Marielitos with their first socialization into U.S. sexual categories and identities. Whereas in Cuba the distinction between active and passive homosexuality was key (passive homosexuals were the real homosexuals and the corrupting force), it is unlikely that U.S. authorities adopted this distinction. However, by the end of the resettlement process, government officials were actively trying to ascertain how many homosexuals remained at the camps, basing their estimates not on identity or same-sex behavior per se but on gender-transgressive expressions that impeded resettlement. Ironically, although the Cuban and U.S. state gazes were differently grounded, in the end, both targeted the same population—gender-transgressive, "obvious" gay men.

Despite inconsistencies and imprecision, the state's fractured gaze has real material consequences for those it identifies as deviant. For the Mariel *locas,* U.S. identification as a homosexual did not necessarily lead to exclusion, but it opened up this possibility and thereby contributed to their ambiguous standing in U.S. society. In this sense, the fractured gaze disguised the workings of state power at the level of subjectivity by constantly reiterating subject categories (criminal, homosexual, black) while allowing for fissures in its inconsistent applications. Although the worst-case scenario of the exclusion of all homosexual Mariel entrants did not materialize in this case, the state's refracted gaze still asserted power in its flickering recognition of supposedly negative characteristics.

3 CULTURES OF GAY VISIBILITY
AND RENARRATING MARIEL

IN MANY WAYS, 1980 was a year of urban anxiety that marked a transformation in Miami's urban, racial, and sexual landscapes. Cuban Americans who had immigrated prior to 1980 were fearful that the Mariel immigrants, often referred to derogatorily as Marielitos, would tarnish their reputations as "golden exiles." African Americans and other non-Latino black Miamians worried that their opportunities in a declining economic situation were diminished by more Latino immigrants. Anglo Americans feared that the city's culture would never be the same, that Miami would be forever Latinized. Anita Bryant and her followers must have been equally horrified by the clearly celebratory performance of gender transgression that many Mariel gay men exhibited in their new homeland.

Although gender-transgressive homosexual men received a great deal of media attention, they did not represent all homosexual men and women who entered as part of this migration. However, as I try to reconstruct here, a particular culture of gay visibility did emerge with this generation, a culture of visibility that can be understood as a reaction against historical conditions (e.g., the targeted persecution of visible homosexuals by the Cuban state). This culture emerged as a response to perceived, if not real, conditions in the United States (e.g., the belief that the United States was the land of gay freedom). In particular, this culture of visibility was constrained by the material realities of the impoverished immigrants who created and embodied it. As is reflected in the cases of "broken sponsorships" I describe in this chapter, many gender-transgressive Mariel migrants could not rely on the economic support of family and friends; simultaneously, their gender expression limited their opportunities for socioeconomic advancement.

The evidence of the gay culture of visibility established by Mariel immigrants is both sparse and controversial. The attention garnered by the Marielenas, as one of my respondents referred to the gender-transgressive Mariel population, worried many, including Cuban American leaders who sought to break the association between the Mariel boatlift and unsavory populations. According to (perhaps) well-meaning leaders, the media was simply interested in sensationalizing stories (such as those focusing on the criminal element and homosexuals), and their focus simply worsened the condition of Mariel immigrants, many of them "normal" people who would have to fight against the stigma of Mariel for many years to come. My intention is not to belittle the urgency of the battle against the stigma of Mariel. As someone who lived in Miami both before and after the Mariel boatlift, I remember how viscerally non-Cubans (re)acted toward Cubans after 1980. The English Only efforts of the 1980s that I discuss in chapter 4 are but one electoral manifestation of the anti-Cuban and anti-immigrant sentiment that festered during this period. I also remember how passionately Cuban Americans reacted and how many sought to distinguish between the good Cubans (those who came before 1980, who spoke Spanish "properly," had been raised with "good" morals in pre-Castro Cuba, and were mostly white) with the bad Cubans (the Marielitos who were clearly corrupted products of the revolution, did not speak Spanish "properly," and were much more dark-skinned than the "golden exiles"). Within this binaristic context, the only way to speak favorably about Marielitos was to argue that *they* were not all that different from previous generations, but they were just like *"us,"* the golden exiles.

With the benefit of over thirty years of hindsight, I propose a different argument here: the Mariel homosexual generation was different—not inferior, but different. To pretend that there is no difference is to erase the history of this generation's persecution and the political significance of their identificatory practices. Moreover, such an erasure homogenizes diverse Cuban American histories. As I argue in the previous chapters, what was most harshly persecuted in Cuba during the 1960s and 1970s was not homosexuality in general but the gender-transgressive public display of male homosexuality. Given that male homosexuality was associated with effeminacy, a wide array of gender-transgressive behavior was believed to demonstrate one's sexuality, including wearing women's clothing, letting one's hair grow out too long, or wearing tight pants or colorful shirts. In Cuba, speech patterns, mannerisms, and even the people one associated with could cause suspicion and apprehension.

Precisely these expressions blossomed in Miami's post-Mariel gay world. Young, poor immigrants who grew out their hair and then bleached it and wore housedresses in public in broad daylight reinvented gender-transgressive homosexuality, drag, and transvestitism. They created a visible gay Mariel culture in 1980s Miami, primarily concentrated in neighborhoods like South Miami Beach and Southwest Miami. Clearly, not all gay men who migrated during Mariel participated in this segment of gay culture; in fact, only a small minority of the gay men who emigrated during Mariel identified with this subculture. Nevertheless, the men who did choose the path of gender transgression added a new face to Cuban Miami and helped create the gay and transgender Miami that exists today. In this chapter, I gather the fleeting evidence of the gay culture of visibility that emerged in Miami after 1980. This very important moment in Miami's racial and sexual history is difficult to document: ephemeral, it faced a concerted effort to silence any documentation of its existence. In the spirit of Eduardo Aparicio, whose efforts at documenting the *rastros,* or traces, of post-Mariel gay culture I discuss in the introduction, I track the shifting responses to gender-transgressive Mariel migrants—from outright rejection and silencing in the 1980s to fairly open acceptance by the turn of the new millennium.

1980: "Tent City"

In chapter 2, I discuss the different paths Mariel entrants took toward sponsorship. Some immigrants found sponsors while still in South Florida, but others were sent to resettlement camps around the country while they waited to be paired with unrelated volunteer sponsors. Unfortunately, for some Mariel entrants, being paired with a sponsor did not lead to the expected transition to independent life in the United States.

According to Cuban–Haitian Task Force documents, the sponsorship of an immigrant did not constitute a legally binding contract, but rather a moral commitment to "aid an entrant in resettling in a new community," an undertaking designed to assist "the individual or family [in] adjust[ing] to living in the community and finding housing, food, clothing and employment."[1] When a Mariel Cuban was handed over to a sponsor, the sponsor was asked to sign a release form that included basic information about the entrant. Although the release form transferred to sponsors "responsibility for the person or persons they take in," a memo about processing procedures in South Florida clarifies that "it [did] not obligate them to keep those they sponsor."[2] Siro del Castillo, then director of South Florida's Krome North processing center, reportedly urged family sponsors in particular to "be aware of their responsibility toward the entrant and not to 'leave him in the street' if the sponsorship breaks down.'"[3] Del Castillo issued this warning not out of an exaggerated sense of doom but because many sponsors—inside and outside Miami, familial and volunteer—*were*, in effect, deserting their Mariel charges.

As early as June 1980, sponsorship problems were becoming obvious for certain populations among Mariel entrants. One FEMA document reported that a significant number of Cubans were being "abandoned by their sponsors."[4] Broken sponsorship cases, "sponsorship breakdowns," or "returnees" (as they were labeled in U.S. government documents) included those who were abandoned or those whose relationships with sponsors had otherwise soured without a successful transition to independent living.[5] Federal records estimate that 30 percent of resettled Cubans had "broken sponsorships." Another estimate found that 60 percent of Mariel Cubans were not living at their sponsor's address by the end of the summer of 1980.[6]

Broken sponsorships posed tremendous challenges for local areas where sponsorless Cubans were located. If all the Mariel immigrants were stigmatized, broken sponsorship cases represented the most marginal of the marginal. To deal with this population of displaced Mariel Cubans, who were sometimes homeless and wandering the streets, the City of Miami established two temporary holding centers to provide makeshift housing and food. The first was established in Miami's Orange Bowl, which had previously been used as a processing center. When that facility closed on July 25, 1980, city officials moved the remaining 650 Cubans to a new holding center at Latin River Front Park, which was situated under the I-95 interstate highway near Southwest Fourth Street. Although funded by the federal government, "Tent City," as it came to be known, was run by "14 harried city of Miami employees."[7] Before it closed on September 30, 1980, 4,000 to 4,700 Cubans were processed through Tent City, with 500 and 600 Cubans staying there at any given time.[8]

By the time Tent City was opened, the mainstream press had already printed stories about the large percentage of homosexuals in the unsponsored Mariel population. Since Tent City was conspicuously located in Miami's city center and afforded its residents only minimal privacy, the encampment provided a media spectacle. Here semihomeless Cubans from already stigmatized groups in Cuba and the United States—homosexuals, blacks, and formerly incarcerated people—cobbled together lives and cultures with only tents to veil their every movement. Soon, obvious homosexuality was noted by the press, visitors, and local residents.

Early reports from agencies working with Mariel Cubans reveal the extreme marginalization of broken sponsorships. Discussing the Orange Bowl situation, FEMA director John W. Macy noted that "many of the group are considered to be in the hard to place category and finding employment and permanent housing for them will be a long and difficult process."[9] While Macy used the umbrella category "hard to place" and avoided mentioning any specific characteristics, the press and other observers more precisely defined what made placing this population "difficult." For example, a *Miami Herald* article described Tent City as "Miami's first Cuban ghetto" and included a carnivalesque description of the camp involving a "midget," a boxer, threats of rioting, and a nearly naked woman whose clothes had just been stolen. In the story, two men identified by the journalist as homosexuals are quoted describing the conditions in the camp and its treatment of homosexuals. The writer casually introduces the first man as "one of the Cuban homosexuals who lives there," language that suggests that the presence of homosexuals in Tent City was well known to readers. In the article, twenty-seven-year-old Juan Puente described arriving at the airport from one of the resettlement camps, presumably to meet a sponsor, and finding no one waiting for him. After "'walking and asking people questions . . . they took me to the Orange Bowl. From there I came here.'" A fifty-four-year-old homosexual wearing a "wrinkled felt cowboy hat" affirmed that the overall conditions in the camp were not good but that "'homosexuals aren't persecuted here. . . . Police have treated us very kindly.'" This quotation suggests that it was common knowledge among Tent City residents that "homosexuals" were a distinct group whose treatment by the state needed to be monitored.[10] More specifically, the article's description of the cowboy hat hints at the aesthetic cobbled together by the gay men who tried to construct temporary homes in Tent City.

Miñuca Villaverde's documentary film *La ciudad de las carpas (City of Tents)* provides a much more thorough description of this aesthetic and the quotidian practices of homosexual residents at the camp.[11] Filmed with a 16 mm Bolex camera during the days before Tent City shut down, the low-budget film documents a fleeting moment in early post-Mariel Miami, providing a glimpse of the temporary communities that emerged in the camp and the outwardly directed performativity of its gender-transgressive residents. Villaverde's gaze is undeniably attracted to gender transgressions, as her narration vacillates between sympathetic and judgmental portrayals. Moreover, her film demonstrates how both visible gender transgressions and the voyeuristic gaze form key elements of Cuban American gay male culture.

For financial and logistical reasons, the video and audio were not recorded together, which gives the documentary an eerie, surreal quality. *La ciudad de las carpas* presents images of camp residents with lips moving to no accompanying dialogue. Voice-overs by Villaverde and some featured residents provide sparse commentary on the population, the camps, and Castro's Cuba. While the documentary references black Cubans, Afro-Cuban religious practices, and former criminals (visibly marked with tattoos), the documentary's central focus is a group of gender-transgressive homosexual men. We learn a little about the paths that brought them here. Like one of the men quoted in the *Miami Herald* article, two of the film's protagonists had formerly been housed in resettlement camps. In voice-over, they describe gender transgressions in distant camps where homosexual men put on cabaret shows, and "the 'girls' dressed like women and they got married and everything."[12] The narrator adds that some of Tent City's gender-transgressive residents had relatives in the Miami area; however, "their parents do not accept their lifestyle. They have different morals. There is a breach between them. Many moral tenets have disappeared, and in their place lies an amoral indifference."[13] It is unclear whether Villaverde suggests that the Miami residents who had spurned their newly arrived relatives were amorally indifferent or whether the gender-transgressive homosexuals were the amoral ones. Regardless of Villaverde's intent, for many Cuban American Miamians, the outward gender performance of the Mariel generation clearly manifested one chasm between the golden exiles and the Marielitos. As was the case with the Cuban state's persecution of homosexuals, it was not homosexuality per se that marked this chasm, but the obvious shamelessness of this homosexuality that seemed so alien and amoral.

Amid the austere conditions of the camps and faced with the gaze of Villaverde's lens, the gender-transgressive Mariel migrants of Tent City perform for the camera and seem to enjoy their performances with no evidence of either shame or discretion. One still from the documentary—strikingly similar to the image of the Fort Indiantown Gap resettlement camp included in chapter 2—captures the campy poses of Tent City residents. In this image, Luisito, the most youthful in appearance, with his distinctive (*llamativo,* a Cuban might say) hair color, holds the stuffed animal that became the group's mascot. The other men exhibit different degrees of gender transgression—slightly sticking out a hip, wearing a pair of woman's sunglasses, or combining a more obvious gesture with wearing a woman's halter-top.

Four gender-transgressive men emerge as primary characters in the documentary. In addition to the young Luisito, Villaverde highlights José Antonio, who we meet as he is getting his hair dyed in one of the tents; El Flaco, nicknamed for his slim figure; and 10½, identified by the logo on his T-shirt. One scene reveals how this group of men created

Miñuca Villaverde's documentary *Tent City* chronicled the experiences of a group of Mariel refugees held in an improvised camp in an area below I-95 in Miami's downtown.

a performative aesthetic with very limited resources. As Villaverde writes in her script, with only sheets as props,

> José Antonio, 10½ and others help El Flaco wrap himself in a colorful mantle. He spins and poses. He opens his mantle and then wraps himself again. . . . El Flaco sits on the bed, wrapped in his mantle. He lies down, imitating sultan poses. He gets up and starts dancing to the rhythm of the drums. He spins and uses the mantle like a great cape. . . . His face, wrapped in the colorful mantle, is seen very close up. He spins for the camera.[14]

In one of the closing scenes, the coquettish play between the men and Villaverde's camera is also evident. With Vivaldi playing in the background:

> Two young transvestites *[jovencitos transvestistas]*, around twenty years old, pose behind one of the tents. One wears a beaded lace dress with ruffles that fall over his shoulders and the other wears a black spaghetti strap dress. They both position themselves in different poses, one with the other. Facing forward. Back to back. They lean. They both are wearing women's shoes and near them on the floor are two women's straw hats. One covers his mouth with his hand, covering up his possible mustache, while the other brings his face closer.[15]

The descriptive language Villaverde uses in her script reveals particular attention to their gender transgressions. She describes Luisito as walking "with forced gestures *[gestos forzados]*, moving his hips" while he poses for the camera, and El Flaco walking "as if he was a lady." She makes reference to their "delicate fingers," their poses, and the way in which they embrace with "affected gestures" *(gestos amanerados)*.[16]

Because the documentary highlights gender transgressions some believed should be kept private, Villaverde had to defend her focus. In an article, she justifies her interest and suggests that the men themselves stole the show: "Perhaps they, because they were the most discriminated against amongst the homeless, touched my sensibilities more than others, and I dedicate a great part of the film to them. Or was it they who took over the film?"[17] Both Villaverde's gaze and the agency of the homosexual men (did they take over the film?) are evident throughout the documentary and in the more widely available printed script. Although the film provides a mostly sympathetic portrayal of the camp's residents, Villaverde-as-narrator does not directly challenge the negative characterization of Marielitos.

These are youths, products of the revolution. With whom did they mix in Cuba, isolated from the exterior world, to become lumpen, scum? We do not need to blame them for being scum, if that is in fact what they are. Or for their lack of teeth or for desiring things that they never had.[18]

Villaverde, therefore, leaves the question of whether the Marielitos are scum unanswered, but asserts that if they are scum, only the Cuban government can be blamed. This message—clear in its attack of Castro's government but ambiguous in its assessment of the camp residents—is ultimately overshadowed by the much more interesting accounts and visual representations of the men themselves.

Sex in the City

A promiscuous and visible gay Mariel culture developed in urban Miami after 1980. Some believed that Mariel gay men were more extroverted in the United States because they believed this was the land of unrestrained gay freedom. Armando, who arrived in the United States via Mariel, explains his initial perceptions of gay life in the United States:

> Como es natural uno llega, se deslumbraba por el simple hecho de que hubiera una discoteca para hombres gay na'más, que tú entraras y todo el mundo era gay, y no venía la policía a recoger a todo el mundo y llevárselo. Ya eso era un cambio tremendo.

> Naturally, when you get here you are blown away by the simple fact that there's a disco exclusively for gay men, that you go in and everybody's gay, and that the police don't come and carry everybody off. That in itself was a tremendous change.

Certainly the lack of certain types of persecution created new opportunities for gay expression (as did the severing of some immediate family ties upon migration); however, defiant sexual cultures had been developing within Cuba well before Mariel. As Reinaldo Arenas reminds us, it was during the most severe period of Cuban repression of homosexuals that "homosexuality began to flourish with ever-increasing defiance."[19] The combination of the perceived freedom in the United States with the defiant cultures that had already been developing in Cuba created the context for the immigrant gay culture that developed in 1980s Miami.

What was that immigrant gay culture like? When I asked René, a fifty-year-old Cuban man who lived in Miami before and after 1980, what the Mariel time was like, he told me about radical changes in Miami's sexual life:

> Oh my god, era así. Yo podía recoger seis personas en las carpas, en la ciudad de las carpas o en el Orange Bowl. El sexo era tan, tan, tanto sexo, tanto, tanto, tanto, tanto, tanto, como esta ciudad nunca ha visto.

> Oh my God, it was like that. I could pick up six people in the tents, in Tent City or in the Orange Bowl. The sex was so, so, so much sex. There was so, so, so, so, so much, like this city had never seen.

René suggested that Mariel made Miami more sexually open. When I asked him to clarify how he thought migration changed Miami's sexual life, he explained:

> RENÉ: Por ejemplo el cruising, en las áreas abiertas, en la calle, etc. Los gay americanos se volvieron locos. Hacían cola . . . con el carro para recoger gente.
>
> SUSANA PEÑA: ¿Por qué era sexualmente más abierto?
>
> R: Era porque eran sexualmente más divertidos, creo yo. Porque los americanos son mucho menos extrovertidos en el sexo. O sea, ellos pueden estar sintiendo mucho. . . . Tú te das cuenta de que ellos terminaron ya . . . tú no te habías enterado. O sea, eso pasó y nadie te avisa, ni nada, no. En Cuba se decía, la gente decía, "a mí hay que gritarme el palo." El palo es el sexo, y es esa cosa de decir lo que sientes en el momento que estás teniendo el orgasmo, de gritar, de decir, ¿qué sé yo? Y yo creo que eso a los americanos los enloquecía. Los americanos son tan fríos, tan aburridos.

> RENÉ: For example, cruising in open areas, in the street, etc. Gay Americans went crazy. They would get in line . . . in their cars to pick people up.
>
> SUSANA PEÑA: How was it sexually more open?
>
> R: I think it was because they [Mariel gay men] were sexually more fun. Because Americans are much less extroverted during sex. They could be feeling a lot. . . . You realize they've finished . . . and you hadn't noticed. I mean, it happened and no one tells you or anything, no. In Cuba there's an expression, *a mi hay que gritarme el palo* (you have to scream your orgasm at me). *El palo* is sex, and it's about saying, yelling, saying what you feel in the moment you're having an orgasm, I don't know. I think that drove the Americans crazy. Americans are so cold, so boring.

The concept of "gritar el palo" reveals one irony about the interrelationship between visibility and silence: it is those men arriving from a country that persecuted public displays of homosexuality and public sex (a country, in addition, whose material conditions made privacy a luxury) who embody this notion of announcing one's orgasm. I see in the yelling, in the announcement of ejaculation, the direct response to systematic efforts to muffle homosexuals and underground sexual cultures. The silencing and the screaming, the persecution and the defiant announcement of sexual pleasure, depend on one another.

1990: Still Too Early to Embrace the "Spectacle of Blatant Male Homosexuality"

Ten years after Mariel, in April 1990, the *Miami Herald* staff writer Elinor Burkett once again focused media attention on the gay men who came to the United States during Mariel. Rather than simply report a number of gay migrants (as Warren Brown's controversial *Washington Post* article did), her human-interest story provided in-depth accounts of the migration of ten gay Cuban men.[20] The story documented forms of persecution in Cuba, the motivations of gay men coming to the United States, the types of lives this particular generation of gay men developed, and the devastating impact of AIDS on their generation.

The story highlighted the Mariel gay generation and how they shocked other gay men (Cuban and not) who had been living in Miami before 1980. Burkett's description of visible gay cultures describes both Tent City and everyday life in the wider urban environment:

In the late summer of 1980 in Miami, everyone was noticing the gay men of Mariel. They were showing up everywhere, not exactly unobtrusively.

Driving by the refugee Tent City under the I-95 overpass in downtown Miami, you could not miss the men in high heels and makeup, the men strolling with parasols, the men holding hands and kissing.

Customers at women's clothing stores in Little Havana were left speechless as their countrymen in the next dressing room tried to wiggle into size 10 dresses and lace camisoles. . . . The more sedate majority went openly, unabashedly public with their homosexuality. . . . The less sedate went kind of berserk. They were flagrant, outrageous. Even Miami's gay population was appalled.

When the men from Mariel arrived at Miami Beach's Arlequin Club, the old-time Latin transvestites complained loudly about the brazen newcomers who were cheapening the craft by cross-dressing not just onstage, but off-stage, too.[21]

Burkett described how these visible Mariel gay men had an impact at the street level, on daily life. Although gender-transgressive Marielitos were not the first to cross-dress in Miami, they did push the boundaries of acceptable behavior even within gay and drag worlds, as Burkett's account indicates. They were considered controversial precisely because they were public and visible in the context of everyday life, rather than limiting their behavior to specifically "gay" or "drag" settings.

Burkett's article was met with much the same hostility and protest as Brown's. The *Miami Herald* published reactions to Burkett's article from two commentators. The first, signed by Rene V. Murai, chairman of the Facts About Cuban Exiles (FACE), a group that promoted positive and accurate representations of Cuban Americans, was published on April 13, 1990.[22] The second article, authored by Alejandro Portes, was adapted from a report previously authored for FACE.[23]

Portes began his critique of Burkett by focusing on the numbers of gay men Burkett cited in her article, a scenario almost identical to that played out when Brown's article appeared in 1980. Portes refuted two "numerical assertions" made by Burkett. He rejected the claim that 70 percent of the Mariel migrants were young men and denied the assertion that thirty thousand migrants were male homosexuals. Portes noted that a much smaller percentage of the Mariel migration was young men (defined as ages 18–35). More than likely, Burkett misused the 70 percent figure, since that was the percentage of all male Mariel migrants (not just young males); however, Portes did not point this out. Although he recognized the difficulty of accurately estimating the gay population, Portes cited available figures about marriage rates of the Mariel immigrants and characteristics of the different phases of the boatlift in order to contradict Burkett and explain the source of her supposedly inflated figures. Although Portes attacked Burkett's unreliable figures, his estimates of the number of married men and adult males are equally unreliable, for they assumed that only unmarried adult males could be gay.

In addition, Portes argued that the media were responsible for the misleading overestimation of Mariel's homosexual male population because of increased coverage of the migration's second phase. This second phase coincided with "stepped up efforts by the Cuban government to discredit the refugees by forcing an increasing number of 'anti-socials' to board the ships": people who arrived during the second phase were more likely to be held in camps. According to Portes, this media focus "included the spectacle of blatant male homosexuality."[24] Therefore Portes contended that the focus on male homosexuals drew primarily from the media's tendency to portray this more deviant phase of the migration. However, the media's focus on the later phase of the migration actually excluded gay migrants who had been reunited with families during the first phase; thus Portes's figures likely underestimated the total number of gays in the entire migration.

In all fairness, Portes correctly pointed out that the media played a pivotal role in shaping negative opinions of Mariel migrants among U.S. residents. Portes did attempt to counteract a common tendency in relation to perceptions about Marielitos, the generalization of the experiences and characteristics of one subgroup of the migrants onto the 125,000 men, women, and children who arrived in 1980. However, his concern with how the overestimation of the gay Mariel population might stigmatize the whole Mariel population was also problematic.

Portes stated that, because of the slanted media portrayal, "it was difficult to remember that the majority of new refugees—including those in the first phase and many detained in the camps—were just ordinary persons seeking a new way of life in the United States."[25] The implication here is that the blatant homosexuals Burkett interviewed were not "just ordinary persons":

> When a quarter of any given group is portrayed as socially deviant, the entire group is tainted by extension. By advancing these figures, unsupported by reliable evidence, the author transformed a "human interest" story concerning the personal misfortunes of some Mariel refugees into a general statement about the common path followed by many members of this group—a homosexual career that ends with AIDS and death.[26]

Portes was concerned that the stigma associated with blatant male homosexuality was generalized to all the Mariel migrants. In short, Portes failed to catch on to Burkett's goal of destigmatizing this population by speaking openly about them (rather than silencing them) and giving weight to their pursuit of liberty, their challenges to the Cuban state and Miami's exile values, and their own transnational cultures of resistance. For Portes to have maintained that Burkett wrote only about the "personal misfortunes of some Mariel refugees" was simply inexcusable. Sexuality is not only a personal matter; moreover, we know that "misfortunes" such as disease and stigma are socially distributed in particular ways. Burkett's article revealed a great deal about state persecution in Cuba, cultural views about homosexuality, the myth of the (gay) American dream, and the local impact of the AIDS epidemic. Although her figures might not have been accurate, the thrust of her article was not really about the number of gay men who were part of the Mariel boatlift; rather, it dealt with their cultural impact on Miami. In clinging to a quantitative high ground, Portes avoided asking questions about the sociological significance of the gay Mariel migration.

The visibility of Mariel gay men after 1980 made the numbers game played out in the media almost irrelevant because even if there were few gay men, as some claimed, it was clear that those few had an impact on street culture, drag, and other Cuban Americans. The conflicting accounts about their numbers further confirm the significance of Villaverde's documentary, Burkett's account, and my own childhood memories. If an official story could not be told about the impact of the gay Mariel generation because of the lack of substantiated estimates, what was left were images of a fleeting subculture that affected a city's daily life.

The 1990s and the New Millennium: Incorporating Homosexuality and Transgender in Miami's Memories

The year 2005 marked the twenty-fifth anniversary of the Mariel boatlift. Events commemorating Mariel proliferated throughout Miami. Film screenings, commemorative newspaper issues, and television news stories participated in remembering and renarrating the Mariel moment. By 2005 Miami and its Cuban American community were ready to remember Mariel as a positive event and to approach the issues of male homosexuality and male-to-female transgendered women with less anxiety than before. In these retellings, homosexuals and transgender women appeared as positively recognized members of the migration. Given the negative reaction against marginalized Mariel immigrants in 1980 and echoes of attempts to silence the issue of Cuban American homosexuality in 1990, what is perhaps most surprising about this coverage was how male homosexuality and transgender issues were seamlessly incorporated into the 2005 commemorations. For instance, Lisandro Pérez-Rey's 2003 documentary, *Más allá del mar (Beyond the Sea),* includes the story of the Mariel immigrant Roberto, who had been imprisoned in a UMAP, and the transsexual actress Alana Inda, who discusses being imprisoned under the Law of Dangerousness for "ideological diversionism" *(diversionismo ideológico).*[27] The *Miami Herald* created a time line of Mariel events for the anniversary. It also prominently featured issues of sexuality and gender identity. The *Herald*'s website presented twenty "personal stories," including that of Alana "La Gata de la Habana" Inda, who declares herself

> the American dream personified. Meow! La Gata de la Habana! I changed my life and my destiny, and 100 percent my sex. I am physically and mentally a woman. I like to spread out on my Arab couch so you can see me. The only thing we need for that regime in Cuba to blow up is to fly me over there and put me on the Tropicana stage.[28]

The same website also included editorials and stories on new leaders, artists, Mariel immigrants living outside Miami, and "Gays & Lesbians."

Of course, much had happened in Miami since the 1990s that could help explain this new rendering of the gay—and transgender—Mariel story. In the 1990s the same southern Miami Beach neighborhood that had been home to a concentration of gender-transgressive Mariel migrants became an internationally recognized gay neighborhood and tourist destination. As I discuss in chapter 7, South Beach became identified with a racialized and highly desired Latino gay masculinity. If the fact that gender-transgressive Mariel gay men were concentrated in the same neighborhood soon to become the hot gay spot suggests a historical continuity, it is important to note some sharp discontinuities exist as well.

The most prominent of these discontinuities is how gay Mariel appeared (or more often, did not appear) in Cuban American gay men's accounts of gay life, gay identity, and gay community. Luis, whose negotiations with masculinity I analyze extensively in chapter 7, was an elementary school student in 1980. He describes his memory of gay Mariel men:

> [I remember] seeing, you know, flamboyant, gay, you know, they weren't necessarily drag queens or transsexuals. I mean they were very effeminate gay men with brightly colored, brightly dyed orange hair. They were expressed in a more feminized way, but they weren't necessarily trying to pass as women specifically. Maybe in a place where gender roles are a lot more specific, they feel that in order, if . . . they're not going to pass as straight

men who happen to have sex with other men, then they're going to express
their gay way by looking more feminine and some were like drag queens
or transsexuals. . . . If anything maybe I felt like a fear, maybe there was a
part of me that, that part me that was trying to fight with what I had been
accused of my whole life was like: I didn't want to be associated with that;
I didn't want to be that; that was not what I was, even though I had maybe
a subconscious fear that that's what I was being told I was.

The first adjective Luis used to describe the gender-transgressive gay
men of Mariel is *flamboyant*. Even in childhood, Luis could recognize
the transgressions of feminized ostentation that were stigmatized in
Cuba as well as in Miami. Luis's account demonstrates how he interpreted Mariel gay expressions through his own emerging boyhood notions of sexuality and gender and how he interprets that feminization
as an adult. As a boy who was beginning to suspect his own attraction
for men, Luis confronted the new models of gay life—as embodied
by "feminized" Mariel men—with fear rather than identification. The
Mariel gay men transgressed gender and class definitions of appropriate behavior. As Luis confronted the gay men with only a partial
understanding that he too might be gay, he wanted to distinguish between his type of gay and their type of gay. As a young adult looking
back on Mariel, we see Luis place the need for feminine expression in
a historical context, distinguishing between Mariel gay men's "feminized" expressions and the emulation of women. Also, he situates these
"feminized" expressions in a cultural context that defines them as gay.

Luis articulated a vivid picture of his relationship to one sector
of gay Mariel. Within the context of my interviews, this type of explicit discussion of gay Mariel was unusual. Typically, the Marielenas
slipped out of most men's accounts. Men rarely mentioned this sector
of Mariel unless directly asked. Given the dramatic impact Mariel had
on all aspects of life in Miami in general and on gay life specifically,
I was surprised by these silences. In chapter 7, I place such silences
in dialogue with fears of effeminacy articulated by Cuban American
gay men and more broadly expressed in the celebration of masculine
physiques that characterized gay culture in 1990s Miami.

I interviewed Luis in the late 1990s in South Beach, the same
neighborhood where many Mariel migrants concentrated shortly after
1980. By the time of our interview, this neighborhood had been dramatically changed by the emergence of gay male commodity culture.
Unlike the *locas* who had lived here in the 1980s—many of them poor

immigrants—more affluent, professional, and generally more masculine gay men began to flock to this area as occasional tourists, regular
visitors, and residents. While gender transgressions and drag were not
absent from South Beach, the rules of the neighborhood's market-
driven economy slowly pushed away all gender transgressions that
did not fit within particular types (star drag performers, for example).
Working-class men, like Luis, who had grown up in this neighborhood
found it increasingly more difficult to afford rents, even in the tiniest
of apartments.

Throughout the rest of the city, the Cuban American community
had also changed. Much of the anxiety caused by Mariel—will Cubans
ever be seen as golden exiles again?—had passed as a powerful Cuban
American elite gained an unexpected degree of economic, political, and
cultural power. In the 1990s, the Cuban American community began
to show an internal diversity in terms of race, political generation, and
cultural tastes. If the incorporation of the once-stigmatized Mariel
generation played a key role in this diversity, so too did the ongoing
entrance of newer generations of Cubans, including the *balseros,* or
rafters, of the 1990s.

In terms of my research, the literature on Latino gay male sexuality is also radically different in 2013 than when I started this project
in 1995. In the mid-1990s, only a limited number of studies focused on
homosexuality in Cuba, and the few studies on U.S. Latino gay men
focused almost exclusively on active/passive models and HIV and "risk
behavior."[29] Since then, a growing body of literature on Latino/a gay
populations has focused on different national origin groups, the relationship between immigration and sexuality, and the intersections of
race, political economy, and sexuality.[30] My work is also in dialogue
with scholars who employ a queer of color critique that uses a mate-
rialist cultural studies approach to analyze the intersections of race,
gender, sex, and sexuality.[31] Along with queer of color scholars, I hope
to analyze the cultures, experiences, and/or representations of queer
people of color to provide a grounded analysis of how these interlock-
ing hierarchies speak to and about one another. In the following chapters, I complicate this dialogue by focusing on a racial/ethnic group
that often understands itself and is understood in a particular U.S.
local context as white. Rather than take this white racialization at face
value, I analyze how it functions precisely through gender and sexual
discourses in the absence of explicit racial self-identification. My work

is further informed by a broader literature on Latino/a gender and sexualities that points to the relationships among racialized structures that affect gay men and those that affect heterosexual women, lesbians, and heterosexual men.[32]

In dialogue with these scholarly literatures on Latino gay men, queers of color, and Latina/o sexualities, the ethnographic analysis of contemporary Cuban American gay male cultures that follows attempts to make connections between gay cultures of visibility and the silencing strategies that accompanied them. I draw on observations, interviews, and conversations with Cuban American gay men from various backgrounds. Both Cuban-born and U.S.-born men populate my study and the culture it seeks to reflect. I try to place these men in a transnational context that emphasizes both historic continuities (e.g., those bridges between the Cuban state's identification of gender transgression as a problem and the emergence of a gay culture of visibility in post-1980 Miami) and historic breaks (such as the disappearance of the *locas* from men's accounts of gay Miami).

4 *PÁJARATION* AND TRANSCULTURATION

Language and Meaning in Gay Cuban Miami

THE GAY MARIEL MIGRATION is one of many migrations that contributed to (gay) Miami in the 1990s. Other migrations from Cuba prior to Mariel ("Golden Exiles") and post-Mariel ("los balseros"), as well as migrations from other parts of Latin America and the Caribbean, contributed to a transcultural and diverse gay culture in this U.S. city. In this chapter and those that follow, I analyze the Cuban American gay cultures that emerged in transcultural Miami since the 1990s. As a hub of globalized labor, cultural projects, information, and capital, Miami is a site of multilingual gay cultures historically linked to U.S. urban gay life and Latin America. In discussing the globalization of gay culture, scholars such as Dennis Altman have focused primarily on the influence of Western, Anglo gay culture on the third world and developing nations.[1] I prefer the approach of Richard Parker, who in his work on gay cultures in Brazil focuses on how Anglo-European gay culture is selectively used and transformed in non-U.S. contexts. He argues that the "importation of international gay styles and symbols . . . within the Brazilian gay world is a good deal more than just an unconscious extension of international capitalism or a sign on Anglo-European cultural imperialism. The appropriation of such signs and symbols . . . is a far more complex and dialectical interaction than simplistic notions of external imposition would otherwise suggest."[2] He argues that Brazilian gay men "adapt the signs and symbols of international gay life . . . to create a repertoire of symbolic resources that build meaning and make sense of the world around them, and to imagine and ultimately manipulate other worlds in other places."[3] In this chapter, I analyze a different side of these globalization processes—the impact of immigrant, transnational, and minority gay cultures on a U.S. urban setting. Specifically, I use language to discuss the meaning-making and selective adaptation of Cuban American gay men living in Miami since the 1990s and ask how the migration of people from throughout Latin America to the United States through entry cities like Miami influence U.S. gay culture. In this multicultural and transnational context, how is language used to construct gay and ethnic communities?

Through their use of language, we can observe the cultural negotiations and innovations made by different groups of Cuban American gay men. Latino gay men who are monolingual Spanish speakers, monolingual English speakers, and multilingual speakers with different levels of proficiency communicate with one another, have sex with one another, and create communities separately and together. Culture is literally made in and through these interactions. Power is not absent, of course. For example, the choice to speak English or Spanish in a particular setting is not available to monolingual speakers. Not demonstrating cultural competency in a job interview that requires strong English skills can cost someone a much-needed job. In Miami, not speaking Spanish can cost someone a job as well, and there are other cultural costs to limited Spanish-language proficiency.

I explore how Cuban American gay men draw from U.S.- and Cuban-based cultural and linguistic histories and use Cuban Spanish, English, and Spanglish to construct gay communities and transnational identities.[4] I analyze how urban Anglo gay culture and language are incorporated, used, rejected, or rearticulated in a multilingual U.S. city increasingly defined by immigrants from Latin America and the Caribbean. While the influence of U.S.-based ways of organizing and naming homosexuality is irrefutable, I argue that transculturation provides the best theoretical mechanism for understanding the linguistic and cultural transformations in which gay men of Cuban descent participate.

Language Autonomy: Spanish in a U.S. Context

While Spanish had gained a measure of acceptance, if not dominance, in Miami since the 1990s, it is important to situate Spanish-language use in Miami in national and historical contexts. In the national context, the use of Spanish is a highly politicized issue, and the struggle for language autonomy has been a primary battleground for U.S. Latino communities. English Only legislation, antibilingual education initiatives, and informal stigmatization of the Spanish language have all been used throughout the country to veil anti-immigrant attitudes, limit the incorporation of Latino immigrants as citizens, and control their impact on what is envisioned as an otherwise unitary American culture. In various and sundry settings, new immigrants struggle to become fluent in a second (or third) language and are often humiliated and ignored if they speak accented or nonstandard English. Consequently, pan-ethnic Latino communities have mobilized for linguistic autonomy in support of bilingual education, against English Only legislation, and for the right to speak Spanish in the workplace and in schools.

For Spanish-speaking Latinos living in the United States, political battles around language have been central to narrow and wide definitions of citizenship. In the narrowest sense, political conservatives have tried to make English-language proficiency a requirement of naturalized citizenship. In terms of the broader definition of cultural citizenship, Latinos have struggled for language rights in order to claim public space, defend the rights of people of diverse language backgrounds to make claims on the state, and limit the extent to which daily practices are circumscribed by imposed English use.[5]

Perhaps not surprisingly, during the same year as the Mariel boatlift began—a year of mass migration of predominantly non-English-speaking immigrants from Cuba and Haiti—Miami became a battleground over issues of immigration and language autonomy. In November 1980, voters in Dade County overwhelmingly passed an English Only initiative that "made it unlawful to use county funds 'for the purpose of utilizing any language other than English, or promoting any culture other than that of the United States.'"[6] With the Mariel exodus so recent that entrants were still being held in resettlement camps, the success of the county-wide campaign signaled that non-Latino, nonimmigrant voters had reached the limits of their tolerance. In 1988, this sentiment was reinforced statewide when an English Only amendment to the state constitution was passed by 84 percent of Florida's voters.[7]

English Only became the battleground on which Dade County and Florida residents who considered themselves rightful citizens asserted what they believed was their exclusive claim to political rights, social services, and government funding. Perhaps more profoundly, these so-called natives asserted their claim to the cultural core of the city through the English Only battle. Their political mobilization in favor of English Only attempted to ensure that the language (and ethnicity) of the city would continue to be English- and Anglo-dominant.

Although Miami's English Only proponents won several battles in the 1980s, by 2000 it was clear that the language war was lost. In May 1993, the Dade County commission overturned the 1980 English Only initiative. Consequently, signs at government buildings in Miami–Dade County are now posted in English and Spanish as well as Haitian Creole. The worst fears of the English Only proponents have been met. In vast swaths of Greater Miami, one can conduct bank transactions, buy groceries, make travel arrangements, learn about government services, and see a doctor all without ever speaking English.

Several factors contribute to the prevalence of Spanish use throughout Miami. The unique (and relatively privileged) history of the region's Cuban Americans is one significant factor. The continued entry of immigrants from Latin America and the Caribbean coupled with decreasing populations of black and white non-Hispanics have also intensified the Hispanicization of the city. As business interests from throughout Latin America continue to house operations in Miami, Spanish becomes more and more entrenched not only as a language of social interaction but as the language of business.

I place my discussion of the globalization of gay culture within the contexts of battles over language autonomy, Miami's citywide ethnic makeup, and the rights of immigrants to shape local culture. Today, Spanish is a language with great currency in Miami's heteronormative settings *and* Miami's gay worlds. Put another way, English is definitely not the only gay language in Miami. In gay social settings catering specifically to Latino audiences, Spanish is both the language of social interaction and the language of performance. In gay clubs that do not cater specifically to Latinos and whose clientele includes mostly a mix of Anglos and Latinos, which I refer to as mainstream gay clubs, it is common to hear Spanish being used by patrons and, on occasion, by featured drag performers. Bilingualism and language autonomy are facts of life in gay circles in Miami.

Sexual Systems, Language, and Culture

Citing the absence of studies of Latino gay men in the United States, Tomás Almaguer employs ethnographic accounts of male same-sex behavior in Latin America to explain the Latin American sex system that he, in turn, uses to analyze the U.S. Latino gay experience. Although

Almaguer also uses Chicana lesbian feminist writings (particularly those of Cherríe Moraga) to discuss the socioeconomic position of Chicanos with regard to homosexuality and relationship to family, it is his reading of the Latin American sex system that has been taken up most often by scholars of the Latino gay experience. Almaguer contrasts how meanings of gender and sexual practices are organized in the "Mexican/Latin American sexual system" with how those meanings are organized in the United States. He argues that whereas sexual object choice is the primary determinant of one's sexual identity in the United States—where a man who chooses to have sex with another man is defined as gay or homosexual, while a man who desires to have sex with a woman is defined as straight—in Latin America, sexual aim (the desire to penetrate or be penetrated) forms the primary determinant of identity. According to the Latin American system Almaguer describes, the penetrated partner—referred to by terms such as *pasivo, maricón, mariposa,* or *loca*—is much more stigmatized than the active/penetrating man.[8] According to this system, a man who penetrates another man, sometimes referred to as a *bugarrón,* is barely, if at all, stigmatized. According to this typology, *pasivos* will not desire each other sexually, nor will *activos.* Rather, the feminine *(pasivo)* will seek out the masculine *(activo),* and vice versa.

These binaristic sexual roles are assumed to correspond to socially visible gendered manifestations. In other words, in most Latin American social contexts, men exhibiting characteristics socially associated with women or socially defined as effeminate are assumed to be members of the socially marked category of *maricones* and assumed to be passive. On the other hand, men who appear masculine are less likely to be accused of being a *maricón,* more often assumed to be an *activo,* and less likely to be stigmatized as homosexual—even if they have sex with men. Some describe the European American sexual system where all men who desire other men are defined as homosexual and are not differentiated in terms of their sexual roles as more egalitarian than the Latin American sex system.

One premise of the literature on the Latin American sex/gender system is that because sex and gender are organized differently in Latin America than in the United States, we cannot simply translate U.S. English-language categories (like gay) to understand Latin American cultural categories. In what follows, I explore how these sexual taxonomies can inform our interpretation of men's linguistic strategies in a multiethnic U.S. urban context.

In chapter 7, I revisit this typology and discuss some of the ways in which Almaguer's argument has been extended, complicated, and critiqued. For the purposes of this chapter, this generalized typology helps clarify the complicated intersections of different sex/gender systems and the languages we use to discuss them.

Transculturation

A Cuban-born man who has sex with men and has been raised primarily to think of himself in terms of an *activo/pasivo* dichotomy does not simply bring a static system of meanings, pleasures, desires, and languages with him when he immigrates to the United States. Rather, these systems of meanings are transformed by new experiences during that man's life. In what ways does a U.S.-born Cuban American gay man—raised with the values of a Latin American sex/gender system, educated in U.S. schools, and offered unrestrained access to U.S. mass media and gay clubs and culture—understand his own sexual identity? What languages might he use to make sense of his own desires and identifications?

I argue that the concept of transculturation best explains these men's experiences. Developed by the Cuban anthropologist Fernando Ortiz, the term *transculturation* was meant to supplant the use of *acculturation,* a term gaining prominence among U.S. sociologists who analyzed the white immigrant experience in urban settings.[9] For Ortiz, the term *acculturation* emphasizes the acquisition of the dominant culture. He reminds us that this acquisition necessarily implies the loss of the culture of the home country, a process he labels *deculturation.* For Ortiz, the concept of transculturation involves both acculturation and deculturation as well as neoculturation—the creation of a new culture that maintains elements of the two meeting cultures but in the end is quite different from both.

When applying the concept of transculturation to gay culture, Ortiz's theory suggests that immigrants (like the Brazilian gay men Parker discusses) do not simply assimilate into a static U.S. gay culture and adopt its language, symbols, and sexual systems. Rather, U.S. gay culture is itself changed by extensive contact with immigrant, non-English-speaking homosexual men and women.[10] The theory of transculturation also speaks to the importance of the culture of Cuban male homosexuals. Because of the racial, economic, and political power that Cuban Americans hold in Miami (relative to other racial/ethnic groups), multiple spaces exist for the development of Cuban cultural projects—so long as they do not contradict an anti-Castro agenda. Allowed at least a marginal space for development, a hybrid that draws on the experiences of first- and second-generation Cuban American gay men, a Cuban American gay neoculture has flourished. This neoculture holds traces of both Cuban and U.S. histories and represents a new formation made possible only at a specific historical conjuncture.

These processes of gay transculturation are evident in the language and meaning systems of Cuban American gay men. In this chapter, I focus on three linguistic practices that illustrate gay transculturation. The first is Cuban American gay men's use of the term *gay* in both Spanish- and English-language accounts to describe their own sexuality and communities. Although the adoption of this terminology sometimes implies an adoption of a U.S.-based sex/gender system, gay as linguistic marker can also coincide with a gendered sexual identity associated with Latin American sexual structures. I argue that linguistic and cultural markers that suggest a reliance on U.S.-based gay culture are invested with divergent meanings by gay men of Cuban descent and must be interpreted within a bicultural framework. The second practice is the use of Cuban Spanish gay argot in Miami's predominantly Latino gay club settings and, occasionally, in more ethnically mixed gay settings. Use of expressions like *perra* and *loca* reflect both the maintenance of Cuban male same-sex cultures and the incorporation of these linguistic traditions by second-generation Cuban American gay men. The third practice is linguistic innovation that involves a mixture of Spanish and English. Such innovation, I contend, reflects and creates an ethnic, bilingual, bicultural gay culture. The term *pájaration* is but one humorous linguistic invention that joins Cuban Spanish and U.S. English and marks the bilingual listener as an insider to Cuban American gay male hybrid culture.[11]

Linguistic Practice 1: Redefining What "Gay" Means

Homosexual men of Cuban descent often use the term *gay,* pronounced in English and Spanish *(gai)* within the contexts of both English- and Spanish-language conversations. In my interviews, I found that men used the word *gay* to identify themselves, the communities around them, and even same-sex practices in Cuba. In Spanish-language accounts, gay was used both as an adjective, as in *el mundo gay* (the gay world), *la vida gay* (gay life), and *un lugar gay* (a gay place), and as a noun,

as in *los gay* (the gays) and *un gay cubano* (a gay Cuban). In these accounts, gay was sometimes used interchangeably with *homosexual.*[12]

Since the term *gay* is associated with a U.S.-based sex/gender system that can be contrasted with a Latin American sex/gender system,
it might be assumed that the use of the term coincides with an adoption
of U.S. sex/gender categories and meanings. In other words, we might
conclude that those men who use the term *gay* in Spanish-language
accounts refer to all men who have sex with men within the context
of a nongendered notion of male homosexuality. However, this is not
necessarily the case. Although the adoption of this terminology sometimes implies an adoption of a U.S.-based sex/gender system, gay as
linguistic marker can also coincide with a gendered sexual identity
associated with Latin American sexual categories.

The two following examples illustrate how men of Cuban descent
invest the term *gay* with different meanings. Armando, the forty-seven-
year-old man who came to the United States in 1980 whom I discuss
in chapter 1, used a heavy mix of English and Spanish throughout our
interview. He used the term *gay* within the context of both English and
Spanish phrases and sentences. His definition of the term closely coincided with a U.S.-based system of meaning. In the following interview
excerpt, I asked Armando whom he included in his category of gay.

SUSANA PEÑA: ¿Por ejemplo, un hombre que tiene sexo con hombres pero
que no se identifica como gay, [qué] es?
ARMANDO: Para mí ese es un *closet case.*
SP: ¿Entonces sí es gay?
A: Ese es un *closet case, but he's still gay.*
SP: Okay.
A: Pero hay muchos, como te decía, *old gay or the old school* que tienen
que tener un hombre, un hombre que inclusive esté casado y tenga
hijos. Que yo siempre he dicho, bueno, si el hombre está casado y
tiene hijos pero se acuesta con otro hombre *there's something weird
there,* pero a la misma vez, es esa cosa latina. Yo me imagino que tú
habrás encontrado eso mucho. Que hay ciertos hombres que están
casados, tienen hijos, se acuestan con gays, pero ellos son hombres
y tú no. Y entonces pues eso es lo que a mí me molesta. El hecho
de imaginarme que yo estoy teniendo una relación sexual con un
hombre que piensa que es un hombre y yo no. Yo soy un hombre
también, un hombre a quien le gustan los hombres pero soy un
hombre, no soy una mujer, ni soy menos que tú, ni soy ninguna
otra cosa. . . . Ese es el tipo de relación que a mí no me, nunca me
ha convencido. . . . Como se decía en los tiempos antiguos, *and
this is a bad word, I'm sorry I have to use it,* bugarrones. Ese tipo

de relación yo no la entiendo, nunca la he entendido, nunca la he tenido, no me interesa.

SUSANA PEÑA: For example, a man who has sex with a man but doesn't identify as gay is?

ARMANDO: To me, he's a closet case.

SP: Then, he is gay?

A: He's a closet case, but he's still gay.

SP: Okay.

A: But there's a lot, like I was telling you, old gay or the old school who have to have a man, even a man who's married and has kids. And I always said, if he's married and has kids but he sleeps with another man, there's something weird there, but at the same time, it's a Latin thing. I imagine you've come across that a lot. That there's certain men who are married, have kids, they sleep with gay men, but they are men and you are not. Well then that is what bothers me. Having to imagine that I'm having sex with a man who thinks that he is a man but I'm not. I'm a man too, a man who likes men, but I am a man, I'm not a woman, and I'm not less than you, or anything else. . . . I've never been convinced by that type of relationship. . . . As I was saying, in the old times, and this is a bad word, I'm sorry I have to use it, *bugarrones.* I don't understand, I've never understood, never had, and never been interested in that kind of relationship.

In this account, Armando used the term *gay* to refer to all men who have sex with men regardless of their gender identity and preferred sexual role. Such is the meaning of gay in the U.S. sexual system, but Armando superimposed this definition, with which he identified, onto men who identify according to the Latin American sex system as *activos* or *bugarrones.* Armando clearly described the U.S. sex system in which all men who desire men are equally gay as more egalitarian than a Latin American sex/gender system that would define him as "not a man" and therefore inferior to a "real man." He unequivocally distanced himself from this type of meaning system.

René, a fifty-one-year-old Cuban man who left Cuba in the 1970s, also used the term *gay.* During the interview he spoke almost exclusively in Spanish and used the term *gay* often, even to refer to life in Cuba. However, his definition of gay was quite different from Armando's:

A mí no me gusta la gente gay en el sentido que me gustan los hombres, que es el tipo de gente que tú, que yo encontraba en Cuba, y que yo disfrutaba en Cuba. . . . Entonces es muy difícil para una gente como yo porque la gente gay no me, no me llama la atención.

I don't like gay people in the sense that I like men. That's the type of person that you, that I used to find and that I enjoyed in Cuba. . . . So it's very hard for someone like me because for me gay people aren't, I'm not attracted to gay people.

Although René, like Armando, used the term *gay* within his Spanish-language account, he seems to be using gay as almost an equivalent to *pasivo,* the passive category in the Latin American sex system, in the sense that his "gay" refers to nonmasculine men who have sex with men, in contrast with "real men" who have sex with men. Since terms like *maricón, pájaro,* and *joto* are all highly stigmatized terms in Latin American countries, the term *gay* has the advantage of not carrying with it this history of stigma. Therefore, when used in this account, gay refers to a category in the Latin American sex/gender system without embodying the same stigma as *maricón.*

Both Armando and René use the same term, *gai,* in the context of Spanish-language accounts. By using a bicultural framework to interpret their narratives, it is clear that this same term actually refers to different categories of people. I discuss the use of the term *gay* as metaphor for the varied incorporation of U.S. gay culture and gay English by U.S. residents who are not predominantly English speakers. This analysis of the term *gay* suggests that non-Anglo and non-English-speaking homosexual men in the United States do not simply adopt U.S. meaning structures. Rather, they sometimes redefine gay English and U.S. gay culture or infuse it with other ways of understanding and organizing same-sex desires. Additionally, this example also illustrates that Cuban first-generation immigrant men do not all make cultural negotiations in the same way. In the example above, Armando and René, both Cuban-born men living in the United States, use the English-language category gay in contrasting ways and also position their own sexual/gender identity in very different relationships to U.S. and Cuban sexual categories. What René finds desirable and exciting is precisely what Armando describes as demeaning and disempowering.

Linguistic Practice 2: Using Cuban Gay Slang

The use of Spanish is common throughout Miami. The use of Cuban Spanish gay slang constitutes a more specific practice that marks the speaker as not only Spanish-speaking but also particularly Cuban or

Caribbean *and* gay. During my fieldwork, "perra" was one of the most widely used Cuban gay expressions I encountered. Literally, *perra* means female dog in Spanish, but within the Cuban gay context, it is used as a term of praise whose meaning is similar to that of fierce in African American gay male communities.[13] Exclamations of *"¡perra!"* are used to laud a particularly decadent drag queen or even a female singer identified as a gay icon. The first issue of *Perra!,* a Spanish-language gay zine published in Miami in 1995 and marketed to Latino gay men, explains that "perra es en nuestro español caribeño, una palabra de exaltación para todo aquello que sea fabuloso o extravagante. Puede ser perra alguien, una voz, un vestido, un peinado, una canción, un show, un logro, una frase" (*perra* is in our Caribbean Spanish, an exclamation of praise for all that is fabulous and extravagant. Someone, a voice, a dress, a hairstyle, a song, a show, an achievement, a phrase can be *perra*).[14] The use of this simple exclamation as the zine's title implies the language of its content, the sexuality of its readers, and the predominantly Cuban slant of its materials.

Perra is used widely in predominantly Latino gay settings, but I have also heard it used by Latino men at predominantly Anglo gay settings and predominantly heterosexual Latino settings. It is a particularly Hispanic Caribbean exclamation that marks the speaker as gay or at least as having a gay sensibility. In addition, *perra* is grounded in Cuban gay kitsch, requiring evaluative skills that draw on a knowledge of gay Cuban icons and expressions. In other words, the speaker needs to be able to evaluate a particular performance or outfit in the context of a Cuban gay sensibility in order to evaluate whether it is *perra*. While the term is extensively used in Cuban Miami, it constitutes one small example of how Cuban gay language is maintained and transmitted in Miami.

In some cases, the men I interviewed felt that expressions grounded in Cuban gay language and culture more closely captured their experience than English-language expressions. René offered a good example. When I asked him about his coming-out experiences, he rejected the concept of coming out, labeling it as something "raro" (strange and/or unusual).[15]

Cuando una persona es mariquita es mariquita. Tú sabes, no necesita *coming out, coming out* es algo muy raro. Yo por ejemplo lo sé desde que tengo siete, o tres, cuatro años. Yo sabía que ese era mi destino, que yo tenía que enfrentarme a eso en algún momento. O sea, yo podría decir que salí del closet a los trece años, porque me acepté que me iba a acostar con un hombre y fui a buscarlo. Pero, yo eso ya lo sabía.

When somebody is a *mariquita,* they're a *mariquita.* You know, they don't need to come out. Coming out is a really strange thing. For example, I knew since I was seven or three, four years old. I knew that that was my destiny, that I had to face up to that at some point. So, I could say that I came out of the closet when I was thirteen years old because I accepted that I was going to sleep with a man and went to look for him. But I already knew that.

Mariquita is a term used to refer to effeminate gay men. It is related to the term *maricón,* but *mariquita* has a diminutive and feminine-gendered suffix. According to René, the concept of coming out is "strange" because one's queerness is undeniable from a young age. In this account, male homosexuality is naturalized to the extent that it is seen an inborn trait that is, or should be, obvious to others. For René, coming out becomes something of an anticlimactic moment, since it is assumed that those around you can see that you are a *mariquita.*

Instead of the concept of coming out of the closet, René proposes that we talk about "cantar 'La Bayamesa.'" This insider expression is not necessarily recognized by nonhomosexuals. "La Bayamesa" is one of several names for the prerevolutionary Cuban national anthem. It therefore can be literally translated as "singing the national anthem." The expression, therefore, plays off of themes of patriotism and valiant masculinity.

[Él] canta "La Bayamesa." Significa aceptarse. . . . En Cuba, cantar "La Bayamesa" era un individuo que se acostaba con alguien y que no se escondía.

[He] sings "La Bayamesa." It means to accept oneself. . . . In Cuba, someone who sang "La Bayamesa" was someone who slept with someone and didn't hide.

Whereas the concept of coming out emphasizes the declaration of your sexual preference to others, "cantar 'La Bayamesa'" as defined by René primarily emphasizes self-acceptance and *not hiding* one's sexual preference. Likewise, René emphasized when he himself came to terms with his preference for male sexual partners, rather than having proffered any kind of declaration about his sexual preference to others. Similarly, Carlos Decena argues that the Dominican immigrant gay men in his study understood their sexuality as a tacit subject, "something understood, yet not stated." He argues that coming out might "sometimes be redundant," for it is a "verbal declaration of something that is already understood or assumed—tacit—in an exchange."[16] The objective difference between the terms coming out and "cantar 'La Bayamesa'" is not the key issue. We might argue that René's explanation of "cantar 'La Bayamesa'" strongly overlaps with some understandings of coming out. However, for René, these two expressions, an English one drawing on U.S. metaphors and a Spanish one drawing on Cuban metaphors, are distinct. One makes more sense to him and has more relevance to what he identifies as the critical moments of his development as a homosexual man.

The use of Cuban gay expressions and slang is also common among second-generation Cuban American gay men who predominantly speak English. They are among those who yell *"¡perra!"* at drag shows and who sometimes greet their friends at gay clubs with a smattering of Cuban gay slang. Learning and using Cuban gay slang by mostly English-speaking Cuban American gay men marks a transmission of Cuban gay sensibility from one generation to the next. It connects young, second-generation Cuban American gay men with a strand of Cuban culture that celebrates male homosexual expression. For example, Luis, the Miami-born man in his twenties who discussed his childhood distance from the Mariel *locas* in the chapter 3, also described the significance of his relationship with two older Cuban gay men as "a door to a cultural awakening." When he described what he learned from them, he focused mostly on language and gay icons: "There was a whole language. . . . I think in most gay cultures there's a, you know, languages that are, if not specific to them at least typical of them at the time and I enjoyed listening to the gay, the older gay Cuban language 'cause it was new to me at the time." Luis eagerly listened to these two older men. He described being intrigued by the content of their conversations: gay life in Cuba, the iconography of female artists in Cuban gay culture, drag history, and webs of gossip weaved about the sexuality of celebrities. Luis also described being intrigued by the language itself ("the older gay Cuban language"): the slang, the expressions, the intonation, and the pacing of their words provided Luis with a sense of how the Spanish language was used in the context of a gay culture. In a sense, Cuban gay expressions taught Luis how to be gay in Spanish.

Luis spoke about his relationship with these two older Cuban gay men on another occasion. I specifically asked him if he felt he had to struggle to be both gay and Cuban.[17] He responded:

> LUIS: No because I've been exposed to a long history of culture that's both.
> SUSANA PEÑA: Through your friends?
> L: Through older gay Cuban friends. I've been aware that there's been a culture there that existed, that has existed forever. The two things to me aren't mutually exclusive. I think, maybe it's not, while not all the things that are gay about Cuban culture can be easily pinpointed as specifically gay, but maybe there's common trends in things that gay people talked about, people gay people admire. . . . I guess there's traditionally been a gay sensibility that people have, that exists, not that necessarily everybody shares in but, through things like theater and literature and the arts that makes up, like, a gay culture.

The transmission of Cuban gay culture is an important element of second-generation Cuban American gay men's ethnic identity. As I discuss in the next chapter, learning Cuban gay slang and tapping into a rich history of Cuban gay sensibility and icons provide a view of Cuban culture that celebrates male homosexuality and facilitates the creation of integrated Cuban and gay identities.

Linguistic Practice 3: Bilingual Linguistic Innovations

Linguistic innovations that involve a mixture of Spanish and English reflect and create an ethnic and bilingual gay culture. I look to drag performances to illustrate this hybrid language, but these linguistic innovations emerge from a lived context of life in a multilingual city where bilingual neologisms occur often as mistakes. These various kinds of plays on language can be a source of embarrassment and humor, but they can also become the dominant mode of expression. Often they capture Miami's multicultural reality in an utterance. This is true for heterosexual and homosexual speakers of English, Spanish, and Spanglish, but in the case of Cuban American gay men, these linguistic innovations can create a particular insider standpoint: that of a biculturally gay man.

This creation of an insider position is most obvious and easily observed in drag settings. Drag performances in predominantly gay settings provide a good place to observe both the linguistic innovations of Cuban American drag queens and the audience reception and reaction to these innovations. Drag queens often use linguistic mistakes as the basis of stand-up routines and drag humor. The audience members who get the joke are privileged as insiders. In my research, I found that exchanges that occur in drag settings, especially those between drag queens and audience members, form one important site where Cuban gay culture is created and reinvented.

I draw the title of this chapter from one such drag performance. *Pájaration* is a linguistic innovation used by the *trasvesti* performer Mariloly, a Cuban drag queen popular in Latino gay clubs and often featured in local Spanish-language television shows. Mariloly does a series of stand-up routines that play off of her "Cuban, can't speak English" character. Mariloly's emcee acts and performances occur predominantly in Spanish, but she incorporates bilingual elements in ways that highlight the humor of the new immigrant experience. In one typical routine, Mariloly speaks to the audience in Spanish and then tries to speak in English to a monolingual club manager who is imagined to be offstage. As she fumbles through her translation for the manager, she tries to come up with a word to describe the characteristics of the audience to the imagined English speaker. She says, "Here, here," pronounced in a thick Cuban accent and points to the audience members around her. Not finding the right word, she asks herself (as many Spanish speakers do when they cannot come up with the appropriate word in English), "Ay, ¿Cómo se dice?" (Oh, how do you say that? or What's the word?). Then, as many Latinos have done before her, she proceeds to make up a word, using a Spanish-language base word and an English-language suffix. "Here, mucho pájaration. You understand?"

"Pájaration" is pronounced in a thick Cuban accent (pa-ha-RAY-shon). The linguistic innovation plays off of the Spanish-language derogatory slang for gay men, *pájaros,* which literally translates to birds. *Pájaro* is used to denote a homosexual man, most likely an effeminate gay man.[18] The term *pájaration* joins the derogatory *pájaro* with "-ation," a form of the English-language suffix "-tion" that denotes the noun form of a condition or state of being.

I saw this skit performed several times, and every time the crowd erupted with laughter when Mariloly said "pájaration." The joke and its instant crowd response mark the bicultural audience members as insiders. To get the joke, you must know the Spanish noun *pájaro,* know the English suffix "-tion," and recognize the incongruence of combining the two.

This stand-up routine also allows the Latino audience to laugh at the mistakes of an un-Americanized immigrant. However, since this joking occurs in the context of a Spanish-language routine, the assumed listener is more likely to be a person who himself has been in a similar situation.[19] Within this context, what is devalued most is the monolingual English speaker who would not be able to understand the majority of Mariloly's routine and would most likely not get the joke about *pájaration*. Given the fact that this performance occurred in a club catering to Latino gay men, I interpret this poking fun at the immigrant experience as an in-joke, understood best by those who have either experienced it themselves or who have seen close relatives in similar situations.

The use of linguistic innovation in this example points to common experiences that characterize Cuban American life in Miami and emerges out of an intersection between Cuban gay Spanish and English. In terms of my larger ethnographic study of Cuban American gay male culture, *pájaration* as linguistic innovation stands in for all the times men throw together seemingly incongruous elements to create a fusion culture.

Conclusion

In their daily use of languages, people infuse known words with new meanings, make up new words, and use particular expressions frequently while completely ignoring others within their vocabulary. In this chapter, I have examined how language can create a bridge between older and younger, Cuban-born and U.S.-born Cuban American gay men invoking cultural signifiers that are necessarily transformed in their journey. I have explored how Cuban American gay men categorize and systematize desires and identities with language and how assumed linguistic categories do not necessarily correspond to a given system of complex meanings. New expressions emerge in particular multicultural urban settings to reflect a bicultural gay reality. In other words, Cuban gay culture and U.S.-based gay culture transform each other.

Each linguistic practice discussed provides insight into transculturation. Men of Cuban descent invest the term *gay* (along with other cultural symbols of the U.S. gay movement such as freedom rings and pink triangles) with a range of meanings. We cannot assume when we hear a Cuban American man say he is gay that he means quite the same thing as does an Anglo man in the United States. Analyses of the effects of U.S. gay culture on cultures of same-sex activity throughout the globe have to take into account this process of meaning-investment. Although we cannot ignore the cultural imperialism and economic power of U.S. values, we also cannot assume that the rest of the world passively accepts this power without resistance and transformation. In Miami transculturation is actively changing the meanings of identificatory terms such as *gay*.

Young, second-generation Cuban American gay men who might have no direct contact with gay life in Cuba still routinely draw on Cuban gay expressions as a form of cultural exchange. Although this education process might be transformative for the young gay men I interviewed, in their new uses, expressions like *perra* are also transformed. When someone screams "¡Perra!" in a South Beach club to a leather-wrapped drag queen lip-synching to Grace Jones, it has a slightly different meaning than when *perra* is used in a Cuban housing project at *travestis* who have applied eyelashes with shoe glue and are lip-synching to a Sarita Montiel song, as seen in the documentary *Mariposas en el andamio (Butterflies on the Scaffold)*.[20] This change in meaning reflects a change in gay sensibilities and material realities. Although Cuban gay slang is more dominant in clubs that cater to a majority Latino population, it has also seeped into Miami's mainstream gay club and drag activities, particularly mainstream drag events that attract a strong Latino contingent. The presence of Spanish-language elements in mainstream gay locales may serve to make these settings less alienating to Latino gay men, especially Spanish speakers.

And then there is *pájaration*. Cuban American character-oriented drag queens like Mariloly are extremely important social commentators. They have built a following precisely because they are able to document Cuban and Latino gay experiences. They draw from bicultural experiences and through humor are able to touch nerves of connection between different generations of Cuban American gay men. The culture that is both reflected in and created through performance and audience reception illustrates gay transculturation.

My research suggests the importance of looking at languages other than English to understand gay cultures. We must be careful not to equate English (gay or otherwise) and U.S. gay cultures with liberation, egalitarianism, or freedom without also asking questions about how these languages and cultures are experienced by non-English-speaking, non-Anglo homosexual men. The struggles over language autonomy in Miami remind us that in the context of the United States, English-language use is imposed with a series of social, legal, and political strictures complexly intertwined with racism and anti-immigrant attitudes. In this context, the use and maintenance of Spanish and the development of Spanglish also embody elements of resistance, liberation, and freedom. The languages of gay expression and pleasure are increasingly plural and shifting.

In the next chapter, I shift from a more narrow focus on language to a broader focus on cultural narratives about *cubanidad*. As I have argued so far, competing narratives of *cubanidad* circulated in Cuba, among Cuban exiles, and in the dominant U.S. media. These narratives both explicitly and implicitly identified the gendered and sexualized subjects allowed within the narrative nation. In the next chapter, I explore Cuban American gay men's relationship to those narratives.

5 NARRATIVES OF NATION AND SEXUAL IDENTITY

Remembering Cuba

IN CHAPTERS 1 AND 2, I trace how the emerging Cuban state created a narrative of a masculine nation by contrasting it with the assumed weakness, unproductiveness, and effeminacy of male homosexuals. In much the way revolutionary Cuban narratives discredited bourgeois capitalism by associating it with gay male subcultures, mainstream exile narratives discredited communism by asserting its relationship to male homosexuality and gender transgressions. Flavio Risech describes the first time he encountered a representation of a homosexual. The Cuban American exile publication, *Zig Zag,* featured a

> limp-wristed Raúl Castro dressed in fatigues, high heels and a ponytail. . . . To cast the communist Raúl as a *maricón* was to reduce him to an effeminate, stinking wretch posing as a real man. . . . The *maricón,* like women, can be neither *revolucionario* in Havana nor anti-Communist *gusano* in Miami, because both of these identities require unambiguous and unquestioned masculinity for their constitution. . . . As an adolescent and young adult, I understood these rules well, and therefore cloaked my emerging sexual desire for other men beneath an intricately tailored suit that read unequivocally as heterosexuality.[1]

Long before Raúl became Fidel's successor, his supposed effeminacy and questionable sexuality made him an object of homophobic humor among Cuban exiles. To a young Risech, the lessons were clear: to be effeminate and a *maricón* was bad, it made you similar to the despised communists, and it placed you squarely outside the Cuban exile nation. In anti-Castro Miami, to call a man a *maricón* is almost as bad as calling him a *comunista,* and the two epithets are often intertwined in all types of derogatory diatribes. The gay men who immigrated to Miami during the Mariel boatlift entered this urban context.

However, in the two decades that followed Mariel, the narratives that placed homosexuality outside the Cuban nation and the Cuban exile community were challenged by gay cultural projects that articulated narratives of Cuba centering on male homosexuality. From the street culture of the Mariel *locas* to the celebrated visual art of the Mariel generation, from Cuban drag shows and gay Latino publications to the explicitly political work for antidiscrimination ordinances, cultural projects disrupted the circulation of images and words in which representations of gayness were tantamount to a "limp-wristed Raúl Castro" or slurs aimed at a variety of so-called bad people. In these new narratives of gay *cubanidad,* male homosexuality was not foreign to Cubanness but central to it.

Both first-generation and second-generation Cuban American gay men navigated competing narratives of Cuba. In this chapter, I analyze the narratives of Cuba that emerged in men's accounts and cultural projects throughout Miami. To the gay men I talked with, Cuba was configured through narratives of memory, family stories, contact with recent immigrants, and (more rarely) visits to the island. These descriptions of Cuba varied widely from a Cuba remembered as a romanticized site of sexual pleasure to a Cuba structured around familial homophobia and heteronormative demands. The way gay men constructed Cuba and its relation to sexuality directly affected their own ethnic identity and their ability to integrate gay and Cuban American identities.

First-Generation Immigrants Remember Cuba

In 1997 Eduardo Aparicio invited me to present my research to a newly formed group of Cuban American gay men and lesbians, Coalición CUBA (Cubans United for a Better Ambiente). In addition to the other cultural projects (editing the zine *Perra!,* writing a weekly column for one of Miami's free weekly Spanish-language newspapers, and creating public art that highlighted homophobia in Latino communities), Aparicio had organized this group. The meeting took place at the home of one of the members, a Cuban American lesbian, a few blocks away from Calle Ocho, or Southwest Eighth Street, the main artery of one Cuban American enclave. In this case, the politics of location were strategic, for Aparicio later confirmed that he had consciously chosen to claim space within Cuban American communities—not in the recognized gay enclave of South Beach. In other words, the very location of the meeting already articulated a narrative of gay *cubanidad,* one that was not concerned primarily with inserting itself into dominant Anglo notions of the gay community but that sought to feel at home in the heart of the exile community instead.

The group, which had met only a few times before, was primarily male with only three women present (including the host and myself). Everyone spoke Spanish. As the meeting progressed, I learned that the men shared certain characteristics: they were all born in Cuba and now lived in Miami. Beyond that, the group was quite diverse. Some of the men had left Cuba over twenty years ago; at least one had come as part of Mariel; and one had arrived in Miami less than a year before the meeting. The participants included a middle-aged entrepreneur; an unemployed *recién llegado,* or recent arrival, who lived with his aunt; and a working artist approaching fifty.

One of the men, Roberto, greeted all new arrivals with a question, stated loudly for everyone in the room to hear. He asked all the men, "¿Te gustan los negros?" (Do you like black men?). Roberto tempered his question by explaining in pseudoformality that he was taking a survey of how many Cuban men liked black men and identifying himself as someone who did like black men. A few of Roberto's respondents answered in the affirmative, but most did not directly respond at all.

Several things were established in these moments before the meeting officially started. One was a mood of *relajo,* an informal or unruly atmosphere that would not be contained for the rest of the afternoon. Roberto's question might be considered inappropriate, and it did seem to put off some of the attendees, for they simply ignored it. The tone of his remarks eventually did rub off on others, however, as the conversation flowed between serious topics, laughter, and jocularity—a tone I associate with Cuban American culture in particular.

Another important thing was established by this exchange. The assumptions underlying Roberto's provocative questioning began to construct a narrative of Cuba where black masculinity was a taboo object of desire. The association between blackness and virile masculinity has a long history in Cuba and the United States. This imagined black masculinity/virile sexuality is sometimes perceived as an object of desire (as Roberto's question suggests) and other times as a dangerous sexual threat. In addition to objectifying black sexuality, this conversation seemed to assume that no one who would attend the meeting was, in fact, black-identified. The specter of *el negro* was a taboo and a tantalizing object of desire for some, but he would remain, it seemed, outside this particular Cuban community. Therefore this community-building meeting began, as many do, with informal definitions of who was assumed to belong to the community. Although the skin color of meeting participants ranged in tone, all fell within the acceptable range of Cuban/Miami whiteness, and the exchanges between Roberto and the other men present reinforced that racial identity.

Although Aparicio had hoped I would give a formal presentation of my research, an informal tone had already been set. As I began to discuss the interviews I had previously conducted with mostly young, U.S.-born sons of Cuban parents (or second-generation immigrants), the Coalición members interrupted me and eagerly told me how they were different from my respondents. The young men I interviewed were American-ized, they explained. They, on the other hand, were Cubans and told me how gay life in Cuba differed from that in the United States and what being Cuban meant to them. They proceeded to paint a picture of their experiences and their narratives of gay *cubanidad*.

Interestingly, some of the men reversed the commonly held valoriza-tion of gay life in the United States as somehow freer or better than gay life in Cuba. For example, one man said, "Hay una espontaneidad en Cuba que aquí la han perdido" (There is spontaneity in Cuba that has been lost here). What others would label as progress and liberation is recast in this account as a loss. One attendee, Raúl, added that while people often discuss the repression of homosexuals in Cuba, he had found that there was an incredible amount of repression in the United States. He noted the patrolling of cruising areas and stated that he had been detained for flirting with a man on the beach in Miami. One man added that Cuba had a long history where "la sexualidad" (sexuality) was tied to "lo prohibido" (the prohibited) and "el miedo" (fear). René, whom I would interview later, cited authors such as Virgilio Piñera and Carlos Montenegro as examples of the long Cuban literary his-tory that reflected this *sexualidad*. René and others lamented that the mystery of this *sexualidad* was also lost in the openness of U.S. gay life.

Roberto spoke warmly about "sustico," the threat of fright that char-acterized the pursuit of possible partners in Cuba. This fear emerged from not knowing exactly who would be receptive to a sexual advance. To illustrate his point, Roberto described going to a movie theater on a recent trip to Cuba. A young man sitting next to him subtly brushed his leg against Roberto. Roberto describes thinking to himself: "Is he? Or isn't he?" He ended his story by remarking that this whole pursuit "era muy inocente" (was very innocent). Miguel jumped in, incredulous, "¡Parece mentira que tú digas que eso era inocente!" (I can't believe you would say that was innocent!). It remained unclear if Miguel emphasized the fact that Roberto was making this remark (I can't believe YOU would say that was innocent)—let's remember Roberto's less-than-innocent opening question—or whether this incident could be innocent at all (I can't believe you would say THAT was innocent). Although part of the excitement of the theater encounter emanated from navigating the unknown intentions of the man in the next seat, Miguel's interruption drew attention to the fact that Roberto did know more than he let on. In Cuban and other gay narratives, the movie theater is a recurring site for anonymous encounters. There were and are recognized codes for cruising that men looking for sexual encounters (and those not looking) know. The brushing of the leg, sustained eye contact, and perhaps the use of a particularly suggestive but not widely known phrase were/are forms of communication used to express sexual interest. Miguel's remark highlighted that the *sustico* relies on sustaining an unknown that everyone involved already really knows. In defense of his position, Roberto compared his Cuban movie theater encounter with gay life in the United States where everyone walks around naked with a towel wrapped around them, and it's all out there. In comparison, he maintained, there was more of an innocence to the Cuban experience. Although clearly referring to sexual encounters in baths, Roberto used this example to generalize aspects of U.S. gay life that he found unexciting. In the United States, he suggested, you know where everybody stands and what everybody wants. The aspect of pursuit and the excitement of discovery are completely lost even if their existence in Cuba relied primarily on a suspension of disbelief.

In the narrative of Cuba described by Roberto and other Coalición members, the island is a romanticized site of sexual pleasure. In this narrative, male homosexuality is far from foreign to *cubanidad*; in fact, it is figured as central to or even constitutive of *cubanidad*. Many Cuban gay cultural projects also explored the connections between sexuality, desire, and *cubanidad*. In a separate interview, Aparicio argued that homosexuality has a central place in Cuba's defining cultural expressions: he claimed a central, and not marginal, understanding of gayness in Cuba. He used the case of the composer Ernesto Lecuona and his foundational composition "Siboney"—a song often interpreted by Cuban American drag queens—to make his argument.

> Entonces no es solamente que digamos que, bueno, hay una sensibilidad gay en la música. No es cuestión de eso. Es que tú coges, y una vez más te repito, lo que quizás sea la principal composición que se ha tomado de una zarzuela de Lecuona que es "Siboney" y te encuentras el canto de un hombre a otro hombre. . . . "Siboney," que es definitoria de la cultura cubana . . . pero que al mismo tiempo es un canto de amor de un hombre a otro. Entonces por eso yo digo que la sensibilidad gay y la cultura gay son centrales a la cultura cubana porque tienes obras claves en las que las dos se están definiendo al mismo tiempo. O sea, no es marginal. No es que Lecuona haya escrito canciones de Cuba que no tenían nada que ver con la homosexualidad y tenía escondidas tres o cuatro canciones de [amor] que ahora las descubrimos. No es así. Es que está haciendo las dos cosas al mismo tiempo y que logró hacer las dos cosas al mismo tiempo. Lo mismo la obra de Lezama, de Lezama Lima, lo mismo la obra de Reinaldo Arenas. Lo mismo la obra de Virgilio Piñera, la obra de Servando.

> Then, it isn't just that there is a gay sensibility in the music. It isn't about that. It's that you take, and I repeat, what is perhaps the most important musical composition of a *zarzuela* by Lecuona, which is "Siboney," and you find a song sung from one man to another. . . . "Siboney," which defines Cuban culture . . . but at the same time is a love song from one man to another. And that's why I say that a gay sensibility and a gay culture are central to Cuban culture because there are key works that define both simultaneously. So, it is not marginal. It's not that Lecuona has written songs about Cuba that have nothing to do with sexuality and then he had these three or four hidden songs that we have recently discovered. It isn't like that. It's that he's doing both things at the same time. The works of Lezama, Lezama Lima, the works of Reinaldo Arenas, the works of Virgilio Piñera, and the works of Servando are the same.

Through this narrative of Cuba, Aparicio and other Coalición members were firmly rejecting the notion that homosexuality was foreign to *cubanidad*. On the contrary, they argue, some of the most recognized articulations of Cuban nationalism in music, art, and literature are infused with a gay sensibility.

The narrative of gay *cubanidad* also provided Coalición members an avenue for critiquing U.S.-style gay liberation. By constructing a nostalgic narrative of another cultural form of sexual pleasure, they discount the notion of U.S. gay life as the most progressive form of homosexual relations. Rather, this narrative of Cuba suggests a "gay structure of feeling" different from that dominant in the United States.[2] Raúl first challenged the notion that gay life in the United States is "free" by pointing out the ways in which his life as a gay man continued to be monitored and controlled by state agents. More profoundly, these men articulated the loss of a mode of experiencing sexual pleasure and interacting as homosexual men. Although he took an extreme position among group members, René stated that he never fully integrated to gay life here. "No siento que pertenezco" (I don't feel like I belong), he told us, even though he had lived in the United States longer than almost anyone else in the room.

Cuban-born gay men's narratives of Cuba are far from homogeneous, and not all the men in this meeting remembered Cuba as a site of (lost) sexual pleasure. Miguel argued that the rest of the group was romanticizing gay life on the island. In addition to challenging Roberto's claims of innocence, Miguel argued that sex was so predominant on the island because men had no other way to explore relationships with one another. For him, because of the extreme repression of homosexuals, gay life in Cuba could only be sexual. In the United States, however, gay men were allowed to live well-rounded lives that also entailed other obstacles like paying bills and maintaining a job. He argued against the notion that life in the United States was more repressed than life in Cuba: repression in the United States was really auto-repression where people censor themselves. In this narrative, Cuba's repressive social system and state mechanisms defined the limits of sexual life. This narrative of Cuba led to his valuing U.S. gay life and critiquing the others for not fully enjoying the freedoms it brings.

Although the men at the meeting disagreed about their visions of gay Cuban life, they agreed that *theirs* was the true authentic gay Cuban life, whereas that of my U.S.-born respondents was (uncomplicatedly) Americanized. They argued that men who came of age in the United States would not comprehend being gay in a Cuban context and would, therefore, understand themselves differently. As the meeting progressed, I was struck by how unquestioningly this group of men saw themselves as purely Cuban, uncorrupted by the almost twenty years of life in the United States some of them had experienced. As I pushed them a little on how their experiences in the United States had affected their narratives of Cuba, they began to admit that many of the manifestations of their *cubanidad* had, in fact, been learned or relearned in the United States. One man at the meeting coined the term *recubanización* to describe this process of relearning, reinventing, and redefining Cubanness. Although these men distinguished themselves clearly from U.S.-born Cuban Americans, they described a similar process of coming to terms with being Cuban. Because their narratives of Cuba centered on the authenticity of their experience, they veiled the constructedness of their Cuban identities.

One example of *recubanización* came from Roberto—obviously a very active participant in the meeting. He talked about how he had learned to dance *guaguancó* (a genre of Cuban rumba music) in the United States, something he would have never done in Cuba. Although *guaguancó* has been incorporated into mainstream Cuban popular music, it is not irrelevant that this form of dance draws from African rhythms and instrumentation. Roberto's point about *guaguancó* suggested that cultural markers associated with blackness came to mark Cuban ethnicity in the United States, but in the process became disassociated from a black racial identity. As these spokesmen for Cuban identity actually learned how to be Cuban in the United States, they also began to experience themselves as racialized beings. For example, at one point René began to explain how he actually felt less Cuban in Cuba than he did in the United States, but Raúl finished his sentence by stating "aquí te sientes negro" (here you feel black). The Coalición meeting was an unusual moment in my fieldwork in the sense that the racialization of Cuban American experience was explicitly discussed. Throughout my fieldwork and other experiences in Miami, I have found that light-skinned Cubans rarely refer to themselves in racial terms, and if they do it is usually to mark themselves as white.

Narratives of Cuba were also inscribed in the men's appearances. To reinforce his *cubanidad,* Raúl announced, "Tuvieran que tumbar todas la palmas de Miami para que yo pare de ser cubano" (They would have to cut down all the palm trees in Miami for me to stop being Cuban). Although he admitted to some shifting cultural standards, he felt that generally his Cubanness had not waned in the seventeen years he had lived in the United States. Raúl wore his hair buzzed short. He had on a white tank top and black and white jeans with a print reminiscent of Andy Warhol's silk screens. Another man at the meeting remarked that when Raúl walked in, he thought Raúl had lived in the United States a long time (based on Raúl's appearance alone). They went back and forth a while because Raúl did not accept this assessment of his appearance. He maintained that his clothes were not a sign of his Americanization but rather just "a look." Although Raúl wanted to assert that he was uncompromisingly Cuban, others contested his claims and read U.S. influences into his stylistic choices. This exchange highlighted how the men read ethnic/national identity through style, clothing, and hairstyles. It also revealed how the meanings of these styles and their relation to national and ethnic identity are contested within the group. I found myself having more questions. Namely, what narrative of Cuba is embedded in a *guayabera*?[3] What about those funky Andy Warhol pants Raúl donned?

The discussion at the Coalición meeting illustrated how different narratives of Cuba define Cuban American ethnicity even as they frame gay life. Most evident were the contradictions of Cuban racialization. At the same time that the Cuban American micro community (Coalición attendees) was defined as white (or at least not black) through the invocation of *el negro* as desired object, the Cuban American experience was defined as becoming black or becoming marked by racial otherness. Although this paradigm might appear contradictory, I believe it reflects the dialectical relationship between Cuban whiteness and nonwhiteness. Being marked by racial otherness is centrally about desire in this context. The invoked but absent *negro* is an object of sexual desire. The same desiring, othering gaze Roberto invoked to question the desirability of *el negro* has been focused on men like Roberto himself. As Cuban American men see themselves as exotic others in the eyes of Anglo men (as I discuss in chapter 7) and as they experience life as immigrants, they experience their own racialization. This is a partial process that does not integrally challenge notions of Cuban whiteness.

In the case of this meeting, *lo cubano* was defined not only by race but also by birthplace. The authentic Cuban experience was understood as that of Cuban men born and raised on the island. There was no audible disagreement on this point. Nonetheless, when pushed further on what defined Cuban authenticity, these men made clear that it was at least partly constructed in the United States through *recubanización*.

There was disagreement on the content of this narrative. Was/is Cuba primarily a site of sexual pleasure or repression for homosexual men? The answer to this question leads to different methods of evaluating gay life in the United States. For those who view Cuba primarily as a site of sexual pleasure, this narrative serves to critique the limits of U.S. gay liberation. For those who view Cuba primarily as a site of sexual repression, the story serves to critique Cuban and Cuban American heterosexism and homophobia.

Second-Generation Cuban American Gay Men and *Cubanidad*

Cuban American gay men who were raised in the United States construct narratives of Cuba quite differently than the Cuban-born Coalición members. The Cuban-born gay men described above developed narratives of Cuba that rested on a claim to authenticity derived from their Cuban birth and Cuban memories. As nôted above, even with these claims to authenticity, it is clear that their definitions of Cuba were transformed in Miami. However, second-generation Cuban American gay men were denied the myth of Cuban authenticity because of the place of their birth or upbringing. Rather than recall personal memories, they drew on a montage of information that José Esteban Muñoz calls "exilic memory":

> I have lived through the auspices of memory. By this I mean to say that exilic memory has reproduced Cuba for me. Cuba, for this Cuban, is a collection of snapshots, disembodied voices over the phone line, and most vividly, exilic memories. The ephemera and personal narratives that signify "Cuba" for me resonate as not only possessing a certain materiality, but also providing a sense of "place."[4]

The Cuban American gay men I spoke with who were raised in the United States drew from family stories, exile narratives, contact with recent arrivals, and (more rarely) travel to Cuba to construct their own Cuba narrative.

Cuba as Parents' Homophobia

One group of second-generation Cuban gay men I interviewed understood Cuba primarily through its reflection of their parents' and grandparents' homophobia. These young gay men, who did not have any direct experience of the island, constructed a narrative that drew almost exclusively on their observations of their parents or other older, heterosexual Cuban immigrants. The presence of families of origin in narratives of Cuba is not surprising given the physical proximity and regular face-to-face contact of respondents with biolegal relatives. It was difficult for this group of men to reconcile their gay identities with heterosexist narratives of Cuba. For example, when I asked Javier, a Miami-born gay man in his midtwenties, if he knew what life was like for gay people in Cuba, he drew on his own experience with his family and other Cuban people of that generation. They "have a very negative image of Cuban gay people . . . so I guess it might have been a very hard or underground thing." I asked him if he felt this negativity informed his experience: "Yes, because I grew up with parents who were Cuban. So yeah, their sense of limitation and prejudice kinda affected me." Javier associated being Cuban, or the "Latin mind-set" as he called it, with his upbringing and his family, and he identified more with "American concepts."

> A lot of my upbringing and family programming comes from that whole Latin mind-set and I find it very limiting, so I guess I don't want to have anything to do with it. Like the American concepts seem more liberating, more open. . . . Slowly but surely some attempts at reform in terms of, like, accepting sexual differences and stuff is there, but the Latins, or the Latin contingent of it, still seem pretty close-minded.

Javier had lived his whole life in the Miami area surrounded by Cuban Americans and other Latinos, and our interview took place in his grandparents' home in a predominantly Latino neighborhood where he was living at the time. He told me toward the end of our interview, "I don't think of myself as Cuban at all. . . . It's not a big deal to me." I asked him to elaborate: "Well I don't go out looking for other people that are Cuban, or try to go to Cuban events, or talk Spanish a lot, or listen to Cuban music." He told me he does not feel a connection with people based solely on ethnicity.

For men who developed a narrative of Cuba as an embodiment of their parents' homophobia, Cubans were referred to as "them" as opposed to "us." In these accounts, respondents described Cuban Americans as a clearly defined group from which they could distinguish themselves. Several men distinguished themselves so much from Cuban Americans that they were not sure if they should participate in my study at all. One respondent admitted that he would not have agreed to the interview if his boyfriend had not insisted. I asked him why he did not feel he should be a part of a study of Cuban American gay men: "I was born in Miami. I was raised in Miami. I've been raised in the United States, and my background is Cuban, but I don't consider myself a Cuban. I'm an American with a Cuban background. I don't consider myself a Cuban." In this way, some respondents rejected association with other Cuban Americans and identified American and Cuban as mutually exclusive cultural categories. It is clear that many of the respondents who rejected Cubanness constructed their notion of a Cuban almost exclusively from an older, first-generation immigrant experience.

In addition to othering and, therefore, distancing themselves from their descriptions of Cubans, most of these men characterized Cuban American culture in particular ways and directly linked their ambivalence to Cuban American culture with their lives as gay men. For example, several of the men characterized Cubans as generally antigay, homophobic, and misogynist, as did Javier. These traits, defined as specifically Cuban, were seen to conflict with participating in gay life.

Narratives of a Gay Cuba: Raised in the U.S.A.

Unlike Javier, other Cuban American gay men raised in the United States without direct experience of being gay in Cuba drew on different sources of information to develop their narratives of Cuba. Rather than draw exclusively on parents to develop an idea of Cuba, some respondents drew on information from first-generation Cuban gay men or other sources who described gay life on the island. With access to a Cuban gay aesthetic, these 1.5- and second-generation Cuban American gay men were able to make positive connections between their gay lives and their narratives of Cuba. As a result, Cuba stopped being the domain of homophobic parents, and gay Cuba became part of their own exilic memories.

Juan was in his midthirties when I interviewed him. Born in Cuba, he came to the United States when he was only seven years old.[5] During his upbringing in Miami, Juan had gone through Americanization and a subsequent process of *recubanización* that drew heavily on his relationship with more recently arrived Cuban gay men. For example, in the context of telling me how the Mariel migration had little direct impact on his life in 1980, Juan discussed his relationships with gay men who arrived in Miami as part of Mariel.

> They started to tell me stories of how it was in Cuba, and how being gay in Cuba was like, and going to eat ice cream at Coppelia or all these things. Now this movie that I saw, *Fresa y chocolate [Strawberry and Chocolate]*,

all brings that to life. I think that was a very good movie because, all the things I had heard of many years before now, I see how it all, how being gay in Cuba was, and everything was on the sly, on the sneak, and he touched your knee, whoa, wow, and that kind of thing.

Juan learned about the *sustico* and gay life in Cuba both from the accounts of first-generation Cuban American gay friends and from contemporary film depictions. When I asked Juan if he felt that gay life in Cuba was connected to his life, he responded, "I think everything that has to do with being Cuban is directly tied to my life." In the context of telling me how he engaged with and distanced himself from the barrage of Cuban political information available in Miami, he again drew on the importance of a friend who immigrated during Mariel:

JUAN: I remember the first friend I met from Mariel, I thought he was very interesting, extremely, he was *so* educated, he spoke French, this guy was exceptional, he was artistic, he was whatever, and I was just like wow. And that's the thing when I started to meet people like that I wanted to be even more and more Cuban, I was just like wow, they really have it going on. I don't know what I thought was going on there before, but yeah when I finally put, when there was an actual person . . . so it was just that other incentive. . . . Now I had friends from there and who grew up in [post-1959 Cuba] and it was all very realistic, but I guess it did affect me on some level, if anything it gave me a push to rediscover my roots, more than anything. We have another friend that he took it farther than me.

SUSANA PEÑA: What did he do?

J: He started making trips to Cuba. . . . He took it that much farther, and I don't know where he's at right now. . . . He also helped me out a lot because he would explain things to me, "oh this is this" and "this is that."

SP: Like what kinda things?

J: Like anything from poems to artwork, "this is what he means by this," and "this represents this," and music he would say, "this is a *guaguancó.*" Another friend of ours, he's really into Cuban music. As a matter of fact, [he's a] Marielito, now that I think about it. He's so Americanized that you wouldn't think about it twice, but he's really into Cuban music, and when we go over to his house there's this whole explosion of like La Lupe and Olga Guillot, and I'm like, "Oh, my god, I remember some of that stuff hearing before in my house," a lot of the stuff actually, but then there are other things that you have to really be into Cuban music to really know about it, but he's from Mariel and . . . he hasn't wanted to lose his thing either. He's made it a point not to.

Although Juan did not physically bridge the chasm between Cuba and the United States, as did his friend who "has gone much farther," he built symbolic bridges between two parallel gay experiences. As he met men his own age who had grown up in Cuba, he was surprised by how much they "had it going on," and he was also reintroduced to Cuban culture. It was a Marielito, like Roberto from the Coalición meeting, who became the educator about *guaguancó* and the world of gay Cuban icons. Juan described a feeling of surprise when being reintroduced to the music he had heard as a child in his parents' house, music reinterpreted through a gay lens that highlights particular performers' diva status (La Lupe, Olga Guillot). Juan's *recubanización* was mediated primarily by first-generation Cuban American gay men. Juan spoke of Cuban American culture as something that was uniquely his, as opposed to belonging to an older generation or a more conservative segment. For him, Cuban American culture was a living culture that he associated with the language he chose to speak, the music he listened to, and the people he befriended. Like Luis, whose relationships with older Cuban gay men opened "a door to a cultural awakening" that allowed him access to a gay Cuban sensibility, Juan also described the influence of personal relationships with Cuban American gay men who had grown up in Cuba in his *recubanización*. As they learned more about gay *cubanidad,* they developed narratives of Cuba in which they could situate themselves as gay men. They saw no contradiction between an ethnic Cuban identity and male homosexuality. On the contrary, they sought out particular Cuban forms of gay expression.

Perra!

In addition to these men's accounts, I found evidence of narratives of gay *cubanidad* in cultural projects throughout the city. I have already mentioned *Perra!,* a predominantly Spanish-language publication produced between May 1995 and March 1998 geared to gay Latinos in Miami and distributed in stores and gay clubs. Although Eduardo Aparicio hoped for a circulation of 3,000, an average of 1,500 copies per issue were printed. *Perra!* was a small-scale, sometimes sporadic publication. Its issues focused on wide array of topics including gay life in Cuba, model Latino gay and lesbian marriages, Latino gay icons, growing up Latino and gay, nationality, and homosexuality. *Perra!* tried to represent Latino gay cultural life as complex, historically influenced, and not always sexy.

At the beginning of this chapter, I discussed Risech's first encounter with homosexual representations in an exile publication, *Zig Zag.* *Periodiquitos,* as such publications are known in Miami, often circulated pejorative and mocking representations of male homosexuals. *Perra!,* in contrast, directly challenged heteronormative narratives of Cuba. Although it sometimes billed itself as a Latino gay publication, *Perra!* was overwhelmingly Cuban, not Latino in general. Except for the centerfold section and discussions of Latino clubs catering to a multinational clientele, most other content tended to be Cuban-specific. All regular contributors were Cuban themselves. Discussions of gay life and history in the home country and relations between more recent and older immigrants were mostly discussed in relation to Cuba and Cuban Americans.

As discussed in chapter 4, the title of the publication itself invoked a narrative of Cuban gay sensibility. In the second anniversary issue, Aparicio further conveyed the zine's meaning and tone. In his editorial, he wrote of his baby *perrita,* abandoned by her mother at such a young age, raised by her *madrinas, tías adoptivas,* and father.[6] This *perrita* had traveled the world, making stops in Miami, Miami Beach, Hialeah, New York, San Francisco, and Havana.

> La perrita ha metido su hociquito en muchas partes: ha querido ser marie-lita, balsera, refugiada y hasta husmeado a algún o otro recluta. Todo por el bien de la cultura y el amor de la patria. Perra! no es sino una perrita sata y peculiar que adora toda clase de pajaritos.[7]

> The little dog *[perrita]* has stuck her snout in many places. She's wanted to be a *Marielita*, a rafter, a refugee, and has even snooped out one recruit or another. All for the good of our culture and love of our country. *Perra!* is nothing more than a peculiar mutt that loves all types of *pajaritos.*

In his witty style, Aparicio revealed much about the way he imagined the publication. In his play on the magazine's title, the Cuban gay expression *perra* again connotes dog, in this case a small or young female-gendered dog, *perrita.* Through the dog's travels, we learn a bit more about the magazine's history, its intended audience, and the narratives of Cuba that would dominate its content. *Perra!*'s Cuban roots were never far from the surface. In the story above, the *perrita*'s travels through Havana and Miami were clearly meant to suggest her Cuban heritage. The references to the "good of our culture" and "the love of our country" implied a relationship between this gay publication and Cuban nationalism. While playing with the recurring theme of Cuban patriotism, Aparicio pointed to a heterogeneous Cuban American gay community, one that embraced men who came during the Mariel boat-lift, those who had recently come on rafts ("balseros"), and those from varied class backgrounds.

Perra! explored a variety of Cuban gay experiences—discussing different migration generations, gay life on both sides of the Florida Straits, and both masculine- and feminine-identified gay men. For example, an early contributor to *Perra!* writing under the name Corin Desentellado explored the sexual travails of a *loca* living in today's Havana in a serialized novel. With sexual explicitness, humor, and drama, Desentellado discussed everything from cruising for a real man on Havana's famed sea wall, el Malecón, to the sexual awakening of a young *guajiro,* to a glimpse at life in the UMAP camps.[8] Desentellado's short installments highlighted culturally specific forms of sexual desire and sexual conquest. While remembering the tactics of the UMAP camps, these articles highlighted the cultural expression of *locas* under oppressive conditions to dramatize their sexual power and conquests.

In the issue devoted to *balseros, Perra!* included short testimonials from *balseros, recién llegados,* and their admirers. These accounts examined gay expression in the Guantánamo camps and the way Cuban Americans perceived *recién llegados.* By exploring differences between and connections among the experiences of men who were held in the UMAP camps, Cuban Americans raised in the United States, drag queens and young couples living in contemporary Havana, refugees in the camps at Guantánamo, and men who came during the Mariel boatlift, *Perra!* constantly disrupted a homogeneous interpretation of gay *cubanidad.*

The political goal of exploring the experiences of diverse groups of Cuban gay men was often achieved in a deceptively simple way, through discussions of personal relationships. In an advice column, a "reader" asked about his American boyfriend, another asked if his *balsero* boyfriend took advantage of him, and Julie Mastrossimone wrote regularly about her Cuban love. The exile experience in these pages was not that of an established Cuban American middle class in Miami. Without the tone of political diatribe, *balseros,* Marielitos and Marielitas, *habaneros,* and Cuban Americans provided a jagged and provocative picture of Miami, where common nationality formed the basis of unity and the backdrop for emotional and sometimes painful discussions.

By producing a publication where both Cubanness and gayness

were central, *Perra!* directly challenged the idea that these were competing identities. In his regular column titled "Dime que te pica" ("Tell
Me Where It Itches," or, colloquially, "Tell Me What's Bothering You"),
the psychotherapist Jorge Arocha dealt directly with the question of
identities in flux. A "reader" wrote to say he felt he had been living
two lives: one Cuban and another gay.[9] He asked how he could reconcile these two lives. Arocha responded that the tension between the
Americanization of gay culture, which gives the impression that being
gay is a uniquely U.S. phenomenon, and the "frozen exile culture,"
which holds in place 1950s homophobia, contributed to a feeling that
Cuban and gay lives are mutually exclusive. Almost directly responding to the issues raised by the Cuban Americans I interviewed who
distanced themselves from Cuban culture, Arocha continued:

> Lo que más te puede ayudar a reconciliar estos dos mundos es fijarte en la
> tradición cubana gay, que es tan netamente gay como cubana. La cultura
> y la historia cubana están llenas de grandes figuras gay. . . . A pesar de la
> homofobia causada por el machismo y el catolicismo, los cubanos tenemos
> una fuerte tradición gay, que mucho ha enriquecido nuestra historia. Por
> lo cual, te digo que sí, que sí puedes ser gay y cubano. ¡Y a mucha honra![10]

> What can most help you reconcile these two worlds is to focus on the gay
> Cuban tradition, which is just as gay as it is Cuban. Cuban culture and his-
> tory are filled with great gay figures. . . . In spite of the homophobia caused
> by machismo and Catholicism, we Cubans have a strong gay tradition that
> has greatly enriched our history. And because of this, I say that yes, you
> can be gay and Cuban. And that's something to be proud of!

The cover of the April 1997 issue of *Perra!* specifically dedicated to
cubanidad featured a picture of a drag queen with a dress bearing the
image of the Cuban flag (similar to one Celia Cruz used to wear) and
a young masculine-looking man with a Cuban flag cap.[11] Posing in
front of Havana buildings, blue ocean waves, and more flags, these figures embodied exaggerated kitsch. This issue in particular engaged in
queering Cuban nationalism. Liván, the macho, copped a tough pose
with a cigar in his mouth, and gazed aloofly at the ground. On the other
hand, Yoko, in her fabulous flag dress, looked directly at the camera
with her hip slightly cocked to the side to show off the immense red
platform heels that left her towering over her Liván.

This queering of Cubanness actively mocked hegemonic and heterosexist *cubanidad,* but this issue did not just critique patriarchal, heterosexist Cuban culture because such a critique would, in and of itself,

The April 1997 issue of *Perra!* magazine focused on *cubanidad.* Copyright by Eduardo Aparicio; reproduced with permission.

have also assumed that gay culture and Cuban culture were mutually exclusive. Instead, *Perra!* reclaimed a Cuban nationalism that is gay to the core. In his editorial introduction to the issue, Aparicio explained his vision:

> Cubanidad y homosexualidad son palabras que riman. ¡Y vaya qué rima! La trayectoria de la cubanidad se puede ver no sólo como sincretismo de lo español y lo africano, sino como una íntima y mutua sincronía de masculini-

dades que se buscan, desean y compenetran, forjando así al moderno *homo cubanus*. . . . Cubanidad. Homosexualidad. Libertad. ¡Y vaya qué rima![12]

Cubanidad and homosexuality are words that rhyme. And what a rhyme! The trajectory of Cubanness is not only seen in the syncretism of the Spanish and the African, but also in the intimate and mutual synchronization of masculinities that search each other out, that desire one another, that interpenetrate each other, forging the modern *homo cubanus*. . . . *Cubanidad*. Homosexuality. Liberty. What a rhyme!

Perra!'s rejection of marginality and its assertion of a central claim to *cubanidad* functioned as community validation and cultural reinterpretation. *Perra!* reclaimed icons, used jargon, claimed some of the most important artists in Cuba's history, and deployed Spanish as the vehicle to convey these messages. It strove to provide Cuban and gay role models flamboyant and mundane, to write the history of gay Cuban life, and to explore how real relations between different types of gay Cubans might work themselves out. For some of *Perra!*'s readers, this project was, of course, something they already knew, already spoke, already believed, and already were. For other readers, however, it spoke volumes about the possibility of an integrated community of Cuban gay men with acknowledged differences sharing a common history and validating their experiences.

SAVE Dade

In the late 1990s the Miami–Dade County Commission (previously known as the Dade County Commission) once again considered including homosexuality in an antidiscrimination ordinance. As discussed in chapter 1, when a similar ordinance was passed and subsequently repealed because of Anita Bryant's Save Our Children campaign in the 1970s, gay rights activists made a strategic decision not to target Cuban Americans because they were believed to be so socially conservative that bringing this issue to their attention could only hurt the gay rights cause. Twenty years later, the leader of the gay rights effort was a Cuban American, and discourses of gay *cubanidad* echoed in this campaign. Gay activists of the 1990s were able to integrate *lo cubano* with gay life and culture in their political campaign.

The first time the Human Rights Ordinance was introduced, it was flatly rejected, and four Cuban American commissioners voted against the measure.[13] In response, two gay rights organizations banded together as SAVE Dade. Cuban-born Jorge Mursili, who was often ethnically identified in media reports, became the group's visible and vocal leader. Mursili, often pictured in a business suit, presented a respectable image of Cuban American masculinity. In fact, he was able to gain the support of the Catholic Church partly because of his own religious credentials as a practicing Catholic. In a 1998 *Miami Herald* article, a lawyer was quoted as giving the following assessment of Mursili:

> The knock on the [gay] movement in the past has been it's too aggressive, too far out of the mainstream. . . . In Jorge Mursili, the movement had a leader who laughs easily, learns quickly, listens earnestly, labors tirelessly and looks like the boy next door.[14]

Symbols of Cubanness emerged in public mobilizations for the ordinance. During Miami's 1997 gay pride march, demonstrators expressed their support. The *Miami Herald*'s coverage of this march noted that about half the participants were Hispanic.[15] The pictures documenting this rally in the *Herald* include one with several signs in Spanish, including one designed by Aparicio. This sign was also reproduced on the cover of *Perra!* and on the public art billboard Aparicio designed. In a simple font, the sign read simply that homophobia equals dictatorship. In the context of Miami, a reference to dictatorship is often quickly associated with Fidel Castro and Cuba, so this manifestation of public art especially resonated with Miami's Cuban American community. In the same newspaper picture, another man held a sign for Coalición CUBA. The two men holding the signs donned straw hats that referenced tropicalized notions of *cubanidad*. These images directly disrupted a heteronormative narrative of Cuba and presented a narrative of gay *cubanidad* that equated the struggle for gay rights with the struggle against Castro's totalitarian government. They suggested that if you oppose Castro, you must also oppose homophobia.[16]

When the ordinance passed in 1998, the images published by the *Miami Herald* demonstrated the extent to which the gay rights struggle had become intertwined with Cuban iconography.[17] Mursili was pictured in one corner, dressed in suit and tie, obviously celebrating the success. In the background, someone was waving a Cuban flag. The success of gay rights was repeatedly marked by signs of Cubanness: a Cuban American man, a Cuban flag. The fact that Cuban men embodied SAVE Dade's gay rights struggle helped displace long-held

PERRA!
L A   R E V I S T A

HOMOFOBIA
=
DICTADURA

G A Y
CUBANO

FOTO: APARICIO

Vida y cultura *gay* de Miami
Año 3. Número 25. Septiembre de 1997

This photograph, shown here on the cover of *Perra!* magazine's September 1997 issue, was taken at a demonstration in support of the Human Rights Ordinance that took place outside the Dade County Commission offices on July 8, 1996. The sign stating Homofobia = Dictadura was also featured in a *Miami Herald* article about Miami's 1996 Gay Pride celebrations. Copyright by Eduardo Aparicio; reproduced with permission.

formulations of gay as synonymous with white men and gay rights as antithetical to Cuban cultural values.

I do not want to overstate the case. In the final vote, the majority of Cuban American commissioners still voted against including sexual orientation in the antidiscrimination ordinance. However, two Hispanic commissioners (one Cuban American and one Puerto Rican), Miami–Dade county's influential Cuban American mayor, and a few vocal voices throughout the Cuban American community spoke publicly in favor of gay rights.[18] The struggle over gay rights in Miami–Dade County made some redefine or at least temporarily reconsider their heterosexist claim of what it meant to be Cuban in Miami.

The hypervisibility of Cuba in Miami in the 1990s and the new millennium should not be underestimated. Narratives of Cuba were not simply nostalgic longings for a lost nation, but rather played an active role in dialectically constructing Miami for both first-generation and second-generation Cuban Americans. This visibility of the ethnic nation coincided with the politics of sexual visibility. Whereas homophobic depictions associated visible or "obvious" homosexuality with its communist enemies, Cuban gay men worked to challenge these associations. In some cases, they challenged these depictions by using the visibility and cultural centrality of male homosexuality to claim a right to the core of the Cuban nation.

As this chapter demonstrates, there is no singular narrative of Cuba. As Cuban American gay men from different immigrant generations negotiated narratives of *cubanidad* and sexual identity, the importance of families of origin kept emerging as an important site where *cubanidad* was learned and negotiated. In the following chapter, I analyze Cuban American gay men's relationship with biological family or families of origin and how these relationships intersected with the politics of visibility.

6 FAMILIES, DISCLOSURE, AND VISIBILITY

WHEN RUBÉN WAS TWELVE YEARS OLD, he told his family he liked boys and not girls. He had heard his parents talk about their love of freedom, a freedom they lost in Cuba and had found again in the land of opportunity. They talked about freedom of speech and the freedom to make one's own choices. Thus twelve-year-old Rubén did not censor himself when proclaiming his attraction for the same sex. He explained: "When I was twelve, I just told everybody I was gay. I don't even know if I knew 'gay' or 'homosexual,' I just knew what I was."

Rubén learned an important lesson that day about Cuban exiles' love of freedom: his psychiatric treatments began almost immediately after his announcement. He had not yet had a sexual experience, so his parents were incredulous: "They were like, 'How could you know?' I don't know. . . . They took it very badly, and they took me to a psychiatrist for three years, once a week, to try and turn me around." Rubén explained his parents' reaction as related to their Cuban upbringing: "My parents . . . left Cuba when they were twenty-five, twenty-six. Their feelings about gay people, the reason why it's so difficult for them to accept me, is because of their Cuban upbringing. That's affected my life a lot."

At the time of our interview, Rubén was a twenty-five-year-old college student who worked part-time. He had been born in the United States and had lived in Miami since he was one year old. He told me the story about his parents' reaction to his declaration early on in the interview; nevertheless, throughout our conversation, he emphasized how much he valued his current relationship with his parents. Although it had been ten years since his last trip to the psychiatrist, Rubén and his parents did not talk about the fact that he was not "cured." In fact, they did not discuss his sexuality at all. He described their stance toward his gayness as "silent acceptance." Given their original reaction, his years of "treatment," and their silence about the issue, it might be surprising that Rubén still lived with both of his parents. His choice to live at home, however, could be explained by economic necessity, for he was trying to pursue his studies. Nonetheless, he spoke of his family only in the warmest terms. Although Rubén's parents did not completely accept that he was gay and did not know about his boyfriend, the family was "close in other ways." They discussed all aspects of his life, except his sexuality. They ate meals together, "hung out," and provided him with a sense of security.

This chapter focuses on the complicated dynamics between Cuban American gay men and their families of origin. Compared with my other respondents, Rubén told a story both unusual and typical. His parents' harsh medicalized response to his declaration was unusual but, unfortunately, not unique in my sample. His explicit, verbal declaration of his sexuality was not the most common strategy employed by the men I interviewed. Nonetheless, Rubén did have much in common with the majority of my respondents. Like Rubén, most respondents discussed how they valued their relationships with families of origin and the ways their lives were concretely structured with family needs in mind. One-third of my respondents lived with parents, grandparents, or siblings. This percentage included young twenty-somethings, but also older men who shared their homes with family members and sometimes served as primary caretakers for their mothers and grandmothers. While my sample is not representative, my research suggests that the relationship between sexuality, family, and migration for Cuban American gay men is distinct from the dominant narrative of gay identity in the United States.

Family and Migration

The dominant story about the emergence of modern homosexual communities in the United States tells a particular story about the role of family and migration. John D'Emilio argues that changes produced by urbanization and industrial capitalism created the possibility for men and women to organize their lives outside a heterosexual family unit. For men in particular, D'Emilio maintains, the forces of industrial capitalism removed them from a household economy and made the heterosexual family an affective group rather than the only means of economic survival.[1] Allan Bérubé argues that the internal migrations caused by World War II played a key role in the development of a gay group identity in the United States. Men and women who enlisted in the military left their heterosexual family units, entered sex-segregated environments, and later returned to port cities and metropolitan areas after military service. In these new locales populated in large part by internal migrants like themselves, men and women relied primarily on commercial establishments, rather than family, to organize their social and sexual lives. An increase in divorce rates, greater sexual permissiveness, and the increased commercialization of sexuality and leisure time also contributed to the possibility of organizing one's life outside the heterosexual family.[2]

D'Emilio and Bérubé rightfully emphasize the role of structural factors in organizing gender/sexual identities and communities. Their analyses, however, most strongly account for U.S.-born Anglo men and women. What is the impact of international migration (as opposed to domestic migration) on families of origin? How does race figure into these analyses? In his study of "gay" Mexican immigrants to the United States, Lionel Cantú Jr. has noted that "in the case of international migration, family-economic interdependence may continue to play a role in relations and identity even while reconfigured through migratory processes and while new systems of support are created."[3] In other words, whereas decreasing dependency on families of origin coincided with domestic migration for the men D'Emilio and Bérubé discuss, international migration can increase dependency on families of origin and extended families. The racialization of some immigrants and the loss of citizenship rights can also further increase dependency, for international migrants cannot necessarily rely on the state for support and might enlist family networks for economic and social support and, indeed, protection from the state.[4] In these cases, heterosexual families of origin continue to be necessary sources of economic survival and can provide a valued space for cultural resistance against forms of racial discrimination even as they may reinforce heteronormativity. In addition, Cantú documents how gay Mexican immigrants who manage to gain social and/or economic status in the United States find that their families are dependent on them. In this case, he argues that "economic interdependence . . . may actually facilitate familial acceptance."[5]

Although Cuban Americans in Miami are unlikely to discuss their families in terms of resistance to racial discrimination—most do not see themselves as a nonwhite racial group—Lisandro Pérez has shown that, at least for early immigrant waves, family structure was related to economic success. The majority of Cuban immigrants prior to 1980 either had close relatives living in South Florida or had arrived with biological family. Analyzing 1980 census data, Pérez found that Cuban Americans had lower fertility rates, were more likely to have three-generation households, and had a higher percentage of women in the labor force than other Latino groups. In addition, grandparents contributed to family income directly through government aid and indirectly by providing in-house child care, an advantage that in turn facilitated Cuban American women's participation in the paid labor force.[6] These demographic data indicate that a particular type of Cuban American family (three-generation, dual-income, with few children and possible government aid) was intrinsically linked with the dominant success story narrative, as proved by high family income. Also, members of these types of family were more likely to be successful entrepreneurs, the common protagonists of the success story. Therefore the pooling of resources involved in multigenerational households constituted one important factor in the economic positioning of Cuban Americans.

Research on gay families has noted differences between Anglo and non-Anglo respondents.[7] For example, in her foundational study on "families we choose" based on interviews with gay men and lesbians living in San Francisco, Kath Weston acknowledges that people of color were more likely to draw "connections between sexual identity, race, class, ethnicity, and kinship" and to privilege "blood" families over "chosen" families.[8] In his more recent study of gay families, Christopher Carrington also notes that

> Latino/Asian/African-identified lesbigay families recurrently report more extensive connections to biolegal relatives than do Euro-American families, and further, they more often than not conceive of family in strongly biolegal terms. For instance, they report greater exchange of money and material goods with biolegal relatives.[9]

Both Weston and Carrington quickly explain away these differences. Weston is unwilling to grant that people of color really do have different relationships to their families and to the coming-out process than do middle-class, nonethnically defined whites. Carrington attributes the differences in his study to the geographic proximity to families of origin as opposed to race/ethnicity. In fact, 90 percent of Carrington's Anglo respondents grew up outside the state and subsequently migrated to California. The "wide majority" of non-Anglo respondents, on the other hand, had grown up in California and because their "biolegal kin live in the area, kin relations become more extensive and more pressing."[10] Rather than attribute findings to geographic proximity or race/ethnicity, I would ask why it is that although 90 percent of Carrington's Anglo respondents moved from out of state to San Francisco, the majority of people of color grew up and remained in California? One possible explanation is that the developmental pattern of moving far away from families of origin in one's early adulthood is more common (and likely) for middle- and upper-class, college-educated Anglos than in it is for others. If that is true, then how do working-class people, people without higher education, and people of color develop gay lives and cultures with their families of origin in their figurative (and sometimes literal) backyards?

In his popular book about gay life in America, Frank Browning shares an observation of a gay male couple, Luna and Gilberto, that might shed some light on how Cuban American families adapt to gay sons and their partners. According to Browning, Luna has been "taken in as a member of the family" by "Gilberto's large traditional family . . . who knew that Luna and Gilberto were lovers."[11] Browning states that "in no other place in America had [he] seen such close ties between gay men and their families—a closeness made all the more remarkable by the fierce conservatism of Cuban Miami."[12] In his discussion of Cuban American and Puerto Rican gay men in Miami, Stephen P. Kurtz also notes that whereas Puerto Rican men chose to leave their biological homes when confronted with the gendered, heteronormative expectations of their families, the Cuban American gay men he interviewed did not consider this option.

> Cuban men in this study felt extremely constrained—much more than the Puerto Rican men—to meet parental expectations. For all of them, developing strategies that enabled them to hide their homosexuality while remaining within the family circle became of paramount concern. To this day, all of the Cuban men (and none of the Puerto Rican men) live in the same cities as their close relatives.[13]

Kurtz argues that Cuban American gay men living in Miami strive to live gay lives that do not preclude them from involvement with and proximity to biological family, and some of them achieve this balance by adopting masculine identities and appearances.[14]

Because I interviewed Cuban American gay men in Miami—the metropolitan area with the highest concentration of Cuban Americans in the United States—my study foregrounds the experiences of men who have chosen to stay in an area with a large population of co-ethnics and are more likely to live near their families of origin. If in D'Emilio and Bérubé's analyses, domestic migration moved men and women away from their families of origin and offered distance from family surveillance, in my study, the most significant migration in my respondents' lives was an international migration (theirs or their parents') from Cuba to the United States. The extent to which families of origin figured in the daily lives of the Cuban American gay men I interviewed formed a surprising characteristic of my sample. The majority of the men I interviewed maintained strong relationships with their families. Apart from the one-third of respondents who lived with their families of origin, most of the remaining respondents maintained regular contact with their families and expressed a special valuing of these relationships. Some of these were Generation X men who lived with heterosexual family because they could not afford to live on their own. Javier, for example, understood that the inability to afford to live alone characterized his generation: "In better economic times I live on my own. If I fall short, like, I guess most of the quote, unquote 'slackers' or 'X generation' do, they end up going back home to their parents after they're in their early- to mid-20s like I have."

Even men who did not share a home with families of origin maintained regular physical contact with family members. Most of my respondents described a commitment or obligation to their families of origin. The value of family was not only symbolic or abstract. Rather, it was grounded in men's everyday lives and included significant time commitments devoted to family responsibilities. For example, one respondent visited his mother every week to help her with any translation she needed; another visited his grandmother weekly in a nursing home; another ate dinner with his parents once a week; and another took regular vacations with his parents. I would not argue that these Cuban American gay men valued families of origin over chosen families, as Weston claims for her sample. Rather, I would argue that, especially in the case of men in long-term relationships, chosen families and families of origin interpenetrated one another.

While a Cuban American family structure might in fact serve as a form of economic support, as Pérez's research suggests, few men discussed their connection with their families in these terms. A couple of men, like Javier, did admit that they lived with family members for economic reasons. In general, though, respondents emphasized non-economic modes of familial support that are less easy to measure than financial rewards. Respondents explained that families provided them with emotional support as well as a sense of home and a reliable source of advice. While he indicated that his family was "very overprotective," Michael, who lived with his parents, added:

> You know, when we're young we tend to think, "Oh god these fuckin' Cuban parents," but as I get older I realize I have it good, and I have a great family, and I really can't complain. I see a lot of my American friends, who are not from here. Their families are all spread around. It's different, so I'm lucky in that sense.

Rather than describe physical distance from family in positive terms, Michael reframed this distance as a loss. Although he was a gay man living with heterosexual parents who did not know about his sexuality, he considered himself "lucky" to be near them.

Relationships with families of origin affected the way these men valorized disclosure and visibility. My research suggests that the relationship between financial status, family structure, migration, and gay lives that D'Emilio and Bérubé highlight operates differently for Cuban American gay men in Miami. This difference, in turn, affects the kinds of family relationships that are both possible and desired by my respondents.

None of the men I interviewed completely hid their homosexuality in all spheres of their lives. In fact, most respondents participated actively in many aspects of public gay cultures. Most also strongly valued maintaining relationships with their families of origin. However, most families of origin did not acknowledge or fully accept my respondents' homosexuality. How then did the men manage to maintain strong family relationships while participating in a gay world? Most of the Cuban American gay men I interviewed employed strategies of nondisclosure in relation to families of origin. In other words, dominant narratives of coming out do not fully explain how the relationship between gay life and families of origin was negotiated by this sample. For instance, in her discussion of coming out, Weston found that almost all her respondents "viewed disclosure to family as desirable."[15] What seemed most desirable to most of the men I spoke with was to maintain family relationships whether or not that prohibited the disclosure of a gay identity, in their opinion. Although representing an extreme position, Miguel, a Cuban-born man in his late thirties who came to the United States as a young boy, told me he felt his younger Cuban American gay male friends were making the "biggest mistake of their lives" coming out to their families because their families "would never be able to accept it." Weston reports that most of the people she interviewed believed that "deception has a negative effect on social relationships, undermining the trust considered a prerequisite for 'close' connections."[16] My respondents did not simply equate nondisclosure with deception. Nondisclosure sometimes coexisted with a profound incorporation of gay partners, as was the case for Luna and Gilberto described by Browning.

Those Cuban American gay men I interviewed who did not verbally disclose their sexuality to their families of origin did not necessarily identify their own nondisclosure as deception, nor did they necessarily understand themselves to be "in the closet." As I argued in chapter 4, for some men, narratives of coming out made little sense to the way they understood their sexuality: because they understood their sexuality as visible and obvious, these kinds of declarations seemed redundant. Several men believed they were able to maintain relationships with their biological families because they never explicitly discussed their sexuality. Moreover, some assumed that their families knew they were gay. For example, Juan, a Cuban-born man in his midthirties who came to the United States as a young boy, explained that he was not "completely out and open" with his parents. If he were, "things might be different, but I've never made a decision because I don't know how it's going to turn out, and I don't want to take the chance, and since things now aren't bad, you know, why provoke a situation?" Although Juan had never discussed his sexuality with his mother, he believed that "she realizes it already. She might not want to deal with it . . . but she realizes it already. . . . She's smart enough not to ask me something she doesn't want to know the answer to." Although this lack of explicit discussion of sexuality might be interpreted as deception, it is important to note the extent to which Juan's partner, Jacobo, had been incorporated into Juan's family of origin. In fact, Juan and his boyfriend shared a one-bedroom condominium. They had dinner with Juan's parents regularly. Moreover, both men and their respective families had all celebrated the previous *nochebuena* (Christmas Eve) together: the shared holiday was significant because Christmas Eve is traditionally spent with extended family of origin in Cuban culture.

At one point in the interview, Juan did invoke the language of deception, saying, "to this day, to an extent, I live a double life." As he continued, the complexity of the relationship among Juan, Juan's parents, and Jacobo emerged:

> I'm sure [my parents] know what's going on. I haven't talked to them about it. I haven't sat down and told my mom, "Look, this and this and this is going on. And this is Jacobo. This is what Jacobo is." But they're not stupid. We've been living together for four years, and it's a one-bedroom apartment, and there's only one bed. Initially when we first moved in together, I had a sofa bed, and the story was Jacobo slept on the sofa bed and I slept on the bed. But later on the sofa bed went, and they never said anything. My parents never said a thing, so it's just like that: it's kinda understood, and it's not talked about.

We discussed not only the relationships among Juan, his parents, and Jacobo but also the relationship between Juan's family of origin and Jacobo's family of origin. After discussing how well both sets of families got along during the Christmas holidays, I asked Juan whether sharing time with both families was important to him. He replied:

> Yeah, it's very important to me because that way it just simplifies everything. There's no headache that comes from when the in-laws don't like each other. Or, let's say my mom didn't like [Jacobo]. That would be terrible on me because my mom is the most important thing.

Similarly, Miguel, who believed young Cuban American gay men were making the "biggest mistake of their lives" by coming out, was living in his parents' house with his partner at the time of our interview. However, Miguel did not consider his cohabitation with his boyfriend in his parents' house a "mistake" like that of the younger men he had chastised because his was not a direct, open declaration. In his estimation, he and his boyfriend made an effort to maintain appearances, an effort that involved the performance of accepted masculinity, as I discuss in chapter 7.

In situations like those of Juan and Miguel, where long-term partners are incorporated into the family of origin, partners were often referred to by the euphemistic "amigo" (friend) as opposed to "novio" (boyfriend) or "marido" (lover or husband). In other words, Miguel's mother would likely introduce her son's boyfriend as "el amigo de Miguel" (never "el novio de Miguel" or "el marido de Miguel"), although this euphemism could be understood to imply a relationship more intimate than that of mere friends.[17]

Unlike Juan and Miguel, Martín had spoken directly to his mother about his sexuality. He did not volunteer information, but his mother had read a journal in which Martín had described a liaison with another boy. Subsequently, Martín came home to find his mother setting his journal on fire. After this incident, she only rarely acknowledged knowing about his sexuality: "She chooses to have selective memory about my sexuality. So you know, she has to deal with it her own way I suppose. To this day we have conversations and I clearly tell her, and, you know, she just won't acknowledge it, a complete block out." Martín added that physical distance and financial independence from his family allowed him to come to terms with his gay identity: "becoming independent in other ways, becoming financially independent, living on my own" facilitated his "being comfortable" with being gay. That being said, Martín lived only fifteen minutes away from both of his parents. When I asked him about his average week, he described spending his Saturdays visiting his grandmother, his sister, and the rest of his family. Therefore, even migrations away from the family often entailed only short trips that could be easily bridged by return visits and, in the case of this sample, did not usually involve cutting off close ties. Like Martín, other respondents had spoken explicitly with their families of origin, most often their mothers, about their sexuality. However, such explicit instances of coming out were often followed by a continued silence on the topic. Some interpreted these silences positively as "silent acceptance," while others read them negatively as "selective memory." Although the story with which I opened the chapter exemplifies a startlingly negative response by parents to a son's disclosure—they sent him to psychiatric treatments to try to "cure" his homosexuality—Rubén insisted that although he and his parents no longer spoke about his sexuality, they "were close in other ways": "We talk about school. We talk about my other friends. . . . We hang out a lot, we have dinner all the time, we're close."

In a published interview, Eduardo Aparicio discusses the differences between "acceptance" in Anglo versus Cuban American contexts:

In the Anglo culture, you verbalize all these things, you talk publicly about sexuality, you demand your rights through laws, you give testimonials on TV . . . but in Latin families, what occurs is an acceptance without talking about the issue. That, however, doesn't mean there is a rejection. On the contrary, there is almost a sheltering, a need to protect others. That's why your mother will tell you, "It's OK, but don't tell your cousin or your uncle."[18]

Hugo, a respondent who had disclosed his sexuality to his family, echoed this point. Hugo argued that Cuban American families in general are more accepting than people think: "They could accept [a gay son]. Cubans here in the States are more, I feel like they're closer because they're not home. . . . They're united family wise more. So they're probably like, 'He's gay, but so what?,' you know." Scholars and popular commentators have argued that immigration has made Cuban Americans and other immigrants more socially conservative because they are trying to re-create a static culture from their past. There is certainly ample evidence of this trend, and the Cuban Americans who supported Anita Bryant in the 1970s are but one example. However, Hugo points out, immigration or being "not home" might have also made Cuban American families more flexible and increased their ability to accept or incorporate gay sons into their midst.

Culturalist Evocations of the Latino Family

In my study, I found that families of origin and families of choice interpenetrated one another to produce a complex web of family disclosures and nondisclosures, closeness and distance. To be clear, public and explicit verbal acknowledgment of homosexuality by families of origin was highly uncommon. On the other hand, the extent to which long-term gay male partners were incorporated into families of origin and how men of all ages maintained regular, physical contact with families of origin were striking. How do we make sense of this apparent paradox and what conclusions can we draw about Cuban American gay culture and families?

Putting this study in dialogue with other works about Latino gay men that discuss families helps address this question. For example, there are interesting parallels and differences between my findings and Rafael Díaz's 1998 study on Latino gay men and HIV. As in my study, Latino gay men in Díaz's sample said relationships with family of origin were central to their lives; some of the men interviewed in his study describe families of origin in positive terms, as a "haven of security"; most of the men in his study did not openly discuss their sexuality with families of origin; and most of the men believed that participation in families of origin required silence about their sexuality.[19] Although there are several commonalities in our empirical data, Díaz and I come to quite different conclusions.

Díaz argues that men who did not openly discuss their sexuality with families of origin necessarily had to segregate gay friends and partners from families of origin. He says, "For those individuals who remain in close connection to their families, identification with and participation in family life requires that their sexual lives, their sexual partners or lovers, and their gay friends be excluded from the social, affective network of family membership."[20] This assumption that non-disclosure of sexuality coincides with segregation between families of origin and gay friends and partners seems contradicted by Díaz's own evidence (and is not the pattern I found either). For example, one of Díaz's respondents told the interviewer that he believed his family of origin knows about his life, "but we don't talk about it." When asked about how he knew that his family understood, he responded:

> RESPONDENT: I think I was a very effeminate little boy and I don't ever remember my family putting me down for just being who I was, and as I developed into adolescence I think I stopped being effeminate but I was more in touch with my own desires and sexuality. And when I was sixteen years old, I started my gay life and I was never ashamed or embarrassed to bring my gay friends home and sometimes they were pretty obvious. So to me the indicators were like my family sees me surrounded by these very unusual type people and yet they don't put it down or anything. They just kind of allow me to be myself.
> INTERVIEWER: But it's never been openly discussed?
> R: It's never been openly discussed.[21]

Far from an account of a family life that required exclusion of gay community, this account seems to stress the incorporation of gay friends, an emerging adolescent gay community, and gender-transgressive expressions of male homosexuality into families of origin. In Díaz's analysis, however, this evidence in the respondent's account is completely overshadowed by the final question and answer that reveal that the respondent did not openly discuss sexuality with his family of origin. For Díaz, "true acceptance" by families of origin requires open discussion and explicit, ongoing verbal communication about sexuality. Even if respondents asserted the importance of family support, if this type of communication did not accompany them, Díaz classifies them as "stories of tolerance and non-abuse rather than true acceptance."[22]

This logic is not Díaz's alone. As discussed in chapter 1, since the 1970s, the mainstream gay and lesbian movement in the United States had privileged a strategy of "coming out, asserting homosexual visibility as a basis for basic rights," and Díaz's model for a healthy gay identity is clearly "homosexual men in the Western industrialized world."[23] For this group, he argues that membership in gay community "requires a shift of referent group from the family to the peer group, which is a re-working of social support systems and personal loyalties away from family of origin."[24] I agree with him that Latino gay men in both of our studies clearly did not fully shift their referent group away from families of origin; many of the men in my study very actively maintained relationships with families of origin in their adult lives. Where I disagree with Díaz is in the assumption that the model of homosexual development so typical in the Western industrialized world (and especially among the white middle-class populations of that world) is the only way in which to lead a healthy and fulfilling life and that any other model is necessarily regressive and inferior.

In his study of sexuality in Guadalajara, Mexico, Héctor Carrillo defines sexual silence as "a widespread method used to keep transgressive sexual behavior under wraps in order to maintain the appearance of normality."[25] While he argues along the lines of Díaz that sexual silence was a "major roadblock for open acceptance of sexual diversity" that came with "a price in terms of the inability to achieve full acceptance of sex, as well as potentially negative psychological effects," he also argues:

> I would be wary of overly pathologizing the use of the strategy. . . . sexual silence also has a productive side, not only in relation to tacit tolerance that it creates but also in terms of sex itself . . . sexual silence also flavors cultural scripts about seduction, sexual passion, and the enactment of sex itself.[26]

In his subtle analysis of interviews with Dominican immigrant gay men living in New York City, Carlos Decena extends this concept of tacit tolerance. Decena uses the term *tacit subjects* to refer to what is assumed to be known but is not discussed. He insists that we should distinguish between "refusing to discuss an openly lived homosexuality and silence. . . . What is tacit is neither secret nor silent."[27] Decena states plainly that "self-realization as a man who loves men does not require moving away from the biological family."[28]

To make his argument, Díaz relies on the concept of familism. Quoting Gerardo Marín and Barbara Van Oss Marín, Díaz states that familism is a "cultural value that involves individuals' strong identification with and attachment to their nuclear and extended families, and strong feelings of loyalty, reciprocity, and solidarity among members of the same family."[29] Díaz asserts that for Latino gay men, familism prevents "homosexuals from denouncing the family's homophobia and demanding acceptance" and "tends to become internalized in a self-punitive way."[30]

I bring a healthy skepticism to such culturalist evocations to the Latino family primarily because the family patterns of people of color in the United States have been characterized as dysfunctional in much social science literature regardless of whether social scientists are pointing out the cohesiveness or lack of cohesiveness of these families. In other words, apparently contradictory evidence is used to argue the same conclusion. As Lionel Cantú Jr. has carefully deconstructed, culturalist arguments tend to homogenize Latino cultures; represent Latino cultures as fixed and static tradition-bound systems characteristic of a past from which the West has already evolved and progressed; and depict Latino culture as an exotic "other" against which the unidentified Western norm can be positively compared.[31] These critiques of culturalist discussions of Latino families have been applied to a literature that has focused mostly on heterosexually organized biolegal families. However, I would argue that this literature also provides lessons for those writing about gay and lesbian chosen families. Although family institutions provide a series of privileges for members, historically only those with the right kinds of families have fully reaped these rewards. Those with the wrong kinds of families—for example, racialized families headed by a strong female with "too many" children—may garner heteronormative privileges, but these privileges are limited and counteracted by the concomitant pathologization of their families. In addition, state intervention and regulation of marginalized populations often occur precisely through the institution of the family. Given the history of how the social sciences and the state have worked in tandem to identify and control deviant families, research on families that are only now beginning to be recognized by the state must be particularly vigilant.

With my research on Cuban American gay men, I bear the brunt of a related concern—that my discussion of these men's daily life inter-actions and economic and social interdependence with families of origin may be interpreted as further evidence of the commonsense assump-tion that Latinos are simply, ahistorically, and essentially family-oriented. While wanting to avoid a culturalist argument that Latino culture values family more highly than Anglos, I also acknowledge the differences my gay male respondents experienced with their families of origin. These differences were related to how the men I interviewed discussed coming out and how they understood the importance of dis-closure, deception, and family. I argue that, taking into account struc-tural and historical factors, this group of Cuban American gay men did have more regular contact with families of origin than has been documented in studies of Anglo gay men. At the same time, the Cuban American gay men I interviewed use strategies of nondisclosure, which is not the same as saying they are in the closet. I am left with the question, How do men who fully participate in public gay cultures, integrate their partners into their families of origin, share a home with their partners, but do not discuss their sexuality with their parents, complicate our discussion of visibility?

The Cuban American gay men I interviewed made concerted efforts to maintain physical and emotional closeness with family. It could be that family provided a place to be Cuban and maintain ties to an ethnic culture that was experienced as less oppressive than other spheres. As I discuss in the next chapter, masculine self-identification also helped ease relationships with families. Men who successfully performed normative masculinity believed that their families and other hetero-normative Cuban American communities accepted them because of this. Their masculinity freed them from further community surveil-lance and reinforced their patriarchal privileges. As men, they were allowed and expected to move through public spheres regularly, and their doing so was not cause for suspicion as it might have been for female members of the family. Their successful performance of mas-culinity also helped them reap a series of masculine privileges in the home—including services like laundry and cooking provided by some mothers and grandmothers to their sons and grandsons. The benefits they received as men helped explain their attachment to masculine gender identification. In the next chapter, I discuss these investments in masculinity and the multiple discourses of masculinity navigated by Cuban American gay men.

7 *LOCAS, PAPIS,* AND MUSCLE QUEENS
Racialized Discourses of Masculinity and Desire

LUIS WAS A MASCULINE-IDENTIFIED, twenty-seven-year-old Cuban American gay man who grew up in South Beach in the 1970s and 1980s. Even though from early childhood he was aware of his own sexuality and engaged in sexual play with other boys, Luis did not begin to understand himself as gay until he was a high school student. However, even during childhood, he felt that the expectations of masculine performance were being imposed on him. Raised by a single mother, Luis indicated that even before he was born, his mother's friends worried about the absence of a father figure and warned her to raise him right so that he would not be a sissy. He recalled being teased by the other Cuban American kids who rode a private school bus with him. Although they did not know he liked boys, they accused him of being a "sissy" and a "fag." Early on, he understood that he was being teased for failing at masculine performance: "I was picked on for being effeminate perhaps but not for liking other boys, you know. Who knows if those other boys were doing things, but that wasn't, like, really an issue." Through explicit warnings and teasing, Luis's schoolmates, his mother, and his mother's friends all taught him appropriate male behavior. Nevertheless, he consistently failed to fulfill these expectations.

> I remember . . . me, like, maybe not being the most masculine little boy. I wanted ballet lessons at three. I wanted to be a ballet dancer which, probably, like you know, made my mom want to kill herself, for me to openly say that around people or whatever. . . . I remember specifically at some age being . . . told how to hold my wrists because I guess I was letting them hang in some stereotypical limp-wristed gay way. And years later when I asked my mom why I had never had piano lessons or if she had ever considered

giving me [lessons], she said she had but that somebody had made a comment about . . . her son turning out to be like Liberace, so she didn't.

Luis's lack of athletic inclinations, his desire to learn how to play
the piano, and his body language marked him as nonmasculine and
further taught him the difference between masculine and effeminate
behavior. These challenges to his boyhood masculinity remained complexly linked to his identity as gay and to his sexual relationships with
members of the same sex. Whereas the taunts of sissy and fag and the
warnings about turning into Liberace all conflated effeminacy and
homosexuality, Luis maintained that his gender transgressions—not
his sexual activities—marked him for ridicule and reprimands.

At the time of our interview, Luis lived an openly gay life in South
Beach, residing a few blocks away from the apartment building where
his mother had denied him piano training. Although at one point in our
interview he had stated, "I don't think I'm overtly masculine," throughout the majority of the interview he clearly contrasted himself with
effeminate gay men and described himself as masculine. He affirmed
that he does "not wear [his] effeminacy" and that this has kept him
physically safe from perpetrators of gay bashing.

One-third of the residents of Luis's building were also gay men, reflecting the demographic makeup of South Beach at the time. Luis
complained about the homogeneousness of the gay South Beach scene
in the 1990s. Though he felt he did not meet the "South Beach standards of the shaved gym-built body," he also explained that he was not
particularly attracted to that physique or style. At the turn of the millennium, "South Beach standards" for gay men's appearance prevailed
throughout the pedestrian malls, clubs, and gyms concentrated within
a few miles of Luis's home. Against this standard, Luis viewed his own
physique as inadequate. At the time of our interviews, a new gym was
being constructed on Luis's block. The three-story structure owned by
a national chain charged nearly $700 a year for the use of its facilities
when it opened in 2001, much more than someone with Luis's salary
could reasonably afford.

Luis's personal history highlights the different discourses of masculinity second-generation Cuban American gay men may confront as
they grow up. Like Luis, many Cuban American gay men navigate their
adult sexuality in the wake of powerful boyhood messages about the
relationship between sexuality and masculinity. As discussed in chap-

ter 4, the Latin American sex system theorized by Tomás Almaguer emphasizes active and passive sexual roles and their relation to gender performance. This conceptual framework explains some of the lessons in masculinity transmitted through child-rearing practices, family messages, and childhood experiences.[1] However, the Latin American sex system does not provide the only definition of masculinity that Cuban American gay men negotiate. Cuban American gay men in Miami live in a transcultural gay culture where they are socialized into, interact with, draw from, and resist several sex-gender systems. Specifically, Cuban American gay men grapple with what I call the *papi* discourse of masculinity that defines Latino men, or hot Latin boys, as virile, hypermasculine objects of gay desire. The *papi* discourse draws on racialized assumptions that depict Latino male urban youth as street-tough and somewhat dangerous even as it eroticizes this danger and makes it safe. In this chapter, I foreground how informants felt alienated by this discourse even as they simultaneously and consciously reenacted its racial and gender markers. Cuban American gay men also position themselves in relation to a hypermasculine ideal of gay Anglo masculinity (an ideal especially prominent in the circuit party scene during the 1990s), what Luis referred to as "South Beach standards of the shaved gym-built body." I maintain that Cuban American gay men, who are often ambiguously situated in Miami's racial hierarchy, also worked within this discourse even as they felt distanced from it. I examine the ways in which Cuban American gay men navigated these three discourses of masculinity. Throughout the chapter, I return to Luis's story and use his complicated relationship to masculinity to highlight the sacrifices and payoffs that these (sometimes competing) discourses of masculinity provide in the realms of family, desire, and men's sense of self-worth.

I examine masculinity in terms of how men self-identify in terms of gender. How do informants describe themselves as gendered beings? How do they describe the development of gender identities, and how does gender identity relate to their personal history of sexual practices? I also examine social expectations about proper masculine behavior. How do Cuban American gay men believe others (their family, friends, coworkers, neighbors) expect them to behave? Via what tangible and intangible channels are these expectations communicated to Cuban American gay men? In what ways do these expectations imply a value-laden hierarchy about what constitutes appropriate behavior for young boys and adult men? I examine the social power of masculinity. What are the benefits gained from a successful performance of masculinity? These might include services and social acceptance provided by family members, a sense of safety, or acceptance in neighborhood and work settings. Finally, I examine the relationship between masculinity and sex. How is gender related to sexual practices? In what ways does masculinity play into men's desires, and how do Cuban American gay men present themselves as desirable to others?

Locas and Machos: A Latin American Typology

Most of the Cuban American gay men I interviewed for this study strongly identified as masculine and explicitly distanced themselves from effeminacy. Although the effeminate, broadly construed, was clearly important in articulating Cuban American gay male culture in sites such as drag performances and gay Latino magazines, in men's stories about themselves effeminacy was nearly always constructed as a source of anxiety. Moreover, Cuban American gay men's masculine self-descriptions commonly took on the form of an insistent claim. For example, one respondent stressed: "I was always a man. I was always very masculine in my way of being. I didn't have feminine things. I think everybody does have feminine things about them, but I was never a queen or a feminine person." Such adamant reiterations of masculinity can be seen as a response to the assumption that gay men are effeminate and not masculine.

Almaguer's discussion of the Latin American sex system helps illuminate this investment in masculinity and concomitant anxiety about effeminacy. According to Almaguer, Latin American men taking the passive sexual role are most highly stigmatized, and these *pasivos* are assumed to be effeminate. On the other hand, *activos,* men who have sex with men but take the penetrating role are less stigmatized and believed to have a masculine appearance. The reverse also holds true in this typology: that is, those with masculine appearances are believed to be real men, whereas those with a gender-transgressive appearance are assumed to be *pasivos.* In summary, in the Latin American sex system, outward gender markers, sexual roles, and social power are highly conflated.

Marvin Leiner describes the enactment of a similar system of sexual and gender meanings in Cuba:

To have sex with another man is not what identifies one as homosexual. For many Cubans, a man is homosexual only if he takes the passive receiving role. And a man is suspected of being homosexual only if his behavior is not macho: if he does not show interest in rough games, or is not physically strong and muscular; if he is gentle or quiet or perhaps has a nurturing sensibility to other people's feelings; if he does not care to control others or to posture and aggressively compete with his fellows.[2]

As Leiner indicates, while discussions of the Latin American sex system often emphasize sex roles, outward gender markers are socially interpreted. In my estimation, the importance of gender roles lies not so much in their correspondence with sexual position, for nuanced accounts indicate that in actual sexual situations many men often desire the opposite of what their outward gender signs might suggest.[3] Rather, the importance of gender markers resides in how they mark or mask sexual difference to others. As Ian Lumsden asserts in his account of Havana in the 1990s:

If you behave "normally," other Cubans will assume that you are basically heterosexual even if you have been known to have had sex with another man. . . . The Cuban equivalent to coming out as a gay person in North America is to refuse to conform to traditional male mannerisms in public, knowing that such behavior will be perceived as "effeminate," as unbecoming a "real man."[4]

In other words, a convincing performance of normal masculinity through outward gender markers ensures social acceptance. The real social transgression is to embrace what is seen as feminine.

The discourse of masculinity embedded in the Latin American sex system intersects with Miami's particular gay history. As discussed in chapters 2 and 3, the hypervisible Mariel gay population was highly stigmatized. Central to this generation's marginalization was not only the gender transgression associated with passive homosexuality in the Latin American sex system but also assumptions about lower-class backgrounds and recent immigrant status. This intersection is most striking in my respondents' self-distancing from the figure of the *loca* or the disparaged combination of outward effeminacy and presumed *pasivo* sexual position within the taxonomy of the Latin American sex system. In this regard, Martín, a light-skinned, Miami-born Cuban American in his late thirties, described his views about effeminacy quite directly.

MARTÍN: I don't necessarily hide being gay, but I don't want to be the
   stereotype of the horrible gay Cuban queen.
SUSANA PEÑA: Which is what?
M: Which is awful. It's awful. You'll know it when you see it. I guess
   in their worst form, I find them overtly effeminate. I find them
   inclined to put on airs of grandeur where none exists, I think. I find
   them uneducated. . . . I think they're low class. They tend to be
   very vicious. . . . I can't really relate to them because I just find that
   they have a whole world of their own, and they remind me to an
   extent of women.

In Martín's account, gender, ethnic, and class markers combine to represent the most feared, disliked, and stigmatized figure in the Latin American sex system. Martín's "horrible gay Cuban queen" bears the stigma of an effeminacy branded as particularly or inherently Cuban. These class-marked "horrible," "uneducated," "low-class" Cuban queens have nothing to do with the world of U.S.-born, professional, masculine-identified men with whom Martín socializes—men who might choose to camp it up when in gay company but who are proud of their achieved masculinity. For Martín, the feminine/*pasivo*/*loca* in the Latin American sex typology represents the type of person he does not want to be: "They remind [him] to an extent of women." His account demonstrates the effects of a fear of the conflation of homosexuality with femininity and/or femaleness as outlined in the Latin American sex system. I would also argue that the "horrible gay Cuban queen" Martín identifies is strongly associated with the widely stigmatized culture of gay men who came from Cuba to the United States as part of the Mariel boatlift, for the combination of ostentation, effeminacy, perceived ignorance, and low-class status negatively marked the gay Mariel migration.

When I pushed Martín further about his feelings toward masculinity and effeminacy, he again interwove gender with class position:

MARTÍN: It comes down to a certain definition of masculinity, and I don't
   see that in some particular Cuban gay men especially, but I guess
   it also depends on education, class and background. . . . I've never
   been into that aspect, you know like the drag aspect. I guess it
   comes down to the fear of being effeminate or too effeminate.
SUSANA PEÑA: So what is being a man to you? What is your idea of
   masculinity?
M: Well I never really thought about that, but I guess there's still a part
   of me that still holds on to the traditional notions, what your dad

always taught you, *ser hombre* [be a man]. . . . And I guess I never
thought about that before, but I guess some of that has stuck into me.

Martín implied that his own class position as a professional and the
son of two upper-middle-class parents may have informed why he has
never "been into . . . the drag aspect" of gay life. In addition, he implied that drag queens and effeminate men are less educated and come
from lower-class backgrounds. Martín's presumptions are supported
by a range of studies throughout Latin America and the United States
that suggest that gendered *pasivo/activo* divisions among men who
have sex with men are more highly entrenched within working-class
populations.[5]

Another key aspect of Martín's tying class position to gender appearance deals with passing and being targeted as gay. Because gender-
transgressive men are more likely targets of discrimination, looking
masculine (or, some might say, passing as straight) provides greater
access to jobs. In addition, other interviewees believed a masculine
appearance made them less likely to be targets of violence. When I
interviewed Luis, he noted that his masculine appearance and his size
were probably responsible for the fact that, in adulthood, he never felt
physically threatened because of his sexuality.

The masculine-identified Martín further discussed learning how
to "ser hombre," or be a man, from his father, and Luis remembered
being taught by his mother how not to be effeminate. Both examples
illustrate how the men I interviewed learned about masculinity and
made use of these lessons in masculinity to navigate adult relationships with families. As discussed in chapter 6, maintaining relationships and regular contact with biological family is important to many
Cuban American gay men across age, migration, and language divides.
Family is the site where many Cuban American gay men negotiate their
relationships to Cuban culture; thus, the men in my sample prioritized
maintaining relationships with biological family in ways that included
regular face-to-face interactions. Most also participated in gay social
settings and same-sex relationships. The Latin American sex system
proves useful in interpreting how these men balanced participation in
family and participation in gay social circles. Commonly, they drew
from the assumptions of the Latin American sex system—that is, that
a homosexual man will look effeminate and that a masculine-looking
man cannot be gay—to maintain their participation in family and gay

spheres. Because effeminacy is equated with male homosexuality, outward masculine markers effectively support presumed heterosexuality. Therefore, these Cuban American gay men routinely assumed that a masculine appearance eased relationships with family members and the Cuban community in general.

For example, Miguel, a respondent in his midthirties who came to the United States when he was very young, explained why his parents fully accepted his boyfriend. Miguel and his parents had been sharing a house when his boyfriend started living with him. According to Miguel, his parents accepted his boyfriend because they both looked masculine and would, therefore, not raise suspicions in the neighborhood. Miguel explained the relationship between sexual practice, gender appearance, and community approval:

> It's not so much with what that person does in bed because maybe that guy will flip over. It's the way he behaves . . . the way he talks is masculine, and he doesn't have a feather on him . . . so immediately the community accepts him as being part of the community even though people might know that he's with another man.

Miguel clearly references the Latin American sex system's understanding of sexual position when he discusses how a guy will "flip over." Flipping over refers to a man who looks masculine and, therefore, is assumed to want to penetrate but who actually desires to be penetrated. The phrase can also refer to a feminine-looking man who will want to penetrate. Flipping over, therefore, makes reference to the assumed correspondence between gender appearance and sexual position while pointing to how the system is undermined in real sexual situations.

Miguel's comments draw attention to the relative importance of gender markers as compared with sexual practices. He referred to a man's choice to behave and speak in an ostensibly masculine way. He suggested that someone who "doesn't have a feather on him" can have access to community acceptance. This reference to feathers derives from the Spanish word *pájaro*, which literally means "bird" but is also used to connote male homosexuality. Here the presence of feathers implies effeminate behavior.[6] Therefore, "not having a feather on you" or appearing unquestionably masculine ensures acceptance in nongay settings. Miguel concisely identified how he employed elements of this meaning system to navigate family and community acceptance. Although he cohabitated with his boyfriend, Miguel bypassed questions about his sexuality and ensured community acceptance by maintaining a masculine appearance.

Because gay men explicitly recognize the consequences of being effeminate, we can understand their deployment of masculinity as strategic. Martín knew that he could not maintain his social-economic position as a professional if he were gender transgressive. Similarly, Miguel believed that he and his boyfriend would not be embraced by his family or accepted by his residential community if either one of them appeared effeminate. Thus Miguel and Martín both consciously evaluated their gender appearances in order to maintain their familial and professional relationships.

Clearly, many elements of the Latin American sex system help explain Cuban American gay men's gender identities, gender strategies, and gender fears. This framework highlights how stigmatized gender and class markers are collapsed. In addition, it draws attention to how Cuban American gay men negotiate their gender and sexual identities with biological family. However, although this typology helps interpret the specific meanings that Cuban American gay men attribute to masculinity, ethnographic accounts of the Latin American sex system are not sufficient to understand the lives of U.S. Latinos. First of all, by collapsing all of Latin America into one cultural system, we homogenize a diverse group of cultures widely differentiated by nationality, race, language, and class divisions. Not all Latin American countries share the same political and social understanding of male homosexuality. Therefore a typology that assumes that all Latin American cultures understand sex/gender in the same way is limited at best. Moreover, several scholars have noted the diversity of sexual systems that exist within different Latin American regions and nations and the extent to which the typology of a sex system, assumed to be self-contained and distinct from other sexual systems, does not fully capture the reality of sexual practices, sexual meanings, and sexual identities in a transcultural world. Various studies note that globalization's effects have made it difficult to discuss the Latin American sexual system and the U.S. sexual system as completely distinct and independent systems. In fact, researchers in Latin American countries have noted the extent to which middle-class Latin American men in urban centers are increasingly identifying as gay and understanding sexuality in terms of sexual object choice instead of sexual aim, in part because of the increased personal and cultural contact between Latin America and the United States. Processes of gay globalization make it more likely for Anglo gay men from the United States to vacation in Havana, Mexico City, and Rio de Janeiro and for men in Cuba, Mexico, and Brazil to watch movies, read articles, and gather information about U.S. gay urban cultures. Likewise, through its attempts to replicate successful U.S. programs to reduce male-to-male sexual transmission of HIV in Latin America, the globalized AIDS industry has reinforced U.S. gay categories in the region. Therefore information about U.S. gay cultures, with the concomitant international economic power and social influence of the United States, is increasingly influential throughout Latin America, especially in urban centers.[7] Just as we cannot accept accounts of a singular or unitary Latin America, we also cannot pretend that Latin American sex and gender systems are easily or unproblematically transplanted to the United States. Latino gay men encounter several competing gender and sexual discourses. It would be wrong to think that a discourse that equates homosexuality with effeminacy is the only or even the dominant system gay men are confronted with as they develop their sexual lives. In Miami alone, various discourses equate Latino males with an erotic toughness and equate male homosexuality with masculine, strong-looking men. In Miami, *locas* are one stereotype of homosexuality, but discourses of *papis* and "muscle boys" are becoming more commonly associated with gay images. In an effort not to conflate Latin American and U.S. Latino lives, we must, therefore, begin to discuss other powerful frameworks that structure gay Latinos' lives in the United States.

Papis or Hot Latin Boys: Latino Masculinity

Another powerful discourse that structures Cuban American gay men's lives is what I call the *papi* discourse. This discourse imagines Latino men as masculine objects of desire. Literally, *papi* means daddy. That being said, when not referring to one's actual father, the term *papi* takes on a sexualized valence that indicates carnal intimacy in the Latin American vernacular—particularly in the Hispanophone Caribbean. Similar to the way baby can be used in English, *papi* can be used informally to suggest familiarity, but variations in intonation or setting can convey a more suggestive, sexualized meaning. In the Cuban American gay vernacular, *papi* is an affectionate term used by gay men to refer to a masculine, attractive man. *Papis* are young, masculine, attractive, "Latino looking" (between white and black), and usually underdressed. They have a prominent but not overwhelming musculature.

Steven Kurtz has found that U.S. gay culture frequently super-imposes these stereotypes of Latino machismo and sexual prowess onto Cuban American and Puerto Rican men in South Florida:

> Having come to despise the *mariposa* they once feared themselves to be, the hypermasculinity of Miami's gay life provided them with an opportunity to perform the machismo they were unable to achieve inside of their ethnic cultural spaces. At the same time, even after coming out as gay men, they found themselves as self-conscious as ever about their ultimate failure to achieve macho sexuality. Their new gay identities gave them no more freedom to express or act upon their desire to be penetrated by other men.[8]

Like *pájaro* and *loca, mariposa* (butterfly) is yet another common term within the Cuban vernacular used to refer to effeminate homosexual men. Kurtz argues that while the derogatory stereotype of the effeminate *loca/pájaro/mariposa* limited the identificatory, sexual, and social possibilities of Cuban American gay men, the stereotype of the masculine penetrating macho also limited what desires they could enact.

Gendered and racialized portrayals of Latino men as *papis* circulate in the dominant media, the social sciences, and the gay media. The *papi* discourse borrows from U.S. popular culture representations of the figure of the Latin lover. This common depiction of Latino (hetero) masculinity combines the characteristics of "eroticism, exoticism, tenderness tinged with violence and danger, all adding up to the romantic promise that, sexually, things could get out of control."[9] The danger and allure of the Latin lover are related to stereotypical historical depictions of a hypersexual and uncontrolled temperament characteristic of Latin Americans, especially those of Caribbean descent. These depictions, in turn, are related to understandings of uncontrollable and virile black sexuality. However, representations of the Latin lover are usually distinguishable from those of black men. First, Latin lovers are always phenotypically depicted as brown-skinned, that is, somewhere between black and white. Second, they are portrayed as only slightly dangerous (as a way to expand their exotic appeal); thus they pose less of a threat than black males. The *papi* discourse also draws on contemporary mass media representations of Latino male youth as dangerous causes of urban social problems. The racialized tough-youth threat softened by Latin lover allure creates a powerful erotic combination.

Social science discourse on Latino masculinity resonates and intersects with these popular representations. In particular, social scientists have uncritically used the term *machismo* as a cultural concept equating patriarchy with Latin America. In his study of masculinities among Mexican working-class men, Matthew Gutmann describes "anthropology's affinity to the Mexican macho."[10] Many ethnographies tend to associate virility, sexual conquest, procreation, bragging, and defying death with Mexican machos. According to Gutmann, Mexican men are used as a

> foil against which other men less concerned with virility are compared. . . . Macho and machismo have become a form of calumny, shorthand terms in social science and journalistic writing for labeling a host of negative male characteristics in cultures around the world.[11]

In this way, machismo and the accompanying notion of the macho become answers rather than questions. In addition, the Mexican macho becomes the negatively valued other against which U.S. social scientists evaluate Anglo U.S. masculinities. Maxine Baca Zinn argues that this tendency to treat machismo as a cultural inheritance from Latin America has been transposed onto analyses of gender relations among Latino populations living in the United States. Chicano men are portrayed as participating in a "rigid cult of masculinity" that involves behaviors including excessive drinking, excessive bravado in fights to prove manhood, the unquestioned power of the father-figure within the family structure, and an uncontrollable virility that leads to extramarital relations.[12]

Social critics such as Baca Zinn, Lionel Cantú Jr., and Alfredo Mirandé have challenged the homogenized concept of machismo from different perspectives. They suggest that when analyzing masculine power within a Latino context, social scientists should take into account the structural position of the men under analysis and the relationship between this structural position and their expressions of masculinity.[13] Here I focus on how the discourse that equates machismo, Latino men, unbridled masculinity, virile sexuality, and sensuality structures how Cuban American gay men imagine themselves and those around them.

Mass media and social science representations of Latino masculinity resonate strongly with the figure of the macho or *activo* in the Latin

American sex system. However, in a U.S. context, the racialized dimensions of these figures crystallize. Whereas in the Latin America
constructed by ethnographers the macho is the dominant figure who
(most) benefits from patriarchy, in the United States the macho is a
racial inferior whose particular type of patriarchal power is criticized.
In part, the macho works to deflect attention from how middle-class
Anglo patriarchy operates across national and class boundaries. Below,
I analyze how this racialization figures into gay representations and
Cuban American gay men's self-identifications.

Representations of young Latino men as virile, highly sexual, and
masculine are common in gay media circles as well. As Christopher
Ortiz argues, representations of Chicano/Latino men in gay pornography primarily marketed to a white gay male audience "act as structures
of desire."[14] According to Ortiz, racial signifiers (conflated with class
signifiers) figure prominently in gay porn videos that feature Latino
men. In this pornographic niche, settings typically are left completely
unidentified (a bed in a bare room) or are class- and race-coded: they
include "prisons, warehouses, restaurants, kitchens and urban areas
that are defined as Chicano/Latino neighborhoods."[15] Likewise, Latino
men are sometimes represented as a "homeboy or street-smart and
tough urban resident, an image of the Chicano/Latino that is widely
circulated in the dominant media." Viewers are reminded of race
through the placement of racial signifiers such as piñatas. Chicano/
Latino men, like black men, are represented as being closer to nature,
having an unbridled sexuality, being "hot blooded," and possessing
uncontrollable desires.[16] Ironically, representations of uncontrollable
Latino men whose desires can be and are satisfied by other men do not
presuppose their homosexuality. Rather, Ortiz explains how gay porn
employs the trope of unbridled sexual desire to exclude Latino men
from gay community:

> One pervasive stereotype in gay pornography is the desire to be fucked by
> the Black or Chicano/Latino stud who does not reciprocate and may even
> be straight. . . . The fantasy of the straight macho Chicano/Latino man who
> fucks "me" (a white man) allows for sexual relations between two men and
> at the same time excludes the Chicano/Latino man from being framed as
> a member of a gay community. For a Chicano/Latino spectator, the identi-
> fication can be a problematic one if he is attempting to articulate a sexual
> experience that may not conform to or may even transgress his own familiar
> cultural codes: macho-chingado/top-bottom. The white man can divorce

himself from the cultural and ethnic implications for the Chicano/Latino of this fantasy scenario; the Chicano/Latino man cannot.[17]

This same trope is used in videos that feature Chicano/Latino men having sex with each other. In these videos, homosexual sex is portrayed as an element of male bonding "attributable to a certain hegemonic notion of Chicano/Latino machismo."[18] In both of these cases, Latino men are portrayed as masculine, sexual, and sexy—but not gay.[19]

My research suggests that Latino gay men also turn to pornographic representations both to fuel their fantasies and to provide a distorted mirror. This particular genre of pornography provides an index of meaningful symbols, possible roles (sexual and social), desirable subjects, and erotic situations that reflect social hierarchies of gender, race, and class. These representations structure the possible desires of viewers. In Miami, gendered and racialized *papi* images are molded to market (and simultaneously influence the content and representation of) particular gay venues. Eduardo Aparicio confronted these marketing strategies head-on when he tried to develop a Latino gay magazine that embraced both masculine and feminine images and voices. In the first issue of his zine, *Perra!,* Aparicio included a "good number" of drag and feminine images. He described the reception of this issue, especially from club owners whose advertising support he was counting on, as *"fatal"* or dismal:

EDUARDO APARICIO: Tú sabes, la cultura gay es, es muy devota de, del, de lo masculino. Entonces poner una loca en la portada no les cuadra. Que haya foto tras foto de travestis no les cuadra.

SUSANA PEÑA: ¿Aún cuando son las travestis, las mismas que estaban trabajando [en esos clubs]?

EA: Aún cuando son las travestis porque es en realidad un imagen femenina. Y lo que quieren ver son machitos medio en cuero.

EDUARDO APARICIO: You know, gay culture is, is very devoted to the masculine. So putting a *loca* on the cover didn't sit well with them. Putting picture after picture of drag queens didn't sit well with them.

SUSANA PEÑA: Even if it was the same drag queen who performed [at those clubs]?

EA: Even when it was those drag queens because in reality it was a feminine image. And what they want to see is half-naked *machitos.*

As Aparicio indicated, owners of Miami clubs catering to Latino gay men wanted to control the images associated with their locales, and

The premiere issue of *Perra!* magazine in May 1995 included various feminine images of both lesbians and drag queens. The cover featured Adora, the popular Cuban American drag queen. Copyright by Eduardo Aparicio; reproduced with permission.

they hoped that gay Latinos would be represented by *papis* or *machitos*. Significantly, Aparicio's choice of the diminutive *machitos* (as opposed to machos) also suggests the preference for youthful, vibrant Latino sexuality. Most importantly, club owners wanted to see *papi* images to the exclusion of other possible representations of Latino gay men. Because Aparicio depended on clubs for advertising dollars and free distribution, he had to cater to their expectations to some extent. He did so by de-emphasizing drag queens and lesbians in the magazine even though *Perra!* always included an element of drag. To appease club owners, Aparicio continued to emphasize the Latino macho in the centerfold section of the magazine, "Papi del Momento" or *Papi* of the Moment, by providing the type of images owners hoped would be associated with their locales.

Latino masculinity, intertwined in the popular imaginary with machismo, is thereby constructed as an object of desire in Miami's gay community. Representations of masculine, young, tough Latino men inform Latino gay men's self-understandings despite the fact that such extreme Latino masculinity is something with which few actually identify. Not simply oppressive stereotypes that portray Latino gay men as objects, these images wield differing levels of relevance to men's lives, desires, and fantasies and are manipulated by men in their own self-interest. Many of the images I discuss are inextricable from sexual desire. Moreover, when a particular brand of Latino masculinity is cast and promoted as more desirable, it can also be used to attract others.

Luis, for example, often used gay phone or chat lines to meet potential sexual partners. In these interactions, he was able to play off of listeners' racial/ethnic expectations. He elaborated on what he thought people expected or desired from Latino men:

> Their ideal, I think . . . it's such an overtly, you know, maybe vulgarly to some people display of masculinity or of male sexuality laced with perhaps a weird little bit of, like, little boy tenderness or whatever. Like, they want . . . a New York or Miami style young homeboy . . . Bangee boy, whatever you want to call it, you know that gang-banger. . . . The image they're drawing in their mind, is of the young dark, you know, not African a hundred percent, but of a young, like, you know, olive to caramel skin tone, you know, with mixed features, goatee.

The "ideal" Luis described has very specific racial, class, style, and regional characteristics, and the "display of masculinity" tops the list of idealized features. Although Luis clearly saw himself as masculine, he did not believe that he fits this stereotype of Latino masculinity in person. Nevertheless, through faceless, semi-anonymous telephone interactions with other men, he was able to perform the Latino *papi*:

> You can kinda create an identity of who you are, so I mean I can put on an accent or a voice that sounds like one of these people that they're either fantasizing about or are merely attracted to, and . . . it's not a persona that,

EL PAPI DEL MOMENTO ... con su rico movimiento *Eric*

Panameño • 28 años • 155 libras • 5'7" de alto • 28" de cintura

Me llamo Eric. Mi música favorita es house music. El desayuno me gusta bien saludable con un buen café con leche cubano. Para mí lo más importante en un hombre es la sinceridad. Soy bailarín de Splash. Ahí me puedes ver, siempre bailando para ti.

FOTO: APARICIO (305) 854-9056

The centerfold section of *Perra!* was devoted to "El Papi del Momento," a photographic layout mostly featuring Latino men, partially clothed—precisely the "half-naked machitos" Eduardo Aparicio believed club owners wanted to see. This centerfold appeared in *Perra!* 2, special issue, August 1996. Copyright by Eduardo Aparicio; reproduced with permission.

I couldn't keep it up in person, you know. I think I'm too complex a person to just be that. . . . I mean if we get further into me and talking to me, you know, I speak both English and Spanish well, I think, or relatively well without any sort of specifically urban inflection.

In short, Luis consciously performed the role of a racialized, young Latino man—a masculine, tough, urban homeboy—in order to be attractive to other men.

Although Luis chose to present himself under the guise of stereotypical Latino masculinity, his statement also suggests a certain distancing from the *papi* persona. Luis recognized that his own "complex personhood" was in no way captured by unitary images of desired Latino masculine men.[20] These enactments of masculinity are perhaps simpler to maintain during short phone conversations, and Luis found this persona difficult to keep up for very long. However, such conversations are often a prelude to sexual contact. When Luis met his phone or online dates in person, he tried to highlight features that might correspond to the stereotypical Latino macho. He continued his performance using "maybe a hairstyle combined with facial hair, you know, and maybe like some like clothes that happen to be baggy." Although Luis did not identify with these Latino macho stereotypes and found it difficult to maintain them for sustained periods of time, he did not hesitate to mobilize these stereotypes in his favor. In his conscious enactment of racial and gender markers, he played with notions of masculinity, but such play has its limits. When analyzing other men's masculinity, Luis relied on naturalized notions of "real" masculinity, most evidently in his evaluation of muscle boys or "typical South Beach guys."

Muscle Boys: Homogenized Gay Masculinity

In the late 1990s when I interviewed Luis in his South Beach apartment, a particular gay masculine look was becoming the dominant aesthetic in this Miami Beach neighborhood. With very rigid and homogeneous definitions of what was attractive, this discourse of masculinity produced a standard of beauty to which young gay men compared themselves. In the 1970s a similar aesthetic, known as the "gay clone" look, dominated U.S. urban centers and privileged a masculine, muscular body and a homogenized working-class uniform. This muscular and masculine gay look was interrupted by the impact of the

AIDS epidemic in the 1980s. As the disease became identified with gay men, media images of gay men devastated by a mysterious wasting syndrome became ubiquitous. Partly as a reaction to and a retreat from this image, a new clone look linked to traveling parties known as circuit parties gained currency in many urban gay neighborhoods of the 1990s. The new look was the antithesis of the thin and frail images of gay men rampant in the mass media. Thus the new gay man in Luis's neighborhood was muscular, pumped up, healthy-looking, and masculine.

According to Michelangelo Signorile, the circuit party subculture promoted a "cult of masculinity" that demanded "conformity to a very specific body ideal" that included a muscular frame with very low percentage body fat and little body hair.[21] Russell Westhaver fleshes out the description of this body ideal: models in materials advertising circuit parties were "invariably muscular, with gym-toned bodies, broad shoulders, well defined arms, v-shaped backs, washboard abdominal muscles, 'bubble butts,' and short cropped hair."[22] Participants in this subculture, commonly referred to as muscle queens, muscle boys, or size queens, had a complex relationship to youth.[23] While this discourse of gay masculinity was associated with youth, it was often embodied and enacted by middle-aged men. Although the markers of youth (a smooth, toned body, for example) were clearly celebrated on the dance floor, in the magazines, and in the sexual market place, many circuit party attendees were older than this ideal.

The circuit parties privileged higher-income gay men who could afford the travel costs, admission prices, and optional drugs associated with these day- to weekend-long events organized in different cities around the world.[24] The politics of circuit parties have been a lightning rod for debates within the gay community, with critics such as Signorile lambasting the parties for promoting unsafe sex, drug use, and unrealistic body ideals and supporters like Eric Rofes celebrating the rites of community building at the parties.[25]

While the militant politics of such organizations as ACT UP marked urban gay communities like 1990s New York and San Francisco, Miami was viewed as "a kind of refuge from the destruction AIDS had wreaked in some American cities."[26] In a short article on the making of a gay community in South Beach, Eugene J. Patron and David W. Forrest argue that this sense of refuge/escape, combined with the "widespread use of steroids to combat HIV-related wasting syndrome" to give men "back their physical strength, fuel[ed] a heightened idealizing of muscle development that corresponded perfectly with the warm weather body conscious environment of South Beach."[27] Miami, identified as it was with circuit party subculture, became a popular tourist destination for gay men. In the late 1990s, minicircuits had developed in Miami, replicating the feel of circuit parties in local weekly club gatherings. Because participation in the minicircuit did not involve travel costs, it was economically more accessible to a broader portion of South Florida's gay population.

National commentators like Signorile and Rofes often note the "whiteness" of the circuit party/muscle queen scene. While the borders between black and white remained quite firm in Miami's interethnic gay culture, Latinos occupied a racially ambiguous and shifting position during the heyday of the circuit party. The presence of Latinos in South Beach's muscle queen culture was undeniable, even if many Latinos assimilated into the circuit party uniform. Recent Latino immigrants and second-generation Cuban Americans made up a large percentage of the clientele, Latino DJs were crucial in developing Miami's house sound, and a bicultural shtick humor by some drag queens was part of Miami's unique charm. The presence of "hot Latin boys" was part of South Beach's marketing strategy that so successfully attracted gay men from throughout the United States. In 1995 Glenn Albin described the desirable ethnic mix at Warsaw, one of Miami's gay clubs, for the national gay magazine *Out*:

> Warsaw's enormous space and DJ David Padilla attracted many of mainland Miami's Cuban-American gay and bisexual men, who showed up for the early explosion of house music.
>
> The combination created a shot heard round the gay world: The new look of love was Latin, and exotic by New York standards. South Beach was hot and the men were hotter. Curiously, class and ethnic distinctions that segregate gay men in most American cities are shed in South Beach nightlife. Because the venues are so large and the dress code is standardized (tank top, jeans, and boots), it's hard to guess who lives with his mother in Hialeah or whose Range Rover key was found by the toilet.[28]

Latino gay men in Miami, who were predominantly Cuban American, were key participants in the emerging gay culture Albin describes. As Albin suggested, in some ways the Latino men simply blended into the huge parties of shirtless, muscular, attractive men. "It's hard to guess," Albin noted enthusiastically, which one of these men "live[d] with his

mother [in the working-class, predominantly Cuban American neigh-
borhood] of Hialeah" and which one was the affluent, (presumably)
Anglo owner of a prohibitively priced luxury vehicle. Of course, if the
Latino men were really that indistinguishable from the Anglo men,
they would not have added "exotic" spice to South Beach's gay culture.
In fact, Albin revealed their visibility. The "look of love was Latin,"
just visible enough to distinguish Miami from other gay urban centers
but not so visible as to threaten the dominance of whiteness.

As Albin suggested, Miami's racial/ethnic categories and hierarchies
differ slightly from those of the rest of the country. Whereas in most
U.S. urban centers Latino men are clearly categorized as nonwhite, in
Miami Latinos are often positioned closer to whiteness. Significantly,
Miami's Cuban Americans typically understand themselves to be
white and do not see a contradiction between participating in Latino
culture, being a member of the white race, and enjoying a dominant
place in U.S. economic, social, and political life. Whereas the Cuban
American gay men I interviewed rarely explicitly identified themselves
as nonwhite, coded racialized meanings emerged in their discussions
about South Beach gay guys or muscle queens.

These identificatory tensions underpinning Miami's racial language—in which the men I studied and the Anglo circuit boys both
staked claims to the same race—framed various questions. For instance, how does this place-specific notion of masculinity compete with
more generalized conceptualizations of Latino masculinity? How did
Cuban American gay men place themselves in relation to the muscle
boy subculture? Many men I interviewed either lived or socialized in
South Beach, the Miami neighborhood recognized as the center of circuit party/muscle boy culture. The Cuban gay men I interviewed who
identified with this scene aspired to achieve its beauty requirements if
they wanted to be competitive in its erotic market. Cuban American
men who identified with this scene did not describe this as racial or ethnic imposition. They simply strove to keep fit and look good. However,
most Cuban gay men, young and old, described feeling distanced from
the South Beach scene. Their critiques were rarely couched in terms of
racial difference: instead, they complained about rampant drug use
in the area, lack of adequate parking, and people being stuck-up. For
men who did not identify with this scene, its expectations were experienced as limiting and confining. Therefore the aesthetic requirements
of the South Beach scene, which I would argue are racialized, were

experienced both as empowering by those who thought they met them and as confining to those who did not.

Emphasized in the following account is a dismissal of the performed masculinity of the muscle queens. When Luis used the expression "typical South Beach guy," I asked him what he meant by that, and he replied that these men are typically

> very body conscious, but at the same time effeminate. Maybe not like consciously effeminate but, like, they can't hide the fact that they're gay. They may be built and huge, but they open their mouths and, you know, as I've heard people from Miami, you know mainland Miami, or perhaps Latin people from mainland Miami say . . . "Oh! One of these South Beach muscle men opens their mouth and you know she's a woman right away."

According to Luis, South Beach gay guys are described as being masculine on the outside but feminine on the inside. Their masculine exteriors are betrayed by the "woman" who is let out when they "open their mouths." The idea here is that no matter how many hours they spend at the gym or how big they get, "typical South Beach guys" cannot conceal what is thought to be their true nature—their effeminacy. For Luis, then, the South Beach look is a farce of masculinity. This masculinity is clearly seen as constructed—the product of regular trips to the gym and steroid use—and, therefore, not natural or real. On the other hand, the Latino macho Luis desired, a Latino meeting many of the criteria he adopted on the phone lines, was seen as more thoroughly and naturally masculine. Latino masculinity was cast as purer in comparison with the hypermasculinity of South Beach gay men. Ironically, in Luis's case, the naturalness of Latino masculinity was described by someone who reinvented that Latino masculinity to attract partners. Luis's own disguise seemed an almost comical construction (a fake accent, stylized facial hair, and baggy clothes), yet the same markers on others seemed more real to him and constituted part of a natural expression of masculinity.

Both constructed and naturalized notions of gender and race interplayed in Luis's own identity, desires, and interpretations of surrounding masculinities. In this account, Luis evaluated the masculinity of the muscle queens and found them lacking. Ironically, the dichotomy of achieved masculine performance and the failure of effeminate men that emerges in the Latin American sex system resurfaces. In an effort to distance himself from the reigning South Beach gay archetype, Luis resorted to the gendered codes of the Latin American sex system.

These competing discourses of masculinity (the *loca,* the *papi,* and the muscle queen) and Cuban American gay men's negotiation of these discourses illustrate the extent to which masculinity is performed in daily life. Masculinity is embodied in men's musculature as well as in how they position their bodies. Masculinity is performed by accessorizing with fashionable signifiers of masculinity. Masculinity can also be performed in a sexual seduction involving the invocation of the Latin lover. Cuban American gay men's masculine performances earn them certain benefits and protections. They described feeling physically safe because they did not "look gay." They described the acceptance they received from their families, an acceptance they believed would have been much less readily forthcoming had their gender appearance suggested their sexuality. Finally, they described the benefits of moving comfortably between different heterosexual and homosexual spheres without repercussions. As sons, they also reaped particular benefits from families of origin who granted them relative freedom from surveillance, particularly as compared with the women in their families. Mothers and grandmothers also helped their sons and grandsons with laundry, housecleaning, and cooking, especially if they shared a home. Even if the successful performance of masculinity involved a strenuous and difficult process, masculinity had its privileges.

Although I have argued that since the 1990s in Miami, discourses of masculinity have been central to Cuban American gay men's self-identifications, I do not mean to imply that gender transgression has disappeared from Cuban American gay culture. In the next chapter, I discuss one important aspect of gender-transgressive Cuban American gay male culture: the staged performance of Cuban American drag queens who gained loyal followings in both mixed and predominantly Latino settings based on a Cuban American shtick that incorporated Cuban divas and ethnic humor. These performances elicited overwhelming responses from Latino gay male audiences that seemed to suggest an identification across varying gender identities and immigrant generation.

8 ¡OYE LOCA!

Gay Cuba in Drag

I BEGAN THIS BOOK by discussing the early decades of the Cuban Revolution. During the 1960s and 1970s, the Cuban state identified gender transgressions as a threat to the new virile subject imagined to be the protagonist of a new socialist society, namely *el Hombre Nuevo* (the New Man). In this chapter, I focus on alternative protagonists. If *el Hombre Nuevo* wore military fatigues and smoked a cigar, my protagonists preferred sequins and fierce pairs of high heels. If the soundtrack to the New Man's story might be one of Fidel Castro's famous speeches, my protagonists preferred another form of highly emotional Cuban rhetoric—La Lupe's wailing songs.

This chapter discusses the cultural work of Cuban American drag queens, *transformistas, travestis,* and other gender-transgressive performers in Miami. In particular I focus on performers who have developed characters or personas explicitly marked as Cuban. In addition to lip-synching, the performers highlighted in this chapter also host theme nights, work as emcees at various events, and perform a particular brand of stand-up comedy. Some notable examples of this type of performer include Adora, Mariloly (discussed in chapter 4), Julie Mastrozzimone,[1] and Marytrini. In my observations of gay Cuban cultural sites, I found that gender-transgressive performers played a key role in articulating gay *cubanidad*: Adora, Julie, Mariloly, and Marytrini embodied and performed narratives of Cuba. On one level, they transmitted information about gay Cuban icons, language, history, and forms of performance and expression that younger and older gay men alike were able to connect with on different levels. Their performances also are spaces in which Cuban gay men and (sometimes) lesbians are hailed in terms of their race/ethnicity and their sexuality simultaneously. The structure of those performances often included unscripted interactions between the performers and their audiences that allowed for those hailed not only to accept this identification passively but actively to participate in constructing it.

In this chapter, I present different aspects of the work of four Cuban American gender-transgressive performers whom I observed during my fieldwork. My goal in this chapter is to analyze the complicated politics of immigrant generation, gender, and race to offer a glimpse of the heterogeneous and changing gay Cuban structures of feeling that permeated these venues during the 1990s and early 2000s.

Adora: Lo tuyo es puro teatro

Popular among both Spanish- and English-speaking audiences, Adora was the most prominent bicultural drag queen in South Beach in the 1990s. In the early part of that decade, she led a fantastically successful drag night at Barrio Restaurant, in what was then an emerging, still somewhat underground, South Beach gay scene. On Monday nights, the small restaurant on Washington Avenue featured an all-drag wait staff while Adora hosted performances by local drag queens and DJ Sugar provided entertainment between sets. It was there that I saw her perform for the first time. With impeccable lip-synching, Adora regularly performed iconic, if somewhat eccentric, Cuban divas, all the while emphasizing their emotive potential through her theatrical performance. Although the performers I discuss in this chapter did not solely lip-synch, the enactment of songs shaped a significant part of their performances. In essence, their choices of artists and songs conveyed specific knowledges about Cuban and Latina divas to younger audiences. For instance, Adora's complex and layered performances were epitomized in her rendition of "Siboney," composed by Ernesto Lecuona and interpreted by the Cuban songstress Xiomara Alfaro, among others. As I discuss in chapter 5, Eduardo Aparicio identified this composition as an example of a Cuban cultural artifact that simultaneously articulates *cubanidad* and a gay sensibility. If Lecuona's composition is somehow intrinsically gay and Cuban, Alfaro's interpretation (said to be Lecuona's favorite) is also queer in its own way. Unlike other Cuban female singers widely known throughout the Spanish-speaking world, Alfaro is more specifically a Cuban icon whose fans are primarily older Cubans. Adora's precisely timed movements, facial expressions, and lip-synching exaggerate the high-pitched tonalities of Alfaro's voice. Adora's persona is also a queered version of a Cuban society lady of the 1950s. Wearing mile-long eyelashes, exaggerated eye makeup, oversized rings, and Technicolor wigs that always perfectly coordinated with her outfits, Adora produced a femininity so queered and hyperbolic as to be almost cartoonish.

In addition to Alfaro's "Siboney," Adora also performed the iconic songs of La Lupe, perhaps the Cuban singer most imitated by drag queens. La Lupe, whose song "Puro teatro" I reference in the title to this section, was known for a raw and emotional style that was jarring (and intoxicating) to many of her contemporaries. La Lupe is the classic tragic Cuban gay diva. After leaving Cuba in 1962, she regained some fame in New York City working with Tito Puente. She eventually died penniless and alone.[2] La Lupe is best known for dramatic performances during which she would kick, cry, scream, and sing. Although recorded performances do not fully capture the unpredictability of her live performances—La Lupe was known for throwing her shoes at audiences—they showcase a vocal delivery both dramatic and honest.

This series of photographs from Adora's performance at Dragboy, a weekly drag night she hosted at a South Beach gay bar in 1999, evinces her emotional performance. On May 15, 1999, she performed "Siboney" as interpreted by Xiomara Alfaro and "Lo que pasó pasó" as interpreted by La Lupe. Photograph by author.

Like other divas, La Lupe sang about lost loves, her vindication, and her reassertion of her place in the world. In performing, identifying with, and reacting to La Lupe and her drag reincarnations, gay men across generations unabashedly celebrated their Cubanness in gay spaces marked as both predominantly Latino and mainstream. La Lupe's songs include exclamations, gasps, and various emotive outbursts. In Adora's lip-synching of these difficult numbers, each syllable, gasp, and exclamation is perfectly timed and delivered so as to exaggerate the already strong emotional impact of La Lupe's songs. Although La Lupe has been recuperated in the last few years, when Adora began performing her numbers, La Lupe's body of work and its relationship to gay Cuban culture was less known to U.S.-born gay men. The processes of gay *recubanización* that I discuss in chapter 5 were partly facilitated by performers like Adora who transmitted a system of symbols, icons, and languages to other Cuban gay generations. Put another way, Adora both recalibrated and amplified La Lupe. She took songs young U.S.-born men might have heard their parents listening to and recalibrated them so that their gay sensibilities seemed patently obvious. When Adora performed "Lo que paso pasó," the pleading "¿Qué te pedí?," or the defiant "Como acostumbro," it seemed as if these songs were intended to be interpreted by a drag queen.

Performers like Adora offered a crucial site for the transmission not only of historical information about these cultural icons but also of their emotional meaning. In chapter 4, Luis discussed how learning about Cuban gay culture from older gay men was a "door to a cultural awakening." While he learned about La Lupe in this context, the first time he saw La Lupe interpreted live was by Adora at an outdoor party on South Beach's Lincoln Road. After that, Luis began attending Adora's Barrio shows fairly regularly and actively seeking out La Lupe's music to widen his understanding of this multigenerational gay Cuban culture. In a more recent follow-up conversation, Luis explained that after not speaking with his older gay Cuban friends for a year or two, he visited their house to tell them about Adora and talk more about La Lupe. He explained, "I thought that was a bit of a circle going back to the 'teachers' with what I'd learned on my own."

Julie Mastrozzimone: "¡Chusma!" "¡Balsera!"

Unlike Adora, Julie Mastrozzimone and Mariloly did not often perform in English-dominant venues and never reached a high level of popularity in South Beach. However, they regularly performed using Spanish and Spanglish in or near mainland Miami's predominantly Latino neighborhoods. I most often saw Mastrozzimone perform during the late 1990s at a midsized gay club located on the border between South Miami and Coral Gables. Situated on US 1, part of which is a busy suburban thoroughfare that runs through Greater Miami, the club was discreetly tucked in behind a protective wall. On Wednesday nights or "Latin night," the club closed off its patio and half of its interior in order to shrink the floor space and give the illusion of a packed house. In this more intimate venue, Mastrozzimone served as emcee, conversed with a lively audience, made jokes, lip-synched, and introduced other drag queens—including those who competed in pageants that she dubbed "las coronadas" (the ones with crowns). In contrast to "las coronadas," who wore expensive-looking, glamorous outfits and more closely approximated idealized feminine beauty, Julie wore simple wigs and light makeup. Her loosely fitting dresses were far from glamorous, and she often joked that she bought them at "el pulgero," the famed Opa-Locka Hialeah flea market. Despite her "cute" features, she did little to embody feminine beauty or a sense of realness. In fact, she regularly disrupted the appearance of femininity with visual or verbal cues to her biological sex. During one performance, she lifted her dress over her head, revealing very unfeminine black male briefs. If Adora's character was a high-society lady, Julie developed a character with more of the aesthetic of a *chusma,* a derogatory Spanish term used in Cuban vernacular to identify someone as low-class and loud or raucous. Julie embraced a working-class immigrant ethnicity by joyfully embodying *chusmería.*

Julie's hosting included relatively little scripted performance and drew heavily from interactive dialogue with an animated, heckling audience. Part of her skill was her "chispa" (literally, a spark) or her ability to respond quickly and humorously to the many comments shouted at her. In almost all the venues discussed in this chapter, the audiences were a vocal and active part of the performance. Audience interaction with drag queens is central to the cultural significance of the performance. In predominantly gay settings, the drag queens often hailed their Cuban gay audiences in explicit (and not the most polite) language. For example, Julie typically began her performance by asking if there were any Cubans in the house. When the crowd responded enthusiastically and positively, she would reply: "Tantos maricones y tortilleras cubanos. ¿Tus padres saben que están aquí? ¡Qué

Julie Mastrozzimone
performs at a banquet
hall venue in Hialeah
in 1999. Photograph
by author.

pena, qué pena para el Sedano's!" (So many Cuban fags and dykes.
Do your parents know you're here? What a shame, what a shame for
Sedano's!). Sedano's, a large Cuban supermarket chain found throughout Greater Miami but commonly in Cuban American areas such as
Hialeah, here became something of a humorous metonym for a larger
Cuban American establishment imagined to be heteronormative and
ashamed of its many gay and lesbian relations. As might be expected
in this gay Latino venue, the crowd's reaction was not one of shame
but of loud, knowing laughter.

Julie Mastrozzimone was featured on the cover of the November 1996 issue of *Perra!* magazine. Copyright by Eduardo Aparicio; reproduced with permission.

Julie's audience typically responded to her in much the same disparaging tone employed by Julie herself. It was common for people to yell epithets such as "chusma" or "balsera" (rafter). Often, "¡Balsera! ¡Balsera! ¡Balsera!" was chanted repetitively to drown out Mastrozzimone and force her to respond to the heckler(s). These epithets mark low-class Cubanness, stigmatized migration status, or both. Although technically not a *balsera,* Julie arrived from Cuba in 1980 as part of the stigmatized Mariel boatlift. She was one of the members of the Mariel gay generation featured in Elinor Burkett's *Miami Herald* article discussed in chapter 3.[3] If the audience sought Julie's mock anger and annoyance, she gave them what they wanted, sometimes deflecting these comments with a pretentious air, claiming to be upper class and not Cuban. Once, when she came across a couple from Cuba, as she was more than likely to do in this predominantly Cuban crowd, she responded with feigned snobbishness, "¡Ay, la misma mierda!" (Oh, the same shit). She went on to apologize and commented that she had heard that Cuba was a beautiful island, but she herself had never had a chance to visit. In that instance, she performed the role of the *cubana arrepentida,* that is, a Cuban woman who is ashamed of her Cubanness and tries to pretend that she is not Cuban and/or better than Cubans.[4] By this time, the crowd had erupted into laughter, and the chants of "balsera, balsera, balsera" momentarily drowned Julie out.

The back-and-forth insults did not reveal a real animosity between performer and audience; instead, they reflected an intimate knowledge about a shared script. Within the boundaries of this imagined community, a member of a stigmatized group could hurl a powerful word, one that had been aimed at him or her in the past, in a playful fashion. When volleyed back, it would not sting as it might have outside this space. Mastrozzimone sometimes made this script visible by breaking character when she was supposed to be very upset and letting out her contagious giggle instead.

Mariloly: Political *Pájaration*

Both Julie Mastrozzimone and Mariloly performed in gay and heterosexual venues that catered primarily to Latinos. Of all the performers discussed in this chapter, Mariloly was probably most embraced by an older, heterosexual Cuban American population. She performed regularly in the drag queen revue Midnight Follies at the Cuban American theater, Teatro de Bellas Artes, which opened in 1983.[5] Both Julie and Mariloly have also hosted evenings at cabaret venues or banquet halls in Latino neighborhoods for predominantly heterosexual Latino audiences. In Miami's Cuban American worlds, drag can be fairly well-received in heterosexual contexts, and it crosses over to quite diverse audiences. For example, Julie and Mariloly performed in a banquet hall in the predominantly working-class Cuban neighborhood of Hialeah, the type of venue typically rented out for *quinceañeras* and weddings. The hall was rented out for a show featuring performances by Julie and Mariloly, and the performances were advertised in local Spanish-language newspapers. The majority of the audience at this type of event appeared to be Cuban American and heterosexual (as imperfectly as one determines either via observation). As demonstrated in the photograph of Mariloly's performance at a banquet hall venue, older men in this predominantly heterosexual Cuban American audience responded enthusiastically to her performance. Although interactions in this type of venue were less likely to feature the exchange of gay codes and sensibilities of Adora's Barrio, they were active interactions nonetheless.

One respondent who was beginning to perform in drag as Gloria at the time of our interview discussed the relative place of drag in heterosexual Cuban American versus Anglo American settings:

Mariloly, in the background, performs at a banquet hall venue in Hialeah in 1999 to an enthusiastic response from the predominantly heterosexual Cuban American audience. Photograph by author.

GLORIA: I mean I think that in shows . . . Latin people are much more
into the show part of it. Like, "Oh my god, there's a drag queen
show," and they don't even care that it's a man dressed like a
woman. They just think it's funny or cute or whatever. And they're
much more artsy about it, much more like, much more advanced
culturally than Americans claim to be.

SUSANA PEÑA: Tell me more about that.

G: Because, like, Cubans are used to a show. I don't think Americans are
like. . . . Like, when I used to go to Lucky Cheng's [a restaurant/
drag venue located on South Beach modeled after a similar venue
in New York City] like, there was people there, like, interested,
but they purposely sought out to find a drag queen—as opposed
to . . . places [that] book like drag queen entertainment at a very
Latin place, like bingo night, at Southwest Eighth Street, you
know? You'd never think it, but no, they're like, no they love it,
it's like a big show. They're much more open about it that way.
But Americans are like, um, I mean middle Americans, I guess,
are more like "Oh my God, that's a drag queen, that's a show,
those are guys and it's all about makeup and stuff!" Where Latin
people are just, like, "so what if it's a guy? It's funny, it's like a lot of
fun." And . . . you see more Latin people at functions, whether gay
or straight, at gay functions, and you see a lot more, definitely more
straight Latin people at gay functions like pageants and stuff like
that than you would straight Americans, middle Americans.[6]

These insights are partly substantiated by my research. I attended several drag performances where the audience appeared to be predominantly Latino heterosexuals. The broad appeal of drag performers might
explain the recent rise of appearances by some gender-transgressive
performers in Spanish-language television shows and theatrical pro-
ductions. Mariloly and Marytrini, in particular, are widely recognized
personalities in Miami's Latino communities and have come to occupy
a significant amount of media space.

Throughout her decades-long career, Mariloly has become especially popular among all audiences because of her enduring creativity,
her well-thought-out performances, and her comic sensibility and timing. Part of Mariloly's appeal to an older, heterosexual Cuban audience
draws from a comedic deployment of anti-Castro rhetoric. For example, in a regular lip-synched routine, Mariloly performs "Sanitario,"
her own recorded song (featuring her voice) about the use of toilet
paper—or the lack of toilet paper—in contemporary Cuban society.[7]
In Miami's Cuban American culture, toilet paper emblematizes the
material goods lacking in Cuba's economy. The toilet paper song is,

therefore, an anti-Castro commentary. In this act, Mariloly, a drag queen, becomes the spokesperson for the Cuban American community, and her popularity with heterosexual and homosexual audiences of both established immigrants and recent arrivals adds legitimacy to this position.

Drag/Race

Adora, Julie Mastrozzimone, and Mariloly are all light skinned and understood to be white in Miami's racial taxonomy. How race emerges in the context of their shows is interesting. In one show, I observed an audience member ask Mariloly to do a particular joke. Her initial response was to scan the audience. Once she had checked out the crowd, she said she could do the joke and proceeded to tell a joke that equated black people with *carbón* (charcoal).[8] After hearing the joke, I understood that she was looking around the room to ensure that there were no black people in the audience, for they were presumed to be the only ones who would be offended by such a joke. The fact that Mariloly surveyed the room raises a few issues. The assumption is that anyone who is not black would not be offended by a joke like this. On the other hand, I question whether Mariloly would not have delivered the joke had she found a black person in the audience. I suspect that she might have delivered the joke with a preamble that engaged the black audience member in the joke. Perhaps if there had been a black (Latino) person in the audience, the joke would have featured Haitians, not simply the more generic category of *negros* (blacks).

Manifestations of joking and communicating that involve an explicit and often (although not always) derogatory employment of racial categories are fairly common in Cuban Miami. Compared with the more coded racism deemed acceptable in Anglo-dominant settings, Cuban American ways of talking about race are much more explicit (and abrasive to those who have internalized U.S. racial etiquette). Both black and white Cuban Americans, especially first-generation immigrants of both races, tend to speak more explicitly about race. Therefore, jokes like Mariloly's that associate black people, dark black people, and/or Haitians (used interchangeably in different contexts) with negatively valued darkness or with something deemed valueless refuse are not uncommon in Cuban Miami. Of course, this makes them no less problematic. Given the way Cuban racisms permeated drag performances, I was particularly interested when a new dark-skinned drag persona emerged as a leading voice in Cuban American gay culture. Marytrini, who would be considered black by U.S. racial standards but would more likely be classified as mulatta in Cuban racial terms, also represents a different generational experience. Although Cuban-born like Adora, Julie, and Mariloly, Marytrini is part of the 1990s Cuban immigrant wave to Miami.

Marytrini: *Pionera Piola* or Race Revolutionary?

Marytrini is a fairly well-known personality in Miami's Spanish-speaking media world. On her website, she identifies herself as Marytrini and Alexis Fernández Mena, "estilista—actor—transformista" (stylist—actor—transformist/drag queen).[9] In this chapter I focus primarily on the live weekly variety/cabaret show she performed accompanied by las Divas del Jacuzzi, Cuban-born Teresita "La Caliente" and U.S.-born Cuban American Sophia Devine, at the nightclub known as Azúcar (2003–10) and Club Sugar. That being said, it is important to note the other kinds of work Marytrini has done. In addition to her cabaret show, she has performed as Marytrini in other venues; opened the Marytrini Boutique in the emerging arts section of Calle Ocho (Southwest Eighth Street); acted in scripted plays such as *Sor-presas*; appeared on the internationally distributed Spanish-language talk show *Laura en América*; appeared in various locally televised variety shows; served as a spokesperson for an HIV prevention campaign; and played a supporting role in the *La flor de Hialeah* airing on América TeVé, a local Spanish-language station.[10]

Azúcar nightclub is located within the city of Miami, caught between the neighborhood of Little Havana and the more affluent city of Coral Gables, in a decidedly Latino section of the Greater Miami area. Just off of Coral Way, the picturesque avenue shaded by banyan and live oak trees, Azúcar occupies a corner lot on a less picturesque cross-street surrounded by a low-rent strip mall and auto shop. Nevertheless, Azúcar is an impressive entertainment business venture. The investment in the show's physical space was evident in monthly updates to everything from expensive lighting and smoke equipment to more mundane elements like tablecloths and trays for wait staff. Every Sunday night, Marytrini and las Divas put on an original show consisting of two ninety-minute-long sets that included lip-synch numbers, skits, comedy segments, dance numbers, visits by local celebrities, and some live singing. The pièce de résistance at Azúcar, however, was Marytrini as emcee and the improvisations between official numbers.

On most Sunday nights, the dance floor filled during intermission and after the end of the second set, typically with equal numbers of same-sex male couples and heterosexual couples. When the performance started, the dance floor cleared and became part of an expanded stage. The seated audience typically included a fair share of women in their fifties and older. Teresita's mother, for example, is a regular attendee. While it was clear that non-Spanish-speaking Americans and Europeans came to the show regularly, the majority of audience members were Latino men. The ideal audience for the show was a Spanish-speaking Cuban who grew up on the island and had spent some, but not too much, time in the United States and perhaps some time in Europe (or at least had some understanding of European popular culture). The range of references and inside jokes in the improvised routines was wide. For instance, references to the televised Russian cartoons of Castro's Cuba, the use of classic Cuban slang as well as the vernacular of those raised in the 1970s–1990s, and references to the popular culture icons of postrevolutionary Cuba peppered the performances. The specific Cuban culture of Marytrini's generation also influenced the choice of lip-synch numbers and dance music played before and after performances. After months of attending the show, I began to hear more of the references that I had not previously understood. It was only after I started attending the show with men who had also lived in Cuba throughout the 1980s and into the 1990s and who were of Marytrini's age that I started to notice how densely populated the show was with references that required a knowledge of Cuba during the postrevolutionary period. When I asked those friends about a short word or phrase I did not fully hear or understand, they could explain a wide network of meanings that involved places, connotations, periods of Cuban social policy, and what was in vogue in Cuba in recent decades. In other words, Cuban Americans of Marytrini's generation were hailed throughout the show with very specific references to their experiences in Cuba.

Although Marytrini appears as a beautiful African goddess in the HIV prevention campaign, in the cabaret/drag performances she often presented herself as someone who denies her blackness. She would often say incredulously, "Yo no soy negra" (I am not black), in a tone that

Marytrini was among the twenty-five Latino celebrities featured in the "25 Mitos, 25 Realidades" HIV prevention campaign. "Sexo Anal–Marytrini" cartel (print), 25 Mitos, 25 Realidades campaign, created by EMS Resources, Hispanic AIDS Awareness Program, in collaboration with Miami–Dade County Health Department and Interart Media.

suggested no one could or should ever think such a thing. Typically, she would continue, "*yo soy* medium brown" (I am medium brown). On other occasions, she would follow her denial of blackness with this clarification: "Esto es un lunar que me cogió el cuerpo entero" (This is a birthmark that has spread over my whole body).

The show's racial politics can be quite off-putting to the uninitiated, especially to someone raised in the United States like myself. When I first saw Marytrini and las Divas perform in 2003, for example, there was a moment when I had the sense that I had walked in on a private joke between the performers and the audience. Of course, in my previous research on gender-transgressive performance in Miami, I had seen many other ongoing conversations, a kind of drag call and response that occurred week after week at given venues. Although I expected this format, I was still surprised because the audience teasing involved throwing stuffed monkeys at Marytrini, who seemed to be in on the joke, if somewhat surprised at the quantity of little monkeys involved. At some point, the floor was littered with what seemed to be obviously racist references to Marytrini's blackness. The monkeys were a gesture almost unimaginable in any other racial/ethnic drag setting.

During my continued observations (primarily in 2004 and 2005), I never saw that many monkeys again, but they did not completely disappear either. For example, one evening someone presented Marytrini with a fair-sized stuffed monkey wearing a leather jacket, and Marytrini commented that she thought the monkey thing was over. In case there remained any doubt about what the monkeys represented, it was often verbally clarified. For example, in a recurring skit that consisted of Marytrini saying something in Spanish and English-fluent Sophia "translating" it to something completely different for comic effect, Sophia once mistranslated one of Marytrini's lines as "Marytrini was born in Monkey Jungle," a theme park in South Florida. On another occasion, after Marytrini had returned from a trip to Brazil and complained that no one from Brazil had come to find her, Sophia brought a framed picture of a monkey from backstage and explained to the audience that the photo depicted the daughter Marytrini had abandoned in Brazil.

Based on these examples, one might decide that the show celebrated racial exploitation, equated blacks with animals, and made a mockery of black culture. This conclusion might not be dramatically challenged by the fact that Marytrini is not only a performer but also appears to be a multifaceted entrepreneur and the creative force behind this and related performances. After all, how many blacks have not profited from black exploitation? This conclusion would not necessarily be off-base, but I would argue that that is not all that is going on. If we look more closely, it is not so clear that Marytrini was inviting the public to unproblematically laugh at her (with her?).

One ongoing example helps illustrate the more complicated readings of Marytrini's performance that were possible. During various performances, she responded to being heckled and called a *piola*. On one occasion, an audience member who did not understand the term requested a definition. Marytrini told the audience that she had to explain the term because there were people in the audience from other countries who did not understand Cuban, and then she explained to the man who had asked that "piola es una negra que le gustan los blancos" (piola is a black women who likes white men). On another occasion, she responded to the heckling with a so-what attitude: everyone knows "que a mí me gustan los blancos" (that I like whites/white men). She added that everyone in Cuba knew she came to Miami (associated with affluence and whiteness in the Cuban imaginary). Did we think she was going to send her mother pictures of her with black people?

"No," of course not, she clarified, "hay que hacer la raza" (you have to make the race). On another occasion, however, she had a more compli- cated response to the *piola* heckling. She began with a statement that emphasized the undesirability of black–black relations: "Dos negros juntos, ¡qué feo! Eso es como la noche sin estrellas" (Two blacks to- gether, how ugly! That is like a night without stars). As the audience laughed as loudly as they often did, she turned the gaze back onto them. She said, "Blancos, ¡no se rían tanto!" (White people, don't laugh so hard!), drawing attention to the racialized meaning of their laughter to that joke. She went on to add: "que dos blancos juntos son como leche y espuma" (because two whites together is like milk and foam). She re- iterated to the directly identified white audience, "no sean tan racistas y mezclen las razas" (don't be so racist and mix the races).

For another number, Marytrini wore a wig with straight hair, and she told the audience to look at her hair: "esto es natural" (this is natu- ral), she exclaimed. How could anyone say she was black? She told the audience that white girls always do "this" and demonstrated by turn- ing her head and flipping her hair from side to side, showing just how straight and flowing it really was. At that point, the skit emphasized her black denial and implied the superior beauty of the straight hair, but her black denial turned quickly to implicate the role whites play in "this." "Si una negra se aparece" (if a black woman comes into the room), and she completes her sentence with a physical demonstration, flipping her hair at a much more accelerated pace, indicating how whites actively try to make blacks feel inferior and/or flaunt the characteristics they believe demonstrate their superiority. If at the beginning of the skit, the audience was asked to find humor in the ridiculousness of a black woman who thinks she is white, quickly the gaze shifts and what is ridiculed are the white girls who overenthusiastically flip their hair to exaggerate their whiteness in an effort to denigrate black women.

While Marytrini often said racist or self-deprecating things, she sometimes actively stopped the same kind of racism when it emanated from her audience. For example, when someone from the audience yelled that there are no "santas negras" (black female saints), Marytrini altered her comedic register slightly, told the person he knew noth- ing about religion, and proceeded to list black saints like Montserrat in Spain and Santa Barbara/Changó in Cuba. In another instance, an audience member made a more serious claim to whiteness than Marytrini's flippant assertions, but Marytrini stopped him short. He was a good-looking man of mixed Colombian and Honduran descent: Marytrini commented that his was an unusual combination and added "pero mira qué mulatico negro más lindo salió" (look what a pretty little black mulatto came from that). After she made a few other comments that included references to him being "negro," he clarified: "No, yo no soy negro. Soy . . ." (no, I'm not black. I am . . .). Since he was not wearing a microphone I could not hear his clarification, but Marytrini jumped in to add "y eres racista también" (and you're a racist, too). He denied this and looked embarrassed by the interaction, but Marytrini did not let it go: "Verdad que hay descarados. Decirme que no es negro con esa piel. Quieren ser medium brown como yo" (Some people are really shameless. Tells me he's not black with that skin. They want to be medium brown like me). While returning to her ongoing joke ("medium brown") and, therefore, literally and figuratively lightening the mood, Marytrini found it important to disrupt the denial (shame) of blackness when not presented within her own loosely scripted persona.

Another part of the show that illustrates a more complicated discussion of race occurred during a skit where Sophia and Teresita played the parts of *locutoras* (news anchors) while Marytrini acted as a sign-language interpreter. The mock news show presented a range of racially charged fictional news stories. As the white anchors went from racist innuendo to outright delighting in racism, Marytrini silently responded through pantomime. When the anchors described someone as a crazy black woman, Marytrini gave them a dirty look. The anchors continued the news story, saying that the woman had left a cigarette on her bed, the house had burned down, her three kids had severe burns, and now they looked like *chicharrón* (Cuban-style fried pork rinds). The anchors continued to describe the children's skin, and Marytrini indicated that she was getting sick of their callous description by pantomiming a gag reflex. Toward the end of the skit, the anchors defined "black" using a slew of negative associations whose English-language equivalents would be things like the black plague or a black widow spider. After the long racist diatribe, the anchors started to say "si ves un negro educado, ingeniero . . ." (if you see an educated black man, an engineer . . .). Marytrini pantomimed her hopefulness that something positive was going to be said about black men, but the anchors continued "entonces están viendo un blanco tostado" (then what you are seeing is a toasted white man). This multilayered skit provokes the question: What precisely is the audience laughing at? Some in the

Marytrini dressed as a *pionera*, wearing the uniform required of all primary school students in Cuba after the revolution, during a skit performed at Azúcar nightclub on Sunday, June 21, 2009. Photograph by author.

audience were likely laughing along with the Cuban American racist humor that devalues blackness, much as Mariloly's audience. On the other hand, this skit could be interpreted as a commentary of bias in Spanish-language news media in South Florida that has very limited and often negative portrayals of blacks. Most importantly, Marytrini's silent "talking back" at these images invites the audience to think about how these pejorative associations to blackness are seen by a black Cuban audience. Marytrini shows a black subject not only as an entertainer for a white audience but also as a cultural citizen who receives, evaluates, and critiques dominant media.

In another skit, the Statue of Liberty (played by the Miami comedian and regular Azúcar guest Zulema Cruz) was being interviewed by a journalist (played by Marytrini). The first component of the joke involved characterizing the statue as a vulgar woman: many men have passed between her legs. After various exchanges in which Marytrini tried to ask a professional question but the statue responded vulgarly, Marytrini turned to leave saying that the interview would not be published. The statue began to plead "ay mulata, no me hagas eso, por favor" (oh mulatta, don't do that to me please). When Marytrini continued to walk off, the statue lost her polite demeanor and went from calling Marytrini a "mulata" to calling her "negra de mierda" (black piece of shit) and adding "tenía que ser negra" (it just had to be a black woman). This exchange highlighted the hypocrisy of white Cubans who often use terms they see as more positive and/or not racially charged (mulatta or diminutives like *mulatica*). However, the skit went on to demonstrate that such a superficial veneer typically rubs right off to reveal an underlying clear disdain for blacks. This skit also can be interpreted in different ways: Is the audience being invited to laugh because we think Marytrini is "una negra de mierda" and we are laughing directly at her? Or, as I suggest above, are we being invited to laugh at the hypocrisy of white Cuban racism? I suspect a little of both is going on, especially when a diverse audience responds and interprets her performance from differing vantage points.

During one show in particular Azúcar was poised to celebrate several huge accomplishments. Marytrini and the club had been featured on the cover of *Viérnes,* the weekend magazine section of the *El Nuevo Herald*; Marytrini and las Divas had just finished filming short promos for the top Spanish-language television network in the country, Univision; and they were set to host the first annual Azúcar Awards, an awards show to recognize South Florida's gay talent. At one point, Marytrini struck a serious tone—something she did regularly. She remembered a time when she was just imagining the possibility of this show, when they had just started performing at the then Concorde Supper Club. She recounted that at a dinner where she was not present, a friend had commented that he thought this venture was a very bad idea, that Marytrini was wasting her time because Miami was a very racist city. She paused the story to rub two fingers over her other forearm, a gesture commonly used in Miami to refer to or signal the presence of blacks. Her friend explained that Miami would never accept a black drag queen as the primary entertainment. Of course, dark-skinned drag queens (black Latinas and African Americans) had worked Miami's Latino clubs but typically performing supporting roles and interpreting the occasional Celia Cruz song—never as emcee or reigning divas. Marytrini told the audience that this set of accomplishments, this show, and this celebration would show that friend that it could, in fact, be done.

This is the kind of moment I looked for in my fieldwork. Part of me wanted to find Marytrini challenging racism, enacting blackness to challenge the inequalities that so permeate the common sense of Miami's Cuban community. However, Azúcar was not quite that comfortable, and this moment was more of an exception than a rule. More often, racism was hyperpresent, highly visible, invited, and enacted by Marytrini, and sometimes but not always it was subverted. The racial politics of Azúcar were complicated by the fact that the stripped-down and explicitly named racism could be delivered and received in different ways. Sometimes the audience seemed to participate in a celebration of racism, by laughing at the monkeys, for example. At other times, the laughter seemed to implicate racist whites and light-skinned Cuban Americans whose racism was revealed to be ridiculous, the butt of the joke. Moreover, the racism was also something that anyone living in Latin Miami long enough, regardless of his or her skin tone, would have experienced or participated in. Marytrini's show revealed the logic that drives many social and professional interactions—a logic that views African Americans and the neighborhoods in which they live as dangerous but that views black Cubans with less fear than superficial and saccharin acceptance. The show also revealed the desire for blackness and the black desire for whiteness—never in politically correct terms, of course.

CONCLUSION

THIS BOOK BEGINS AND ENDS with highly visible forms of gender transgression associated with Cuban male homosexuality. As stated earlier, the *locas* who came to the United States as part of the Mariel boatlift were the original inspiration for this project. Likewise, the *locas* whom I discuss in chapter 8 were important cultural interlocutors that complicated my research questions and shaped my understanding of Cuban American gay culture. Whereas I hope to center these highly visible Cuban American gay social actors, my project also highlights the erasure and reinvention of gender transgressions.

My goal is to complicate our analysis of the politics of visibility as it relates to racialized and queer cultures. As I document throughout this manuscript, visibility played a key role in both the control of and empowerment of Cuban homosexual male populations. In Cuba before the Mariel boatlift, Cuban state authorities identified visible (i.e., gender-transgressive) male homosexuality as a threat to the state, and men who embodied certain visible characteristics associated with effeminate male homosexuality faced persecution. I use the term *state gaze* to discuss how male homosexuality was identified and subject to state control precisely through gendered characteristics believed to be socially visible. Ironically, the Cuban state's persecution made homosexuality more visible to a wider national and international public.

When the 1980 Mariel boatlift occurred, the Cuban state actively encouraged negatively valued populations, among them "obvious" homosexuals, to emigrate. Some in this generation imagined the United States to be a land of unrestrained gay freedom. In the United States during the 1970s, gay identity politics were developing that were strongly invested in a particular notion of visibility. The logic of gay visibility was that group rights could be ensured only through group recognition and group recognition could be achieved only through an explicit and visible articulation of group identity. A backlash against this politics ignited in South Florida, with the help of Anita Bryant, in the late 1970s. The audacity of gay visibility shocked Bryant and her followers who could tolerate closeted homosexuals exhibiting appropriate shame but who were unwilling to accept this new generation of gay activists.

For many in the Mariel generation, the gay freedom they expected to encounter in the United States was one that allowed (and perhaps even celebrated) the expressions of homosexuality that had been restricted in Cuba. For the Mariel generation of *locas,* a strategy of hypervisible gender transgressions was an explicit challenge to the state gaze that had structured their lives prior to migration. If in Cuba they had to be very careful not to exhibit gender transgressions associated with male homosexuality, in the United States they expected to flaunt them. And, many flaunted, celebrated, and expressed their identities in ways that were culturally relevant to them, but they were entering a local area that was far from embracing the gay visibility that many of them embodied. In addition, these expressions of gay visibility did not neatly align with the politics of U.S.-style gay activists. While "coming out" and being proud were key elements of U.S.-style gay activism, the success of this movement also tended to center masculine men and marginalize the kinds of gender transgressions seen in many of the Mariel generation. As Jesse Monteagudo's comments in chapter 2 suggest, even gay Latino activists in the United States did not see the visibility politics of gender transgression as serious, or as "politics" at all.

The Mariel gay generation was visible not only in terms of gender and sexuality. They were also a racialized, stigmatized, first-generation immigrant population. For these reasons, they were both more visible and more eagerly erased. This generation's poverty and detention made them more visible. From the broken sponsorship cases I document in chapter 3 that captured the media spotlight to the young gender-transgressive immigrants who lived in small apartments in what was to become South Beach, this generation seemed visible in ways that challenged gay communities and Cuban American communities that had previously lived in the Miami area. Accounts from the post-1980 period indicate that previous gay residents did not fully appreciate the gay expressions of the Mariel generation. Cuban Americans who had been living in Miami prior to 1980 and cherished their visibility as

"Golden Exiles" worried that the negative visibility that came with Mariel would shatter their placement in the U.S. national imaginary. I argue that the stigma of the Mariel gay generation contributed to its systematic erasure. This study shows how this population was exposed and erased in media contexts. More importantly, however, this study documents how Cuban American gay men from the 1990s to the present largely forgot the Mariel generation.

Although I argue that this stigmatized gay Mariel migration has been recently remembered in positive ways, the sting of the 1980 stigma is far from absent. What I hope to illustrate is how the history of the Mariel boatlift continues to shape the development of Cuban American gay culture in Miami even when (or especially when) Mariel is not mentioned at all. For example, the investment of the men I interviewed during the 1990s in masculinity and their distancing from effeminacy cannot be fully understood outside Mariel's history. I argue this is the case even when they do not mention Mariel in their interview accounts. The silences about Mariel, and the erasure of a highly visible gender-transgressive migration, help structure the identities that are embraced and seem possible for many Cuban American gay men. Men's navigation of family relations is also carefully mediated by visibility. As I discuss in chapter 6, most of the men I interviewed regularly participated in public gay cultures and also sought to maintain relations with families of origin, something most believed required the performance of masculinity. Cuban American gay men believed that successful performance of normative masculinity confirmed their presumed heterosexuality, and therefore eased relationships with families of origin. In other words, if they were visibly masculine, they were assumed to be heterosexual, and therefore, their families would not question their sexuality. Narratives of Cuba, the most hypervisible of Miami's ethnic discourses, are also invoked in the politics of visibility. Homosexuality was visible in Cuban culture. In negative terms, male homosexuals were the butt of cultural jokes and male homosexuality was identified by the state as a problem. This, however, allowed male homosexuality a centrality in Cuban culture. As Eduardo Aparicio argues, Cuban American gay men were able to claim a culture that was both simultaneously Cuban and gay, and this claim could be culturally legible (even if not widely accepted). For some Cuban gay men I interviewed, a U.S. politics of visibility and coming out did not fully capture their self-understandings—not because they were "in the closet" but because

they believed their gender/sexual identity was "obvious," which therefore made "coming out" redundant. By juxtaposing the visibility politics of gay men in Cuba and the United States across time, it is clear
that what is experienced as liberatory, what is politically valued, and
who is in a position to make these valuations shift across national/
cultural boundaries and across time.

This study also points to the complicated politics of racialization by
focusing on a group that is ambiguously placed in local and national
racial hierarchies. Although Latinos are generally considered nonwhite in the U.S. racial consciousness, in Miami light-skinned Cuban
Americans are generally accepted as white. In addition, most self-
identify as white. This study helps reveal the process of racialization
by pointing to the small fissures in this racial identity. The dominant
representation of Cuban Americans from the 1960s to 1980 was that
of the "Golden Exiles." This narrative was interwoven with the "success story" narrative that emphasized the work ethic and related economic success of Cuban immigrants in the United States. The image
of light-skinned Cuban Americans, who were successful and positive
contributors to U.S. society, intertwined racial, ethnic, and economic
discourses. This image of Cuban (white) success was not only central
in U.S. discourses but also dear to Cuban Americans themselves. The
1980 Mariel boatlift presented the most substantial challenge to Cuban
American claims to whiteness. I argue that the stigmas of blackness
and gender-transgressive male homosexuality coincided in this migration. The hypervisibility of this migration—with a focus on dark-
skinned immigrants and gender-transgressive immigrants who were
in state control for some time—scared many Cuban Americans, who
feared that their positive reputation would be permanently lost.

Fifteen to twenty-five years after Mariel, Cuban American claims
to whiteness in the context of Miami have survived. Although all of
the men I interviewed would be considered white in Miami's racial
classification system, I argue that their distancing from muscle queen
aesthetics (discussed in chapter 7) signals a race-based critique that
avoids explicit language of race. If we use census data exclusively, the
percentage of the black-Hispanic population in Miami has not greatly
increased in the last few decades. However, other observations indicate that Miami's Latino (and Cuban American population) is much
more racially diverse and that dark-skinned Cuban Americans are
choosing to remain in South Florida (as opposed to settling in New

York or Chicago) and claiming a visible place in Miami's cultural and media institutions. Marytrini, whom I discuss in chapter 8, is an example of this. Her work as a drag artist illustrates the potential of this more racially diverse generation. Her performances articulate a different perspective that was largely absent or silenced in Miami's Cuban American gay male culture. However, her work also reveals the extent to which brusque racial hierarchies, that sometimes combine the worst of U.S. and Cuban racisms, continue to structure relations in Miami.

Structures and *Rastros*

In the introduction I highlighted Raymond Williams's structure of feeling and Avery Gordon's concept of the "sociology of haunting," both of which stress the importance of analyzing less-articulated ways of being that, although not fully visible and explicitly articulated, still "set palpable pressures and set effective limits on experience and action."[1] This theoretical framework puts the focus on the hypervisibilities and fleeting visibilities that I discuss the throughout the book: the gender-transgressive Mariel generation that was both highly visible yet erased from the official record; the silences in men's accounts; the complexity of racialization without the explicit language of race. This theoretical framework also poses the methodological challenge: How do social analysts analyze structures of feeling? When the traces *(rastros)* of a culture are fleeting, how do you document them? The overall methodological design of this book seeks to address these questions. Interdisciplinary methodological tools were quite helpful in this regard. When I started to push up against the limits of the ethnographic present, a historical perspective that centered the state's role allowed me to address questions that seemed unanswerable. In this way, I shifted both methodologically (from ethnography to archival methods) and from a micro to macro perspective. Juxtaposing what men said in interviews, what I observed in the field, and what I found in archival records helped provide a more complex analysis. Shifting my gaze from the state level to the street level also helped me see what was not always in the official record. This combination of methods and levels of perspectives helps define *Oye Loca*.

Through this method(s), I have attempted to face a methodological challenge posed by cultural studies scholarship in the last three decades. While our theoretical critique and the sophistication of our analysis continue to grow by leaps and bounds, our methodologies have not always expanded in the same ways. This has led to a huge gap between what is seen as "theoretically sophisticated" work and what is seen as "empirical work." I would argue that this divide greatly limits our abilities as social analysts. Theoretically challenging work that has only a fleeting connection to our material world and empirical research that does not push beyond what is visible on the surface has limited utility to those of us who want to write social research that can both accurately diagnose our social context and play a role in creating a better future.

ACKNOWLEDGMENTS

I would like to thank all the men who participated in this study and generously agreed to share their lives with me. This book would not have been possible without their support, their stories, and their time. Although I cannot identify these men by name because of promises of confidentiality, I hope that if they read this text they can sense my appreciation and the respect I have for them.

This project began while I was a graduate student of sociology at the University of California, Santa Barbara. I will always be indebted to Avery Gordon, my dissertation adviser and mentor, and I aspire to be the kind of scholar, writer, and teacher that she is. Other members of my dissertation committee (Beth Schneider and France Winddance Twine) also supported this work. At Santa Barbara, I benefited greatly from the support of my fellow graduate students, including Peter Chua, Darcie Vandegrift, Light Carruyo, and Lorena García.

This research was supported by a Dissertation and Post-Doctoral Fellowship from the Social Science Research Council's Sexuality Research Fellowship Program (SRFP), with support from the Ford Foundation. This program not only allowed me to dedicate myself fully to my research but also connected me to a range of scholars who continue to influence my work. A fellow SRFP recipient, Susan Stryker, first suggested I go to an archive—which led to the transformation of this manuscript. I thank the SRFP for its productive and dynamic annual meetings that encouraged me to meet and develop professional relationships with scholars Susan Stryker, Marysol Asencio, Pablo Mitchell, Christina Hanhardt, Kevin Murphy, and Gloria González-López.

This project matured from a dissertation into a book at Bowling Green State University (BGSU), where I have worked since graduation.

I thank my colleagues in the Department of Ethnic Studies for providing an interdisciplinary home that fostered research that focused on race/ethnicity, gender, and sexuality simultaneously. I was fortunate to work with BGSU's Institute for the Study of Culture and Society throughout my academic career; I benefited from its Scholar in Residence program and developed my work in faculty/graduate student working groups, including the Narrative and Culture Cluster and the Sexualities and Borders Cluster. I would like to thank all those who read versions of these chapters, including Theresa Mah, Robert Buffington, Eithne Luibhéid, Christina Gerken, Joelle Ruby Ryan, Vibha Bhalla, and Valeria Grinberg Pla.

I also thank others who have supported my scholarly work: Tomás Almaguer, Ramón Gutierrez, and Tiffany Ana López. Nancy San Martín spent countless hours discussing and editing this work with me. I thank her for always being there when I needed her. I thank Jason Weidemann, senior acquisitions editor at the University of Minnesota Press, for his patience and guidance. This book is also much clearer due to the feedback from its four reviewers and the copyediting of Paula Dragosh.

Eduardo Aparicio was always willing to talk to me about my research and his various cultural and political projects throughout the city. I am indebted to him for these conversations and for his willingness to share contacts. His cultural projects were inspiring, funny, and smart, and working with them helped me develop ideas that emerge throughout this book. José Davila was a constant throughout this research process: I thank him for a lifetime of friendship and for his willingness to continually challenge me and support me.

I was lucky to have developed this book and related scholarly projects in the company of scholars with similar interests and passion. As a graduate student and assistant professor, I had the privilege of meeting and working with Lionel Cantú Jr., an emerging scholar in Latino/a gay studies. Lionel was an extremely intelligent and gifted researcher, but he was also a funny, kind, and generous human being. His passing was a great loss to our field of study, and it was also a huge personal loss to all of us who knew him during his short life. I value all the conversations I have shared with Carlos Decena and Salvador Vidal-Ortiz. Throughout our careers, we have often participated side by side at academic panels, and the conversations that have occurred around the margins of conferences (which always combined serious academic critique and raucous laughter) have been invaluable.

As I embarked on archival research—something completely new to me—I benefited greatly from the generous support of archivists everywhere I visited. I thank the staff at Jimmy Carter Presidential Library, Cornell University's Human Sexuality Collection, Florida's Moving Image Archive, and Florida International University's Special Collections. I would like to thank Willie Walker of the Gay, Lesbian, Bisexual, Transgender Historical Society of Northern California (now the GLBT Historical Society), who assisted me during my first archival trip, and Shawn Wilson, who helped me on several trips to the Kinsey Archives at Indiana University.

I want to thank everyone who helped me secure permissions for the images included throughout this book, especially Paul Baker from the *Lebanon Daily News* who tracked down an original negative of a 1980 photograph thirty years later.

Pedro Pablo Porbén, my husband and life partner, has consistently supported my work. He has done everything from helping me design the club cards that I used to recruit interview participants to thinking through the arguments in my book; more generally, he has supported my emotional and physical well-being throughout this research project. I am grateful for his generosity and understanding.

I dedicate this book to my mother, Estrella Peña. One of my biggest regrets is that she did not see this book published while she was alive. It would be impossible to list all the ways she supported this book. She was always my biggest ally and a tireless supporter of every endeavor I decided to pursue—whether it was going to a small liberal arts college in New England, going to graduate school in California (she was terrified of earthquakes), or writing a dissertation on Cuban American gay men. She helped this project in tangible and specific ways, like connecting me with Cuban gay men, especially those closer to her age than mine, whom I interviewed. She also contributed more significantly as well, because I would not be the person, scholar, or teacher that I am without her.

NOTES

Introduction

1. *Antisocial,* which literally translates to "antisocial," is a catchall term often used to refer to ostentatious homosexuality (Ian Lumsden, *Machos, Maricones, and Gays: Cuba and Homosexuality* [Philadelphia: Temple University Press, 1996], 83).

2. After Mariel, a scholarly debate emerged about the true nature of the Mariel immigrants, addressing questions such as: What percentage were really undesirables? Were these immigrants really different than previous Cuban migrations? How did these migrants fare economically compared with previous migrations? For more on this debate, see Benigno E. Aguirre, "Cuban Mass Migration and the Social Construction of Deviants," *Bulletin of Latin American Research* 13 (1994); Robert L. Bach, Jennifer B. Bach, and Timothy Triplett, "The Flotilla 'Entrants': Latest and Most Controversial," *Cuban Studies* 11, no. 2 (1981) and 12, no. 1 (1982); Gastón A. Fernández, "Comment—the Flotilla Entrants: Are They Different?" *Cuban Studies* 11, no. 2 (1981) and 12, no. 1 (1982); Eduardo A. Gamarra, "Comment: The Continuing Dilemma of the Freedom Flotilla Entrants," *Cuban Studies* 12, no. 2 (1982): 87–91; Mark F. Peterson, "The Flotilla Entrants: Social Psychological Perspectives on Their Employment," *Cuban Studies* 12, no. 2 (1982): 81–85; Alejandro Portes, Juan M. Clark, and Robert D. Manning, "After Mariel: A Survey of the Resettlement Experiences of 1980 Cuban Refugees in Miami," *Cuban Studies* 15, no. 2 (1985): 37–59; Alejandro Portes and Leif Lensen, "The Enclave and the Entrants: Patterns of Ethnic Enterprise in Miami before and after Mariel," *American Sociological Review* 54 (1989): 929–49. For an analysis of Mariel as a moral epidemic, see Benigno E. Aguirre, Rogelio Sáenz, and Brian Sinclair James, "Marielitos Ten Years Later: The Scarface Legacy," *Social Science Quarterly* 78 (1997): 487–507.

3. Immediately after the 1980 boatlift, the term *Marielitos* was used, often in a derogatory way, to refer to the Cuban Mariel entrants. The term uses the Spanish-language diminutive literally to denote "those from Mariel." The derogatory connotations of the term, especially for the period during and immediately after the

boatlift, reflect the widespread negative perception of this migrant group, including among Spanish-speaking Cuban Americans who originated its use. With time, the stigmatization of the Mariel migration diminished as more members of that generation and Cuban American activists and scholars challenged negative perceptions of the migration as a whole. With this shift in perception, the term *Marielitos* also was redefined as more descriptive than derogatory. Although I use the term here to highlight the racialized and class-based stigmatization of Mariel entrants, in other places in the book I also use the term to mark this migration's distinct identity and experiences.

4. I use the term *Latino* to refer to people living in the United States who trace their descent to the Spanish-speaking Caribbean and Latin America. This is a diverse group that includes people from many different nationalities, including Cuban Americans. When referring to census data, I use the term *Hispanic* to refer to this population because that is the official term used in these statistics. My respondents, like many other Miamians, often use the term *Latin* to refer to this population when speaking in English. Therefore, when I am quoting them, I use this term as well. I understand these terms to refer to a similar population. I use the term *Anglo* (instead of white) to refer to non-Hispanic whites, although this term is not commonly used in Miami. In Miami's racial landscape, many Latinos understand themselves and are understood by others to be white. Therefore, I believe the use of Anglo provides more precision in this context. When referring to census data, I use the terms *non-Hispanic whites* to refer to Anglos and *non-Hispanic blacks* to refer to African Americans and black immigrants from non-Hispanic nations. For more on census definitions of race and ethnicity, see Clara Rodriguez, *Changing Race: Latinos, the Census, and the History of Ethnicity* (New York: New York University Press, 2000).

5. Carlos Ulises Decena, *Tacit Subjects: Belonging and Same-Sex Desire among Dominican Immigrant Men* (Durham, N.C.: Duke University Press, 2011), 115.

6. For a discussion of the relationship between gender-transgressive homosexuality and the term *transgender* in Latino/a communities, see Susana Peña, "Gender and Sexuality in Latina/o Miami: Documenting Latina Transsexual Activists," *Gender and History* 22, no. 3 (2010): 755–72.

7. Carlos Paz Pérez, *La sexualidad en la habla cubana* (Madrid: Agualarga Editores, 1998), 126.

8. Ibid., 62–65. Pérez adds that within gay populations the term *loca* can also have "evident positive validation."

9. José Esteban Muñoz, *Disidentifications: Queers of Color and the Performance of Politics* (Minneapolis: University of Minnesota Press, 1999).

10. I received approval to conduct this research from the Institutional Review Boards of the University of California, Santa Barbara, and Bowling Green State University.

11. When I began preliminary observations in August 1996, I identified social centers crucial to Cuban American gay men's identities and culture. Gay and les-

bian studies scholars have demonstrated how sites such as gay bars, clubs, bath-houses, and coffeehouses are important to social networking, identity formation, and community development. See, for instance, Laud Humphreys, "Exodus and Identity: The Emerging Gay Culture," in *Gay Men: The Sociology of Male Homo-sexuality*, ed. Martin P. Levine (New York: Harper, 1979), 134–47; Elizabeth Lapovsky Kennedy and Madeline D. Davis, *Boots of Leather, Slippers of Gold: The History of a Lesbian Community* (New York: Routledge, 1993); Deborah Goleman Wolf, *The Lesbian Community* (Berkeley: University of California Press, 1979). During initial interviews, I also found that Cuban American gay men navi-gated their sexual and ethnic identities in part through gay club scenes (at least during one phase of their lives).

12. A club card is a promotional card used to advertise a club's activities. The cards are usually 4¼ by 5½ inches and have a colorful and eye-catching design.

13. The support of the Social Science Research Council's Sexuality Research Fellowship Program allowed me to conduct this research and provide compensa-tion to interviewees.

14. This popular expression translates literally to "I am eating a cable." It im-plies difficult economic times when survival depends on what one can find in one's immediate surroundings. I also asked men about their family's class background. Nine men indicated their family background was the same as their own. Three men indicated that their class background was higher than the rest of their family. Six men responded that their own class background was lower than their family's.

15. I have chosen to identify Eduardo Aparicio by his full name because he is a public figure who has published articles and magazines under his name. If I had chosen to give him a pseudonym, anyone with even sparse knowledge of Cuban American gay culture in Miami would be able to figure out who he is. When interviewing Aparicio, I did not promise confidentiality because that would be impossible.

16. See Kath Weston, *Families We Choose* (New York: Columbia University Press, 1991).

17. John D'Emilio, *Sexual Politics, Sexual Communities: The Making of a Homosexual Minority in the United States, 1940–1970* (Chicago: University of Chicago Press, 1983); Allan Bérubé, *Coming Out under Fire: The History of Gay Men and Women in World War Two* (New York: Free Press, 1990). Eric Garber notes the importance of the northward migration of African Americans in relation to the development of gay life in Harlem. See Garber, "T'aint Nobody's Bizness: Homosexuality in 1920s Harlem," in *Gay Roots*, ed. Winston Leyland (San Fran-cisco: Gay Sunshine, 1983), 141–47.

18. D'Emilio, *Sexual Politics, Sexual Communities*, 23.

19. For a critical analysis of the emergence of culture industries in Miami, see George Yúdice, *The Expediency of Culture* (Durham, N.C.: Duke University Press, 2003), 192–213. In discussing the growth of Miami's entertainment indus-tries between the 1980s and 1990s, Yúdice identifies the growth of South Beach's gay culture as one significant contributing factor (199).

20. Raymond Williams, *Marxism and Literature* (Oxford: Oxford University Press, 1977).

21. I elaborate my critique of culturalist analysis of Latino culture in chapter 7. See also Lionel Cantú, *The Sexuality of Migration: Border Crossings and Mexican Immigrant Men,* ed. Nancy A. Naples and Salvador Vidal-Ortiz (New York: New York University Press, 2009); Maxine Baca Zinn, "Chicano Men and Masculinity," in *Men's Lives,* ed. Michael S. Kimmel and Michael A. Messner (Boston: Allyn and Bacon, 1995), 67.

22. Tomás Almaguer, "Chicano Men: A Cartography of Homosexual Identity and Behavior," in *The Gay and Lesbian Studies Reader,* ed. Henry Abelove, Michèle Aina Barale, and David M. Halperin (New York: Routledge, 1993), 263.

23. Cantú, *Sexuality of Migration*; Eithne Luibhéid, *Entry Denied: Controlling Sexuality at the Border* (Minneapolis: University of Minnesota Press, 2002); Luibhéid, "Heteronormativity and Immigration Scholarship: A Call for Change," *GLQ* 10 (2004): 227–35; Eithne Luibhéid and Lionel Cantú Jr., eds., *Queer Migrations: Sexuality, U.S. Citizenship, and Border Crossings* (Minneapolis: University of Minnesota Press, 2005); Decena, *Tacit Subjects*; Martin F. Manalansan IV, *Global Divas: Filipino Gay Men in the Diaspora* (Durham, N.C.: Duke University Press, 2003); Manalansan, "Queer Intersections: Sexuality and Gender in Migration Studies," *International Migration Review* 40, no. 1 (2006): 224–49; Martin F. Manalansan IV and Arnaldo Cruz-Malavé, *Queer Globalizations: Citizenship and the Afterlife of Colonialism* (New York: New York University Press, 2002); Gloria González-López, *Erotic Journeys: Mexican Immigrants and Their Sex Lives* (Berkeley: University of California Press, 2005); Héctor Carrillo, "Sexual Migration, Cross-Cultural Sexual Encounters, and Sexual Health," *Sexuality Research and Social Policy* 1 (2004): 58–70. See also Susana Peña, "Latina/o Sexualities in Motion," in *Latina/o Sexualities: Probing Powers, Passions, Practices, and Policies,* ed. Marysol Asencio (New Brunswick, N.J.: Rutgers University Press, 2010), 188–206.

24. Cantú, *Sexuality of Migration,* 21.

25. U.S. Bureau of the Census, QT-P10, "Hispanic or Latino by Type: 2010." Census 2010 Summary File 1 (SF1). Geographic Area: Miami–Dade County, Florida (2010); U.S. Bureau of the Census, QT-P9, "Hispanic or Latino by Type: 2000," ed. Florida. Census 2000 Summary File 1 (SF 1) 100-Percent Data. Geographic Area: Miami–Dade County (2000); U.S. Bureau of the Census, DP-1, "General Population and Housing Characteristics: 1990," ed. Florida. Census 1990 Summary File 1 (STF 1) 100-Percent Data. Geographic Area: Dade County (1990).

26. U.S. Bureau of the Census, QT-P6, "Race Alone or in Combination and Hispanic or Latino: 2010," ed. Census 2010 Summary File 1. Geographic Area: Miami–Dade County Florida (2010); U.S. Bureau of the Census, QT-PL, "Hispanic or Latino, and Age: 2000," ed. Census 2000 Redistricting Data (Public Law 94-171) Summary File. Geographic Area: Miami-Dade County Florida (2000).

27. U.S. Bureau of the Census, QT-P10, "Hispanic or Latino by Type: 2010"; U.S. Bureau of the Census, QT-P9, "Hispanic or Latino by Type: 2000."

28. Air traffic between Cuba and the United States resumed in the late 1970s.

29. Thomas D. Boswell and James R. Curtis, *The Cuban American Experience: Culture, Images, and Perspectives* (Totawa, N.J.: Rowman and Littlefield, 1983), 45–46.

30. Silvia Pedraza-Bailey, "Cuba's Exiles: Portrait of a Refugee Migration," *International Migration Review* 19, no. 69 (1985): 15.

31. Sheila L. Croucher, *Imagining Miami: Ethnic Politics in a Postmodern World* (Charlottesville: University Press of Virginia, 1997), 103.

32. Benigno E. Aguirre, "Differential Migration of Cuban Social Races: A Review and Interpretation of the Problem," *Latin American Research Review* 11, no. 1 (1976): 103–24.

33. For more on the Cuban refugee program, see María Cristina García, *Havana USA: Cuban Exiles and Cuban Americans in South Florida, 1959–1994* (Berkeley: University of California Press, 1996).

34. After contact and conquest by the Europeans, the indigenous population of the island declined rapidly from 112,000 to fewer than 3,000 by the mid-1550s (Louis A. Pérez Jr., *Cuba: Between Reform and Revolution* [New York: Oxford University Press, 1988], 30).

35. Alejandro de la Fuente, *A Nation for All: Race, Inequality, and Politics in Twentieth-Century Cuba* (Chapel Hill: University of North Carolina Press, 2001), 3.

36. Ibid., 12.

37. Ibid., 335.

38. Mulhare, "Sexual Ideology in Pre-Castro Cuba: A Cultural Analysis" (PhD diss., University of Pittsburgh, 1969), 75.

39. Ibid., 72.

40. Pedraza-Bailey, "Cuba's Exiles," 23.

41. Mulhare, "Sexual Ideology in Pre-Castro Cuba," 73.

42. Although others define Haitians as black, many Haitian Americans resist this label. In fact, the U.S. Census regularly "corrects" the racial self-identification of Haitians and counts them as black even if they do not identify that way on the census.

43. U.S. Bureau of the Census, "QT-P10: Hispanic or Latino by Type: 2010"; U.S. Bureau of the Census, "QT-P6: Race Alone or in Combination and Hispanic or Latino: 2000"; Bureau of the Census, "QT-PL: Hispanic or Latino, and Age: 2000"; Bureau of the Census, "Census of Population, General Population Characteristics, Florida, 1990" (Washington, D.C., 1992).

44. The much-noted black presence of Mariel amounted to only 10 to 12 percent of total migrants. See Portes, Clark, and Manning, "After Mariel," 41; Bach, Bach, and Triplett, "Flotilla 'Entrants,'" 33. Thirty-four percent of Cuba's population identified as black or mulatto in the 1981 Cuban census, as cited by Tomás Fernández Robaina, "Race Relations in Cuba" (paper presented at the Center for Black Studies, University of California, Santa Barbara, February 13, 1997).

45. For research on Cuban American lesbians, see Oliva M. Espín, "Crossing

Borders and Boundaries: The Life Narratives of Immigrant Lesbians," in *Ethnic and Cultural Diversity among Lesbians and Gay Men,* ed. Beverly Greene (Thousand Oaks, Calif.: Sage, 1997); Espín, *Latina Realities: Essays on Healing, Migration, and Sexuality* (Boulder, Colo.: Westview, 1997). See also Lourdes Argüelles and B. Ruby Rich, "Homosexuality, Homophobia, and Revolution: Notes toward an Understanding of the Cuban Lesbian and Gay Male Experience, Part 1," in *Hidden from History: Reclaiming a Gay and Lesbian Past,* ed. Martin Duberman, Martha Vicius, and George Chauncey (New York: Meridian, 1989), 441–55; B. Ruby Rich and Lourdes Argüelles, "Homosexuality, Homophobia, and Revolution: Notes toward Understanding the Cuban Lesbian and Gay Male Experience, Part II," *Signs: Journal of Women in Culture and Society* 11, no. 1 (1985): 120–36.

46. Cherríe Moraga, *The Last Generation* (Boston: South End, 1993).

47. Peña, "Latina/o Sexualities in Motion."

48. All translations are by the author unless otherwise noted.

49. For a visual depiction of *rastros,* see Aparicio's photographic essay, "Rastros/ Traces," in María de los Angeles Torres, *In the Land of Mirrors: Cuban Exile Politics in the United States* (Ann Arbor: University of Michigan Press, 1999), 24–25.

50. Avery Gordon, *Ghostly Matters: Haunting and the Sociological Imagination* (Minneapolis: University of Minnesota Press, 1997).

51. Williams, *Marxism and Literature,* 132; italics mine.

52. Gordon, *Ghostly Matters,* 17.

53. Ibid., 195, 202.

54. Ibid., 195.

1. From UMAPs to Save Our Children

1. Homophobic attitudes and state practices clearly existed in Cuba prior to the 1959 revolution. However, a significant qualitative change occurred after 1959. Ian Lumsden argues that after the revolution, the repression of homosexuals became more systematic and institutionalized; the revolutionary state more efficiently policed private behavior; and homosexuals increasingly were persecuted as a group (*Machos, Maricones, and Gays,* 57–75). Homosexuality in Cuba has been the subject of extensive scholarship; see, for example, Argüelles and Rich, "Homosexuality, Homophobia, and Revolution, Part 1"; Henk van den Boogaard and Kathelijne van Kammen, "We Cannot Jump over Our Own Shadow," in *Coming Out: An Anthology of Gay and Lesbian Writings,* ed. Stephen Likosky (New York: Pantheon, 1992), 82–101; Marvin Leiner, *Sexual Politics in Cuba: Machismo, Homosexuality, and AIDS* (Boulder, Colo.: Westview, 1994); Allen Young, *Gays under the Cuban Revolution* (San Francisco: Grey Fox, 1981). Argüelles and Rich articulate a "countercritique of Cuban homosexuality" that challenges what they see as the "continual scapegoating of Cuban revolutionary homophobia" ("Homosexuality, Homophobia, and Revolution, Part 1," 455, 42). For a discussion of Cuban sexuality in the 1800s, see Abel Sierra Madero, *La nación sexuada: Re-*

laciones de género y sexo en Cuba (1830–1855) (Havana: Editorial de Ciencias Sociales, 2002). For literary/cultural analyses of Cuban sexuality, see Víctor Fowler, *La maldición: Una historia del placer como conquista* (Havana: Editorial Letras Cubanas, 1998); Fowler, *Historias del cuerpo* (Havana: Editorial Letras Cubanas, 2001); José Quiroga, "Homosexualities in the Tropic of Revolution," in *Sex and Sexuality in Latin America,* ed. Daniel Balderston and Donna J. Guy (New York: New York University Press, 1997); Quiroga, *Tropics of Desire: Interventions from Queer Latino America* (New York: New York University Press, 2000); Quiroga, "Boleros, Divas, and Identity Models," in *Cuba, the Elusive Nation: Interpretations of National Identity,* ed. Damián J. Fernández and Madeline Cámara Betancourt (Gainesville: University Press of Florida, 2000); Emilio Bejel, *Gay Cuban Nation* (Chicago: University of Chicago Press, 2001). For recent ethnographic work on male sexuality in Cuba, see Jafari Sinclaire Allen, "Means of Desire's Production: Male Sex Labor in Cuba," *Identities: Global Studies in Culture and Power* 14 (2007): 183–202; Allen, *Venceremos? The Erotics of Black Self-Making in Cuba* (Durham, N.C.: Duke University Press, 2011).

2. Castro, quoted in Lee Lockwood, *Castro's Cuba, Cuba's Fidel* (New York: Vintage, 1969), 207.

3. Argüelles and Rich, "Homosexuality, Homophobia, and Revolution, Part 1," 448. This chapter highlights the historical conditions experienced by gay men who arrived during Mariel; thus, it focuses on the relationship between the Cuban state and homosexuality up to 1980. However, Castro later softened his official stance on homosexuality; subsequently, the degree of systematized persecution of homosexuals diminished in Cuba. There is debate as to when and to what extent conditions for homosexuals improved. Argüelles and Rich, who have a relatively positive view of the Castro regime, argue that life for Cuban homosexual men and lesbians began to improve as early as the 1970s. Leiner states that "life for gay people had improved considerably in the mid to late 1980s" and that discrimination during that decade came from "individual prejudices not official policies." Lumsden defines 1965–75 as the "worst period of homosexual oppression"; agrees that since the 1970s homosexual persecution became less systematic and institutionalized; and argues that "there is little evidence to support the contention that the persecution of homosexuals remains a matter of state policy." However, he calls Debra Evenson's 1994 assertion that "homosexuals are no longer subject to official harassment for simply being identified as homosexual" a travesty. See Argüelles and Rich, "Homosexuality, Homophobia, and Revolution, Part 1," 449; Leiner, *Sexual Politics in Cuba,* 49, 51; Lumsden, *Machos, Maricones, and Gays,* 80, 86, 91; Debra Evenson, *Revolution in the Balance: Law and Society in Contemporary Cuba* (Boulder, Colo.: Westview, 1994), 159.

4. Lumsden, *Machos, Maricones, and Gays,* 57.

5. Ernesto Che Guevara, "Socialism and Man in Cuba," in *Che Guevara and the Cuban Revolution,* ed. David Deutschmann (Sydney, Aus.: Pathfinder, 1987), 246–61. I do not want to give the impression that the revolution solely focused on male issues. On the contrary, it did much to improve the place of women in Cuban

society. However, the discourse of the revolution, especially during this early period, was highly masculinized. For more on women and the Cuban Revolution, see Julie D. Shayne, *The Revolution Question: Feminisms in El Salvador, Chile, and Cuba* (New Brunswick, N.J.: Rutgers University Press, 2004); Lois M. Smith and Alfred Padula, *Sex and Revolution: Women in Socialist Cuba* (New York: Oxford University Press, 1996); Leiner, *Sexual Politics in Cuba*.

6. Leiner, *Sexual Politics in Cuba*, 26–27; Guevara, "Socialism and Man in Cuba," 246–61; Luis Salas, *Social Control and Deviance in Cuba* (New York: Praeger, 1979), 165–67.

7. Samue Feijóo, "Revolución y vicios," *El Mundo*, April 15, 1965. Original: "Este grave vicio es uno de los más nefandos y funestos legados del capitalismo. . . . Contra él se lucha y se luchará hasta erradicarlo de un país viril, envuelto en una batalla de vida o muerte contra el imperialismo yanqui. Y que este país virilísimo, con ejército de hombres, no debe ni puede ser expresado por escritores y 'artistas' homosexuales o seudohomosexuales. Porque ningún homosexual representa la Revolución, que es asunto de varones, de puño y no de plumas, de coraje y no de temblequeras, de entereza y no de intrigas, de valor creador y no de sorpresas merengosas." Various scholars cite this passage. See, for instance, Leiner, *Sexual Politics in Cuba*, 25; Lumsden, *Machos, Maricones, and Gays*, 53–54; Salas, *Social Control and Deviance in Cuba*, 166.

8. Leiner, *Sexual Politics in Cuba*, 30–31; Lumsden, *Machos, Maricones, and Gays*, 65–70; Salas, *Social Control and Deviance in Cuba*, 158.

9. Salas, *Social Control and Deviance in Cuba*, 158. According to Young, when these camps were closed, the government stated that they "did not object to the philosophy behind the camps; they merely disagreed with the way the orders were being interpreted" (*Gays under the Cuban Revolution*, 27).

10. The closure of the UMAPs was announced in 1967; however, they were not finally phased out until 1968 (Lumsden, *Machos, Maricones, and Gays*, 70) or 1969 (Leiner, *Sexual Politics in Cuba*, 31). In a letter published in the United States, Cuban homosexuals assert that in 1970 even after the UMAPs were closed, there were still other "prison farms exclusively for homosexuals" ("Letter from Cuban Gay People to the North American Gay Liberation Movement," in *We Are Everywhere: A Historical Sourcebook of Gay and Lesbian Politics*, ed. Mark Blasius and Shane Phelan [New York: Routledge, 1997], 407).

11. According to Young, homosexuals were excluded from the Communist Party and the Youth Communist Party; arguably then, this exclusion translated into "second-class citizenship of Cuban homosexuals." Both Leiner and Lumsden suggest that homosexuals were not explicitly prohibited from the Communist Party, but in practice homosexuals were denied membership or dismissed if their homosexuality became known. Argüelles and Rich imply that the targeting of homosexual gathering places by the Cuban state—especially after the Bay of Pigs invasion in 1961—was justified because in some cases the state was correct to assume that these gathering areas were "centers of counterrevolutionary activities" (Young, *Gays under the Cuban Revolution*, 28; Leiner, *Sexual Politics in Cuba*, 36–37;

Lumsden, *Machos, Maricones, and Gays,* 93; Argüelles and Rich, "Homosexuality, Homophobia, and Revolution, Part 1," 447).

12. Names of interviewees have been changed unless noted otherwise.

13. For example, laws against corruption of minors in the 1936 code did not specify homosexuality. However, the first article in the corruption of minors section of the 1979 code specifically sanctions anyone who "induces a minor, 16 years old or younger, of either sex, to engage in homosexuality, or go to places where vice or acts of corruption are practiced" (Código de Defensa Social, 17 de abril de 1936 [1938], Jesus Montero [ed.], Obispo, 127, La Habana, Cuba, Art. 486–488, 154; Código Penal, Ley No. 21 de 15 de febrero de 1979, Gaceta Oficial de 1ro. de marzo de 1979. La Habana, Cuba: Ministerio de Justicia, Art. 359, 193).

14. Original: "—Se sanciona con privación de libertad de tres a nueve meses o multa hasta doscientas setenta cuotas o ambas al que: a) haga pública ostentación de su condición de homosexual o importune o solicite con sus requerimientos a otro." The 1936 penal code also included laws against public scandal (Article 490) for those who "habitually dedicated themselves to active or passive pederasty or publicly displayed this vice, or importuned or solicited another for [homosexual] purposes" ("con grave escándalo se dedique habitualmente a la pederastia, activa o pasiva, o haga pública ostentación de ese vicio, o importune o solicite con su requerimiento a otro"). When revised in 1979, the sentence was also increased from a maximum of six months to a maximum of nine months. The maximum fine was increased from 180 cuotas to 270 cuotas (Código de Defensa Social, 17 de Abril de 1936 [1938], Art. 490, 155; Código Penal, Ley No. 21 de 15 de febrero de 1979, Art. 359, 193).

15. Código Penal, Ley No. 21 de 15 de febrero de 1979, Art. 359, 193.

16. Articles 76 and 77, as cited by Salas, *Social Control and Deviance in Cuba,* 153. The drafters of the 1936 code were indebted to the positivist criminologist Enrique Ferri for the concept of dangerousness and precriminality. For more on how lawmakers used Ferri, see José Agustín Martínez, "Relación sobre el proyecto preliminar del libro primero del código de defensa social," in *Código de defensa social,* ed. Jesús Montero (Havana, Cuba: Biblioteca jurídica de autores cubanos y extranjeros, 1936).

17. Translation by Evenson, *Revolution in the Balance,* 157. Original: "Se considera estado peligroso la especial proclividad en que se halla una persona para cometer delitos, demostrada por la conducta que observa en contradicción manifesta con las normas de la moral socialista" (Código Penal, Ley No. 21 de 15 de febrero de 1979, Art. 76, 60).

18. Evenson, *Revolution in the Balance,* 156–57. Evenson emphasizes that homosexuality was never mentioned in the articles relating to social dangerousness (see 159).

19. Lumsden, *Machos, Maricones, and Gays,* 83.

20. For example, see Leiner, *Sexual Politics in Cuba,* 43; van den Boogaard and van Kammen, "We Cannot Jump over Our Own Shadow," 92; Lumsden, *Machos, Maricones, and Gays,* 83; Salas, *Social Control and Deviance in Cuba,* 153–54.

21. Salas, *Social Control and Deviance in Cuba,* 155.

22. For examples of visible markers associated with homosexuality used by the state, see Leiner, *Sexual Politics in Cuba,* 31–32; Salas, *Social Control and Deviance in Cuba,* 155.

23. Leiner, *Sexual Politics in Cuba,* 31.

24. For an English-language translation, see "Declaration by the First National Congress on Education and Culture," in *Out of the Closets: Voices of Gay Liberation,* ed. Allen Young and Karla Jay (New York: Douglas Book, 1972), 246–47.

25. Homosexuals were also banned from medical professions (because close physical contact was possible) as well as army jobs and sensitive government jobs (because they were deemed untrustworthy). See, for instance, Leiner, *Sexual Politics in Cuba,* 37, 46; Salas, *Social Control and Deviance in Cuba,* 158, 60.

26. For an English-language translation, see "Declaration by the First National Congress on Education and Culture," 246–47.

27. Feijóo argues, "This is not about persecuting homosexuals, but rather about destroying their positions, the way they behave, their influence. . . . We will have to eradicate them from their key positions in the spheres of revolutionary art and literature. This is called revolutionary social hygiene" ("Revolución y vicios," 5).

28. Feijóo, "Revolución y vicios," 5.

29. Ley no. 1267, Gaceta Oficial de Cuba, 12 de marzo del 1974, 117–18, as cited and translated by Salas, *Social Control and Deviance in Cuba,* 160. These labor restrictions were formally eliminated in 1978.

30. Paul Julian Smith has referred to the enforcement of these laws as a "trial of visibility" in which men were arrested for appearing homosexual ("Cuban Homosexualities: On the Beach with Néstor Almendros and Reinaldo Arenas," in *Hispanisms and Homosexualities,* ed. Silvia Molloy and Robert McKee Irwin [Durham, N.C.: Duke University Press, 1998], 256).

31. Carlos Alberto Montaner, *Informe secreto sobre la revolución cubana* (Madrid: Ediciones Sedmay, 1976), 176.

32. For another Latin American case that clarifies the dynamic relationship between visibility, same-sex sexual practice, and gender transgression, see Carlos Monsiváis, "The 41 and the *Gran Redada,*" in *The Famous 41: Sexuality and Social Control in Mexico, 1901,* ed. Robert McKee Irwin, Edward J. McCaughan, and Michelle Rocío Nasser (New York: Palgrave, 2003), 139–67.

33. Quiroga, "Homosexualities in the Tropic of Revolution," 134–36.

34. Reinaldo Arenas, *Before Night Falls,* trans. Dolores M. Koch (New York: Viking, 1993), 105–7.

35. I focus on the treatment of homosexuals in Cuba prior to 1980, but there have been dramatic changes in relation to homosexuality and transgender issues in Cuba in recent years. In 2010 Fidel Castro apologized for the persecution of homosexuals in Cuba since 1959 and recognized that this was "una gran injusticia" (a great injustice). Raúl Castro, who was the butt of so many homophobic jokes and innuendos, is now Cuba's formal leader after his brother Fidel stepped down. Raúl Castro's daughter, Mariela Castro Espín, has become an outspoken advocate for

homosexual and transgender rights (or "sexual diversity") in her role as director of the Centro Nacional de Educación Sexual (National Center for Sexual Education) known as CENESEX. Since 2008 Cuba has held a series of officially sanctioned gay pride parades with the leadership of Mariela Castro. How this emerging respect for homosexual and transgender rights will extend to sexual minorities who do not work through officially sanctioned organizations and channels remains to be seen. It is unclear, for example, if the independent group Observatorio Cubano de los Derechos LGBT was able to hold the Paseo LGBT por el Prado habanero (An LGBT Walk through Havana's El Prado) on June 28, 2011.

36. Bérubé, *Coming Out under Fire*; D'Emilio, *Sexual Politics, Sexual Communities*; Barry D. Adam, *The Rise of a Gay and Lesbian Movement,* rev. ed. (New York: Twayne, 1995).

37. John D'Emilio, "Cycles of Change, Questions of Strategy: The Gay and Lesbian Movement after Fifty Years," in *The Politics of Gay Rights,* ed. Craig A. Rimmerman, Kenneth D. Wald, and Clyde Wilcox (Chicago: University of Chicago, 2000), 33.

38. Denis Altman, *The Homosexualization of America* (Boston: Beacon, 1982), 128.

39. D'Emilio, "Cycles of Change, Questions of Strategy," 35.

40. According to James T. Sears, thirty-seven cities, including Chapel Hill and Austin, had adopted some kind of gay rights ordinance (*Rebels, Rubyfruit, and Rhinestones: Queering Space in the Stonewall South* [New Brunswick, N.J.: Rutgers University Press, 2001], 230). Of the twenty-eight cities and counties that adopted gay rights ordinances analyzed by James W. Button, Barbara A. Rienzo, and Kenneth D. Wald, half could be considered college communities. Other cities included Detroit, Minneapolis, San Francisco, Seattle, and Washington (*Private Lives, Public Conflicts: Battles over Gay Rights in American Communities* [Washington, D.C.: Congressional Quarterly Press, 1997], 64).

41. Local laws used to justify bar raids were challenged by those arrested at the Coral Way Bachelor II Lounge on November 6, 1971. Among the six arrested was Enrique Vela. The judge threw out the charges, and the city later repealed the ordinance. The newly formed Gay Activist Alliance–Miami challenged the Miami Beach ordinances against cross-dressing, taking up the battle after the failed attempts of the early gay activist Richard Inman. The presiding judge struck down the ordinances in 1972. The Florida Supreme Court struck down the state-level "crimes against nature" law in 1971 (Sears, *Rebels, Rubyfruit, and Rhinestones,* 125–26). Interestingly, Inman also had a Cuba connection. He traveled to Cuba, owned a hotel that catered to Cuban clientele, and reportedly aided the FBI in surveillance of pro-Castro groups posing as anti-Castro groups (Sears, *Lonely Hunters: An Oral History of Lesbian and Gay Southern Life, 1948–1968* [Boulder, Colo.: Westview, 1997], 255–56).

42. Dade County includes the city of Miami and what is known as the Greater Miami area. In 1997 Dade County was officially renamed Miami–Dade County.

43. The full language of the amended ordinance reads: "Ordinance prohibiting

discrimination in the areas of housing, public accommodations, and employment against persons based on race, color, religion, ancestry, national origin, age, sex, physically handicapped, marital status, place of birth, and affectional and sexual preference."

44. Sears, *Rebels, Rubyfruit, and Rhinestones*, 237.

45. Bryant was SOC president, Green was secretary, and Brake was treasurer (Bryant, *The Anita Bryant Story* [Old Tappan, N.J.: Fleming H. Revell, 1977]). Brake is considered the "architect of the repeal language" (Sears, *Rebels, Rubyfruit, and Rhinestones*, 237).

46. Save Our Children Inc., advertisement, *"A Mother's Day Wish," Miami Herald*, May 8, 1977.

47. Bryant, *Anita Bryant Story*, 146. The SOC campaign was quite successful in focusing the media message on the ordinance as a threat to children, for interviews at polling centers suggests that many who voted for repeal were motivated precisely by this message.

48. Altman, *Homosexualization of America*, 128.

49. Frank Greve and Gerald Storch, "Anita Bryant: Homosexuality Is a Sin," *Miami Herald*, May 29, 1977.

50. Ibid.

51. Sears, *Rebels, Rubyfruit, and Rhinestones*, 231; "History of the Dade County Coalition," *Miami Sunshine* 1, no. 1 (1977): 2. In addition to Campbell and Basker, Keith Davis, Marty Rubin, Lisa Berry (assistant pastor of Metropolitan Community Church), Jay Freier, Alan Rockway, Barbara Bull (Lesbian Task Force), Bob Kunst, Bob Stickney (owner of Candelight Club and Warehouse VIII), and Alexias Ramón Muni were in attendance.

52. Sears, *Rebels, Rubyfruit, and Rhinestones*, 231–32.

53. Carl Hiaasen, "Out of the Closet and Then Some," *Miami Herald*, Tropic Magazine, June 5, 1977.

54. Sears, *Rebels, Rubyfruit, and Rhinestones*, 237–38.

55. Ibid., 238. See also 237–42.

56. Adam, *Rise of a Gay and Lesbian Movement*, 111. In addition to Geto, Jim Foster, Michelle deMilly, and Mike Scott joined the Coalition ("Team of Professionals to Co-ordinate Campaign," *Miami Sunshine* 1, no. 1 [1977]: 1).

57. See, for example, "An Unneeded Ordinance," editorial, *Miami Herald*, June 5, 1977.

58. See Sears, *Rebels, Rubyfruit, and Rhinestones*, 242.

59. Ibid., 232.

60. The issue that prompted Kunst's departure was whether the local coalition should participate in a national boycott of Florida orange juice, since Bryant was the official spokesperson for the Florida Citrus Commission. Gay activists in other parts of the country had called for the boycott to protest Bryant's hateful rhetoric. While other coalition members felt the boycott was a good strategy for homosexuals and supporters outside South Florida, they did not believe they should start a local boycott (Sears, *Rebels, Rubyfruit, and Rhinestones*, 236).

61. Bob St. Aubin, Media Committee, Dade County Coalition for Human

Rights formerly Dade County Coalition for Humanistic Rights of Gays, to Dear Friend, n.d., Harry Langhorne Papers 7304, box 3, folder 21, Division of Rare and Manuscript Collections, Human Sexuality Collection, Cornell University Library, Ithaca, New York.

62. Hiaasen, "Out of the Closet and Then Some," 12; Adam, *Rise of a Gay and Lesbian Movement,* 111.

63. Although *Latinos pro Derechos Humanos* was described as a "small band of gay Cuban activists," the choice of a pan-ethnic name suggests a conscious desire and/or need to work with other national origin groups (Sears, *Rebels, Rubyfruit, and Rhinestones,* 240). Both the Spanish- and English-language names of the organization were used during the campaign. The Spanish term *Latinos* was translated as "Latins," reflecting the local common usage.

64. Bryant, *Anita Bryant Story,* 125.

65. Ibid.; Theodore Stanger, "Gay-Rights Law Is Crushed: Margin of Victory Greater Than 2–1," *Miami Herald,* June 8, 1977.

66. Sears, *Rebels, Rubyfruit, and Rhinestones,* 236. See also Perry Deane Young, *God's Bullies* (New York: Holt, Rinehart and Winston, 1982), 53; Helga Silva, "Bryant Urges Latin Turnout on Gay Rights," *Miami News,* June 4, 1977.

67. Duberman, "The Anita Bryant Brigade," in *Left Out: The Politics of Exclusion/Essays 1964–1999* (New York: Basic Books, 1999), 321.

68. Vanderbilt Compilation of Off-Air Recording, WC06880, Florida Moving Image Archive, Miami.

69. Bryant, *Anita Bryant Story,* 152, 71.

70. Rich and Argüelles, "Homosexuality, Homophobia, and Revolution, Part II," 125–26.

71. A public opinion survey was commissioned and paid for by the Advocate Research and Education Foundation under the leadership of David Goodstein in order to "determine why they voted the way they did." Had this survey been completed, we might have more information on the degree to which Cuban American voters participated in the election and how they voted. Unfortunately, the survey was never conducted in Dade County. Instead, these resources were used to evaluate a similar upcoming vote in St. Paul, Minnesota (David Goodstein, Memorandum on Organization of Advocate Research and Education Fund to Board of AREF, 17 April 1978, Advocate Research and Education Papers 7310, box 5, folder 17, Human Sexuality Collection, Cornell University; Hugh Schwartz, Memorandum on Study—Dade County to David Goodstein, 27 April 1978, Advocate Research and Education Papers 7310, box 8, folder 54, Human Sexuality Collection, Cornell University; Advocate Research and Education Fund, "Report on the St. Paul Opinion Survey: Public Attitudes Toward Homosexuality," Advocate Research and Education Papers 7310, box 5, folder 16, Human Sexuality Collection, Cornell University).

72. Stanger, "Gay-Rights Law Is Crushed."

73. "8 Precincts—and How They Voted," *Miami Herald,* June 8, 1977. In addition to Little Havana (precinct number 657), the following precincts also voted for repeal: Hialeah (110) by 70.6 percent, Liberty City (450) by 55 percent, Kendall

(569) by 68.1 percent, Key Biscayne (817) by 76.2 percent. The following precincts voted against repeal: North Miami Beach (37) by 66.6 percent, Miami Beach (646) by 52.8 percent, and Coconut Grove (832) by 62.6 percent. In Dade County overall, 69.3 percent of voters voted for repeal and 30.6 percent voted against repeal.

74. Juanita Greene, "Inside Look at Gay Vote," *Miami Herald,* June 10, 1977.

75. Rich and Argüelles, "Homosexuality, Homophobia, and Revolution, Part II," 125–28.

76. "8 Precincts—and How They Voted."

77. Ibid.

78. Sears, *Rebels, Rubyfruit, and Rhinestones,* 127.

79. Ibid., 156.

80. Ibid., 127.

81. Ibid., 304.

82. Ibid., 159.

83. Ibid., 285.

84. After becoming a U.S. citizen, Ramón Muni changed his name to Alexias Ramón Muni in tribute to the hero in *The Last of the Wine* by Mary Renault (London: Longman, Green 1956). Because he was hesitant about using his real name, during the 1977 campaign he used a pseudonym, Ramón Ruiz (Jesse Monteagudo, e-mail to author, July 4, 2006).

85. Sears, *Rebels, Rubyfruit, and Rhinestones,* 230. According to Sears, Muni had been a participant in Stonewall, was an active member of the Gay Liberation Front and the Gay Activist Alliance in New York City, and cofounder of Gay Community Services of South Florida.

86. Ibid., 240; Jesse Monteagudo to Robert Roth, November 18, 1977, Robert Roth Papers 7325, box 3, folder 29, Human Sexuality Collection, Cornell University (hereafter cited as RRP). Although the group included gays and lesbians, the great majority of members identified in various accounts I found were men.

87. Robert Roth to Stephen J. Jerome, Esq., April 29, 1977, RRP.

88. Sears, *Rebels, Rubyfruit, and Rhinestones,* 240; *Estudio Uno,* WQBA, March 14, 1977.

89. Young, *God's Bullies,* 53.

90. Jesse Monteagudo, as quoted in Sears, *Rebels, Rubyfruit, and Rhinestones,* 240.

91. Young, *God's Bullies,* 54.

92. Ibid.

93. Jesse Monteagudo to Robert Roth, April 2, 1977, RRP.

94. Sears, *Rebels, Rubyfruit, and Rhinestones,* 240–41.

95. Ibid.

96. Ibid., 373n76.

97. John Katzenbach and David Holmberg, "MD Says Gay Leader Took Drug Overdose," *Miami News,* May 6, 1977.

98. Sears, *Rebels, Rubyfruit, and Rhinestones,* 372n72.

99. Dade County Coalition for the Humanistic Rights of Gays, "Latin Gay Ac-

tivist Car Firebombed," press release, March 22, 1977, Harry Langhorne Papers 7304, box 3, folder 21, Human Sexuality Collection, Cornell University.

100. According to the *Miami News,* police claimed that they had no report of the hotel room attack. According to the *Herald,* police seemed to acknowledge the previous incident but claimed Gómez could not describe his assailants. The two newspapers also disagreed as to whether Gómez had a history of depression. The *Herald* reported that his manager had said he was depressed. The *News,* however, quoted Robert St. Aubin as saying Gómez had not been depressed (Edna Buchanan, "Pill Overdose Caused Coma of Gays Leader, Cops Say," *Miami Herald,* May 6, 1977; Katzenbach and Holmberg, "MD Says Gay Leader Took Drug Overdose").

101. Katzenbach and Holmberg, "MD Says Gay Leader Took Drug Overdose."

102. Buchanan, "Pill Overdose Caused Coma of Gays Leader."

103. Hiaasen, "Vote Is Likely to Settle Nothing," *Miami Herald,* June 5, 1977. These incidents must have rattled the LHR's small group as well as the national activists gathering in Dade County for what promised to be a ferocious electoral battle. National gay rights leader James Foster arrived in Miami the day after Gómez was found unresponsive. Foster was introduced to the Coalition by way of a press conference announcing the attack and reporting that Gómez was unconscious and in critical condition (Handwritten diary, James M. Foster Papers 7439, box 11, folder 46, Human Sexuality Collection, Cornell University).

104. Jesse Monteagudo to Robert Roth, April 2, 1977.

105. Theodore Stanger, "Gay-Rights Campaign Is Unorthodox to End," *Miami Herald,* June 7, 1977.

106. Jesse Monteagudo to Robert Roth, April 2, 1977.

107. Sears, *Rebels, Rubyfruit, and Rhinestones,* 241.

108. Adam, *Rise of a Gay and Lesbian Movement,* 111.

109. White, *States of Desire: Travels in Gay America* (New York: Dutton, 1980), 208.

110. Jesse Monteagudo to Robert Roth, April 30, 1977, RRP.

111. Ibid.

112. Fetner, "Working Anita Bryant: The Impact of Christian Anti-Gay Activism on Lesbian and Gay Movement Claims," *Social Problems* 48, no. 3 (2001): 425.

113. Theodore Stanger, "U.S. Watches Dade's Gay Rights Vote," *Miami Herald,* June 5, 1977.

114. This interviewee, a Cuban American gay man, became disillusioned with gay politics after his participation in the coalition. He goes on to say, "Of course, you never know when there's going to be another repression. Repressions always come when people are enjoying many liberties."

115. Jesse Monteagudo to Robert Roth, March 19, 1978, RRP.

2. Obvious Gays and the State Gaze

1. Michel Foucault's seminal discussion of the medical gaze is found in *The Birth of the Clinic: An Archeology of Medical Perception,* trans. A. M. Sheridan

Smith (New York: Vintage Books, 1975). For more on Foucault's application to the study of immigration and sexuality, see Luibhéid, *Entry Denied.*

2. Most cases of immigrant homosexual exclusion documented in the scholarly literature deal with male homosexuals. Luibhéid's discussion of the case of Sara Quiroz, a Mexican national excluded because the INS determined that she was a lesbian, is one exception (*Entry Denied,* 77–102).

3. García, *Havana USA,* 57.

4. Ibid., 57–59.

5. Castro, "Speech to a Fighting People," May 1, 1980, in *Fidel Castro Speeches: Cuba's Internationalist Foreign Policy, 1975–80,* ed. Michael Taber (New York: Pathfinder, 1981), 278.

6. For more on the construction of deviance of Mariel immigrants, see Aguirre, "Cuban Mass Migration and the Social Construction of Deviants"; Aguirre, Sáenz, and James, "Marielitos Ten Years Later."

7. For example, Fidel Toboso-Alfonso reported that he received a notice to report to "the public order" (police station) at his hometown in Güines, Cuba. At the station, the police chief gave him the choice of serving four years in a penitentiary for being a homosexual or leaving Cuba as part of the Mariel boatlift. Young reports that *Paris Match* contributor Nina Sutton was told that "imprisoned homosexuals were ordered to leave for Florida, and were told that if they did not go they would be given four additional years of imprisonment" (Matter of Toboso-Alfonso, U.S. Department of Justice, Board of Immigration Appeals, 20 I. & N. Dec. 819 [BIA 1990]; Young, *Gays under the Cuban Revolution,* 42). See also Notes on interviews with Mike Tominski, Ray Morris, and James Smith attached to memo by Mario A. Rivera to James Giganti, August 10, 1980, "Tent City," Miami [file 2] folder, box 22, CHTF Public Affairs File, Jimmy Carter Presidential Library, Atlanta, Georgia (hereafter cited as Carter Library).

8. Félix Roberto Masud-Piloto, *With Open Arms: Cuban Migration to the U.S.* (Totowa, N.J.: Rowman and Littlefield, 1988), 100–101; Margarita Garcia, "The Last Days in Cuba: Personal Accounts of the Circumstances of the Exit," *Migration Today* 11, nos. 4–5 (1983): 13–22.

9. Garcia, "Last Days in Cuba," 20. See also Masud-Piloto, *With Open Arms,* 100–101.

10. Garcia, "Last Days in Cuba," 18.

11. Castro, "Speech to a Fighting People," 282.

12. Antonio L. Conchez, *A Gay Cuban in Exile: Memories and Letters of a Refugee* (Los Angeles: Urania Manuscripts, 1983), 28. Original: "cartas acreditativas de que éramos homosexuales, ladrones, mariguaneros, antisociales y contrarrevolucionarios."

13. Ibid., 28–29. Original: "Yo había ido preparado para la ocasión con una vestimenta diamativa *[sic],* el pelo alborotado y un poco de maguillaje *[sic]* en la cara y los ojos, además hablaba con una voz fingida exagerando los amaneramientos para que convencieran que yo era homosexual y entonces le hablé y le supliqué que me dieran esa carta. Dios entonces permitió que así fuera y me dieron la carta,

donde decía que yo era una escoria de la sociedad que no trabajaba ni estudiaba, que había estado preso, que no estaba de acuerdo con el proceso revolucionario y otros horrores y calumnias más."

14. Arenas, *Before Night Falls,* 281. See also Arenas, *Antes que anochezca* (Barcelona: TusQuets, 1994), 301.

15. Arenas, *Antes que anochezca,* 302.

16. Arenas, *Before Night Falls,* 281; Arenas, *Antes que anochezca,* 301.

17. For an example of tensions concerning gay and lesbian issues among Venceremos Brigade, see "On the Venceremos Brigade: A Forum," in Young and Jay, *Out of the Closets,* 228–44. See also Gay Committee of Returned Brigadistas, "Response to Cuban First National Congress on Education and Culture," in *We Are Everywhere: A Historical Sourcebook of Gay and Lesbian Politics,* ed. Mark Blasius and Shane Phelan (New York: Routledge, 1997), 410.

18. For a discussion of the challenges involved in evaluating the extent to which sexuality affects the choice to emigrate, see Peña, "Latina/o Sexualities in Motion."

19. Only the very earliest arrivals from Cuba in 1980 were defined as refugees and covered under the provisions of the U.S. Refugee Act of 1980, a law that allowed for an annual quota of fifty thousand refugees from throughout the world. This quota could be exceeded by the president in consultation with Congress. The 1980 Act adopted the United Nations definition of refugee as anyone who has fled his or her country because of persecution or a "well-founded fear of persecution on account of race, religion, nationality, membership in a particular social group, or political opinion." Previously, a refugee had been defined as anyone fleeing a communist country or a Middle Eastern nation. After the passage of the 1980 Refugee Act, those fleeing communist countries remained more likely to receive asylum. It soon became clear that the scale of the Mariel migration would quickly exceed the quota. A small group of early Mariel immigrants were defined as asylees, but cumbersome asylum applications and review procedures quickly proved too time-consuming. Therefore, the majority of Mariel Cubans were defined not as political refugees or asylum seekers but as economic immigrants. See also Aguirre, "Cuban Mass Migration and the Social Construction of Deviants," 166.

20. Mark Hamm clarifies this status: "Under the terms of the Refugee Act of 1980, an excludable person paroled in the [United States] . . . [is] considered to have no more rights than someone who is stopped at the border of a country. An excludable person on parole has no rights to a hearing and his parole may be revoked at any time. In contrast, a deportable person is entitled to certain hearing rights under federal law and INS regulation" (*The Abandoned Ones: The Imprisonment and Uprising of the Mariel Boat People* [Boston: Northeastern University Press, 1995], 190n4). For more on the implications of the Cuban-Haitian entrant category and the legal repercussions for incarcerated Mariel immigrants, see Mark Dow, *American Gulag: Inside U.S. Immigration Prisons* (Berkeley: University of California Press, 2004), 285–301.

21. Aguirre, "Cuban Mass Migration and the Social Construction of Deviants," 165.

22. Luibhéid, *Entry Denied,* 21. For a historical overview of immigration law in relation to sexuality, see also 31–54.

23. Ibid., 78.

24. Ibid., 23.

25. David Crosland to James Lounsbury, telegraphic message, September 8, 1980, Immigration and Naturalization Procedures folder, box 14, CHTF Director's File, Carter Library. For more on clarified immigration procedures, see Lubhéid, *Entry Denied,* 23.

26. National Gay Task Force, "Immigration Victory for Gays," press release, September 10, 1980, National Gay and Lesbian Task Force Papers 7301, box 36, folder 164, Division of Rare and Manuscript Collections, Human Sexuality Collection, Cornell University Library. Although national gay and lesbian gay rights activists did acknowledge that a real victory would have entailed dropping homosexual exclusion altogether, they still claimed that as a "practical matter" this new policy was "very close to a total victory."

27. Notes on interview with Siro del Castillo attached to memo by Mario A. Rivera to James Giganti, August 10, 1980, "Tent City," Miami [File No. 2] folder, box 22, CHTF Public Affairs File, Carter Library.

28. Notes on interviews with Mike Tominski, Ray Morris, and James Smith; notes on interview with Siro del Castillo; Rachel M. Schwartz and Peter D. Kramer, "Report on the Status of Cuban Refugees at Fort McCoy, Wisconsin," August 1980, Fort McCoy, Wisconsin folder, box 21, CHTF Public Affairs File, Carter Library, p. 8. There are conflicting reports about the intensity of these INS interviews. INS officials in South Florida clarified that there was no intensive interrogation of Mariel Cubans during processing. A report about Cuban refugees awaiting resettlement at Fort McCoy, however, stated, "this [initial INS] interview is designed to be stressful and to obtain information about the individuals' history in Cuba." In procedural discussions, federal officials were careful to insist that Cubans were not being automatically administered applications for asylum. Rather, they clarified that Cubans, like Haitians, were only being administered applications for asylum if they claimed "well-founded fear of persecution" if returned to their home country. Although the 1980 Refugee Act intended to make applications for asylum fairer, preference continued to be given to people leaving communist governments.

29. See Notes on interviews with Mike Tominski, Ray Morris, and James Smith; Notes on an interview with Siro del Castillo.

30. "A Report of the Cuban–Haitian Task Force," November 1, 1980, Misc. Informative Materials [1] folder, box 15, CHTF Director's File, Carter Library, p. 75. The remaining 49.8 percent of arrivals were placed directly with family from one of the processing centers in South Florida.

31. "Report of the Cuban–Haitian Task Force," 70–71; Department of State memo by Frederick M. Bohen to Eugene Eidenberg, November 6, 1980, "Monthly Entrant Report for October," Executive Summaries 10/27/80-11/25/80 folder, box 29, CHTF Data Summaries File, Carter Library, pp. 8–9. After providing the dis-

claimer that "the sociodemographic data which follows was obtained under somewhat imperfect conditions from many sources [including the INS, PHS, and each processing center] and would not fulfill all the criteria for a controlled scientific study," the Cuban–Haitian Task Force Report reported that 8 percent of those resettled directly in South Florida were black and 92 percent were white. The November 1980 memo stated that "roughly" 10 percent of those resettled directly in South Florida were black and 90 percent were white while 50 percent of the camp populations were either black or mulatto. This memo also clarifies that the racial statistics for the camp population are "rough" estimates because "no hard data is available."

32. "Report of the Cuban–Haitian Task Force," 70–71; Department of Health and Human Services memo by Frederick M. Bohen to Eugene Eidenberg, December 11, 1980, "Monthly Entrant Report for November," Executive Summaries 11/25/80-1/5/81 folder, box 29, CHTF Data Summaries File, Carter Library, p. 15.

33. Single adult males made up 93 percent of the postconsolidation population at Fort Chaffee.

34. Notes on interview with Siro del Castillo.

35. Most Mariel Cubans identified as having prison records were released from FCIs. By November 1980, 1,769 remained in FCIs, a much smaller number than the "substantially larger number of Cubans [who] admitted to having prison records in Cuba" ("Report of the Cuban–Haitian Task Force," 55).

36. "Fact Sheet: Release of Detainees from Talladega," draft, Talladega [Federal Correctional Institute] folder, box 9, CHTF Subject File, Carter Library.

37. Ibid.

38. For example, see Homosexuals [File No. 2] folder, box 22, CHTF Public Affairs File, Carter Library.

39. "Report of the Cuban–Haitian Task Force," 58.

40. Ibid., 37.

41. Department of State Memo by Brill to Christian R. Holmes, August 22, 1980, "Negative public reaction," Public Affairs–State Department folder, box 27, CHTF Public Affairs File, Carter Library.

42. *"Mensaje de salud," La Vida Nueva* (Fort Chaffee newsletter), no. 88, 22 agosto 1980, *La Vida Nueva* 8/20/80-9/27/80 folder, box 37, CHTF Fort Indiantown Gap File, Carter Library.

43. Department of State memo by Whitteaker to John Cannon, September 2, 1980, "Security/criminal activities/mental health," [Fort] Chaffee folder, box 21, CHTF Public Affairs File, Carter Library.

44. Garry Lenton, "Cuban Gays in Web: Agencies Caught Up in Alien Laws, Too," *Lebanon Sunday Pennsylvanian,* July 6, 1980, located in News Clippings 6/27/80-7/19/80 folder, box 39, CHTF Fort Indiantown Gap File, Carter Library.

45. Michael Massing, "The Invisible Cubans," *Columbia Journalism Review* 19 (1980): 49–51; Young, *Gays under the Cuban Revolution.*

46. Massing, "Invisible Cubans," 50.

47. For more on the medical gaze, see Foucault, *Birth of the Clinic.*

48. Memo by Bill Schroeder to Nick Nichols, "Discussion with Dr. Harold Ginzburg, Mental Health Services," Mental Health [2] folder, box 38, CHTF Fort Indiantown Gap File, Carter Library, p. 2.

49. Schwartz and Kramer, "Report on the Status of Cuban Refugees," 11, 22.

50. Ibid., 11.

51. Ibid., 14, 15. Also, Ginzburg stated he did not know which Department of Health and Human Services staff was "claiming minors hidden in family compound and being abused" ("Ginsberg's Statement," Fort McCoy [1] folder, box 4, CHTF Subject File, Carter Library).

52. Schwartz and Kramer, "Report on the Status of Cuban Refugees," 15, 16.

53. "Ginsberg's Statement."

54. Schwartz and Kramer, "Report on the Status of Cuban Refugees," 16. Mario Rivera describes this report as a "briefly publicized, then suppressed, internal [Health and Human Services] evaluation by medical officers" (*Decision and Structure: U.S. Refugee Policy in the Mariel Crisis* [Lanham, Md.: University Press of America, 1991], 129).

55. Transcripts of "Fort Chaffee," in *The MacNeil/Lehrer Report* (WNET/ Thirteen), Public Affairs Releases 9/16/80-1/29/81 folder, box 61, CHTF Administrative File, Carter Library, p. 3.

56. Warren Brown, "Cuban Boatlift Drew Thousands of Homosexuals; Thousands of Refugees from Cuba Are Homosexual," *Washington Post,* July 7, 1980.

57. Warren Brown, "Gay Refugees Await Sponsors," *Miami Herald,* July 7, 1980.

58. See, for example, press guidance sheets dated July 7, 1980, September 11, 1980, and September 12, 1980 in [Reading Material Notebk] [3] folder, box 17, CHTF Director's File, Carter Library.

59. FEMA memo by Macy to Eugene Eidenberg, July 7, 1980, "Executive Summary—Cuban Refugee Situation," FEMA Executive Summaries 6/21/80–7/14/80 folder, box 30, CHTF Data Summaries File, Carter Library.

60. Press guidance sheet, September 12, 1980.

61. "Report of the Cuban–Haitian Task Force," 37.

62. Siro del Castillo, "A Plea to Destigmatize Mariel," *Caribbean Review* 13, no. 4 (1984): 7.

63. Schwartz and Kramer, "Report on the Status of Cuban Refugees," 22.

64. Ibid., 11.

65. Memo by Bill Schroeder to Nick Nichols. It is unclear here what behavior verified their homosexuality. Throughout government documents, gender transgression was seen as synonymous with homosexuality.

66. Young, *Gays under the Cuban Revolution,* 54–55.

67. Ibid., 42.

68. Department of State Memo by N. G. W. Thorne to Victor H. Palmieri, July 22, 1980, "Report on July 18 Staff Briefing," Staffing Briefing 7/18/80 folder, box 18, CHTF Director's File, Carter Library.

69. "Report of the Cuban–Haitian Task Force," 5564. The other three groups defined as "problem populations" were the "criminal element," "mental health," and "unaccompanied minors."

70. Press guidance sheet, September 11, 1980. Other sources have argued that the number of homosexuals was an issue created by the media with no basis in reality. For example, Yohel Camayd-Freixas complained of the ongoing effect of the erroneous newspaper figure: "It is interesting to note that this is the only reported estimate—if grossly inaccurate—of a high proportion of homosexuals among the Mariel group. Yet many subsequent articles include the 'homosexual problem' as a characteristic of the Mariel group, even though these reports have no objective bases for such claims aside from this erroneous Herald article" (Camayd-Freixas, *Crisis in Miami* [Boston: Boston Urban Research and Development Group, 1988], III-47). Del Castillo makes a similar argument in "A Plea to Destigmatize Mariel."

71. Underline in the original. FEMA memo by Macy to Eugene Eidenberg.

72. In the semi-retraction printed the day after Brown's article, Judy Weiss from Fort Chaffee asserted that only 94 of the 10,000 Cubans who had passed through her camp were known to be gay. Furthermore, Bruce Brockway reported 900 homosexuals in Fort McCoy and estimated a total of 6,800 gay detainees. Larry Mahoney of FEMA estimated this number at 4,000 (Ethan Bronner, "Camp Personnel Deny Report of 20,000 Gay Refugees," *Miami Herald,* July 8, 1980). After the media frenzy fomented by Brown's article, estimates of the number of homosexuals awaiting resettlement remained low. For example, in preparation for consolidation of the camps some officials estimated only 260 homosexuals awaiting resettlement ("Consolidation Data," Consolidation [File no. 2] folder, box 11, CHTF Director's File, Carter Library).

73. Estimate of 1,000 in "Briefing Materials, Senate Appropriations Subcommittee Hearings," March 6, 1981, Briefing Materials Senate Appropriations Committee 3/6/81 Folder, Box 11, CHTF Director's File, Carter Library. Estimate of 2,500 in "Fort Chaffee Resettlement Plan," attached to memo by Wilford J. Forbush to Jack Svhan, March 10, 1981, Fort Chaffee folder, box 14, CHTF Director's File, Carter Library.

74. "DHHS [Department of Health and Human Services] Role in the Consolidation of Cuban–Haitian Populations into One Camp," draft, August 7, 1980, Consolidation Plans PHS and HHS folder, box 35, CHTF Fort Indiantown Gap File, Carter Library.

75. "Questions on Consolidation: Asked by Cuban Haitian Task Force, Washington," Consolidation [File no. 2][1] folder, box 34, CHTF Fort Indiantown Gap File, Carter Library.

76. "Consolidation Data."

77. Both male and female homosexuals are included in the list of classes, as are the physically and mentally handicapped, the elderly, unaccompanied minors, and those with previous criminal offenses and medical problems (further identified by medical condition). With only four out of seven voluntary agencies providing information, 378 male homosexuals and 8 female homosexuals are counted on this spreadsheet (Department of State memo by Donald E. Whitteaker to Chris Holmes, October 22, 1980, "List of classes at Ft. Chaffee, first very rough approximation," Funding folder, box 35, CHTF Fort Indiantown Gap File, Carter Library).

78. "Fort Chaffee Resettlement Plan."

79. Press guidance sheet, September 12, 1980.

80. Press guidance sheet, September 11, 1980.

81. Massing, "Invisible Cubans," 50.

82. Young, *Gays under the Cuban Revolution,* 54.

83. See, for example, Coordinating Council of Dade County memo by Silvia Unzueta to Eduardo J. Padrón, August 26, 1980, "To Assess Existing Conditions at Ft. Chaffee, Arkansas, and Evaluate Consolidation Plans," Cuban Community folder, box 11, CHTF Director's File, Carter Library.

84. "Fort Indiantown Gap after Action Report," vol. 1, May 11, 1980–October 15, 1980, box 32, CHTF Fort Indiantown Gap File, Carter Library, p. 67. In October, an INS memo recommended that separate facilities and minimal security barracks house "hardcore criminal, insanes, riot agitators, juveniles and homosexuals" (INS Task Force memo by Alfred Saucier to William Lang, Jr., October 11, 1980, "Problems at Ft. Indiantown Gap—Border Patrol Suggestions," AA Today folder, box 33, CHTF Fort Indiantown Gap File, Carter Library).

85. Lenton, "Cuban Gays in Web."

86. The Press guidance dated September 11, 1980, responded to the question "Do you think you will be able to resettle homosexuals?" by stating that gay organizations "have come forward voluntarily."

87. "Lesbian and Gay Community Meets to Form Nationwide Network for Aiding Gay and Lesbian Cuban Refugees," press release, July 8, 1980, National Gay and Lesbian Task Force Papers 7301, box 36, folder 159, Human Sexuality Collection, Cornell Library.

88. "Resettling Gay Cubans," *Christian Century* 98 (1981): 504–5.

89. Ibid.

90. "Minutes from CHTF Staff Meeting," July 28, 1980, CHTF-Staff Meeting Minutes folder, box 34, CHTF Fort Indiantown Gap File, Carter Library.

91. Department of State memo by Barbara Lawson to Christian R. Holmes, September 26, 1980, Camp Consolidation [2] folder, box 1, CHTF Subject File, Carter Library.

92. Memo, Wilford J. Forbush to Jack Svhan, March 10, 1981, and attached "Fort Chaffee Resettlement Plan."

93. Department of Health and Human Services, Office of the Secretary, Cuban-Haitian Task Force, Office of Refugee Resettlement, "Management Tracking System," February 6, 1981, Camp Consolidation—Press folder, box 11, CHTF Director's File, Carter Library.

94. "Resettling Gay Cubans." According to the MCC, the Baltimore house was destroyed by arson before it could open.

95. Frank Zerrilli, e-mail to author, December 15, 2003.

96. National Gay Task Force, "Cuban Refugees' Status Clarified by Immigration Service," press release, February 19, 1985, National Gay and Lesbian Task Force Papers 7301, box 37, folder 6, Human Sexuality Collection, Cornell Library.

97. Ibid.

98. Luibhéid, *Entry Denied,* xi.

99. Margot Canaday, *The Straight State: Sexuality and Citizenship in Twentieth-Century America* (Princeton, N.J.: Princeton University Press, 2009), 4.

100. Ibid., 254.

101. Luibhéid, *Entry Denied,* xi.

3. Cultures of Gay Visibility and Renarrating Mariel

1. "CHTF and ORR Transition Briefing Materials," December 3, 1980, Transition Briefing Book folder, box 19, CHTF Public Affairs File, Carter Library, p. 8.

2. Notes on interviews with Mike Tominski, Ray Morris, and James Smith attached to memo by Mario A. Rivera to James Giganti, August 10, 1980, "Tent City," Miami [file No. 2] folder, box 22, CHTF Public Affairs File, Carter Library.

3. Memo by Mario A. Rivera to James Giganti, August 10, 1980, "Tent City," Miami [File No. 2] folder, box 22, CHTF Public Affairs File, Carter Library.

4. "FEMA Executive Summary," June 25, 1980, FEMA Executive Summaries 6/21/80–7/14/80 folder, box 30, CHTF Data Summaries File, Carter Library.

5. *Returnees* was a term used to refer to broken sponsorships among those sponsored outside resettlement camps.

6. "CHTF and ORR Transition Briefing Materials," 9; Notes on interviews with Mike Tominski, Ray Morris, and James Smith. A portion of the 60 percent not living with sponsors might have been living independently.

7. Guillermo Martinez, "Tense City: Wait Is Endless, Tempers Short for Refugees," *Miami Herald,* August 24, 1980.

8. "A Report of the Cuban-Haitian Task Force," November 1, 1980, Misc. Informative Materials [1] folder, box 15, CHTF Director's File, Carter Library, p. 14; "CHTF and ORR Transition Briefing Materials," 8.

9. FEMA memo by John W. Macy to Eugene Eidenberg, July 1, 1980, "Executive Summary—Cuban Refugee Situation," FEMA Executive Summaries 6/21/80–7/14/80 folder, box 30, CHTF Data Summaries File, Carter Library.

10. Martinez, "Tense City."

11. *Ciudad de las carpas* (dir. Miñuca Villaverde; 1980), 16 mm film. I saw two screenings of the documentary, both attended by Villaverde and followed by question and answer sessions. The first screening was part of the "Made in the U.S.A." series held at the Alliance Theatre in Miami Beach in March 1997. The second screening was held at the Tower Theatre in Miami as part of events commemorating the twenty-fifth anniversary of the Mariel migration in 2005. Although the documentary itself is not readily available, a script and commentary appear in Miñuca Villaverde and Fernando Villaverde, "La ciudad de las carpas," in *Dos filmes de Mariel: El éxodo cubano de 1980,* ed. Jorge Ulla, Lawrence Ott, and Miñuca Villaverde (Madrid: Editorial Playor, 1986), 59–92.

12. Villaverde and Villaverde, "La ciudad de las carpas," 82.

13. Ibid., 80.

14. Ibid., 81–82.

15. Ibid., 88.

16. Ibid., 76, 69.

17. Miñuca Villaverde, "¿Cómo y por qué se realizó esta película?" in Ulla, Ott, and Villaverde, *Dos filmes de Mariel*, 96.

18. Villaverde and Villaverde, "La ciudad de las carpas," 87.

19. Reinaldo Arenas, *Before Night Falls*, trans. Dolores M. Koch (New York: Viking, 1993), 105–7.

20. Brown, "Cuban Boatlift Drew Thousands of Homosexuals."

21. Elinor Burkett, "The Price," *Miami Herald*, April 1, 1990.

22. Rene V. Murai, "Rebuttal to *Tropic* Article on Mariel Gays," *Miami Herald*, April 13, 1990.

23. Alejandro Portes, "Homosexuality among Mariel Men," *Miami Herald*, September 8, 1991. Portes's response was likely included because he was a prominent sociologist, immigration expert, and Cuban American academic. Published more than a year after Burkett's article, Portes's response received its own headline and subheadline under his own byline.

24. Ibid.

25. Ibid.

26. Ibid.

27. *Más allá del mar (Beyond the Sea)* (dir. Lisandro Pérez-Rey; 2003).

28. www.miamiherald.com/multimedia/news/mariel/ (accessed June 18, 2011). Previously at www.realcities.com/multimedia/miami/news/archive/mariel/index .html (accessed October 27, 2007).

29. For studies of homosexuality in Cuba, see, for example, Leiner, *Sexual Politics in Cuba*; Lumsden, *Machos, Maricones, and Gays*; Argüelles and Rich, "Homosexuality, Homophobia, and Revolution, Part I," 441–55; Rich and Argüelles, "Homosexuality, Homophobia, and Revolution, Part II," 120–36. For studies on U.S. Latino gay populations that emphasize *activo/pasivo* models, see Almaguer, "Chicano Men," 75–98; Rafael M. Díaz, *Latino Gay Men and HIV: Culture, Sexuality, and Risk Behavior* (New York: Routledge, 1998).

30. See, for instance, Decena, *Tacit Subjects*; Lawrence La Fountain-Stokes, "*De un Pájaro las dos Alas*: Travel Notes of a Queer Puerto Rican in Havana," *GLQ* 8, nos. 1–2 (2002): 7–33; La Fountain-Stokes, *Queer Ricans: Cultures and Sexualities in the Diaspora* (Minneapolis: University of Minnesota Press, 2009); Cantú, *The Sexuality of Migration*; Quiroga, *Tropics of Desire*; Michael Hames-García and Ernesto Javier Martínez, eds., *Gay Latino Studies: A Critical Reader* (Durham, N.C.: Duke University Press, 2011); Juana Maria Rodríguez, *Queer Latinidad* (New York: New York University Press, 2003); Lázaro Lima, "Locas al Rescate: The Transnational Hauntings of Queer *Cubanidad*," in *Cuba Transnational*, ed. Damián J. Fernández (Gainesville: University Press of Florida, 2005), 79–103; Lima, *The Latino Body: Crisis Identities in American Literary and Cultural Memory* (New York: New York University Press, 2007); Luibhéid, *Entry Denied*; Luibhéid and Cantú, *Queer Migrations*; Marysol Asencio, ed., *Latina/o Sexualities: Probing Powers, Passions, Practices, and Policies* (New Brunswick, N.J.: Rutgers University Press, 2010); Horacio N. Roque Ramírez,

"'That's My Place!': Negotiating Racial, Sexual, and Gender Politics in San Francisco's Gay Latino Alliance, 1975–1983," *Journal of the History of Sexuality* 12, no. 2 (2003): 224–58.

31. See, for instance, Roderick A. Ferguson, *Aberrations in Black: Toward a Queer of Color Critique* (Minneapolis: University of Minnesota Press, 2004); Manalansan, *Global Divas*; Muñoz, *Disidentifications*; Jasbir Kaur Puar, "Global Circuits: Transnational Sexualities and Trinidad," *Signs: Journal of Women in Culture and Society* 26, no. 4 (2001): 1039–65; Gayatri Gopinath, *Impossible Desires: Queer Diasporas and South Asian Public Cultures* (Durham, N.C.: Duke University Press, 2005).

32. Some examples include Gloria González-López, *Erotic Journeys: Mexican Immigrants and Their Sex Lives* (Berkeley: University of California Press, 2005); Jennifer S. Hirsch, *A Courtship after Marriage: Sexuality and Love in Mexican Transnational Families* (Berkeley: University of California Press, 2003); Ramón A. Gutiérrez, *When Jesus Came, the Corn Mothers Went Away: Marriage, Sexuality, and Power in New Mexico, 1500–1846* (Stanford, Calif.: Stanford University Press, 1991); Elena R. Gutiérrez, *Fertile Matters: The Politics of Mexican-Origin Women's Reproduction* (Austin: University of Texas Press, 2008); Pablo Mitchell, *Coyote Nation: Sexuality, Race, and Conquest in Modernizing New Mexico, 1880–1920* (Chicago: University of Chicago Press, 2005); Natalia Molina, *Fit to Be Citizens? Public Health and Race in Los Angeles, 1879–1939* (Berkeley: University of California Press, 2006); Laura Briggs, *Reproducing Empire: Race, Sex, Science, and U.S. Imperialism in Puerto Rico* (Berkeley: University of California Press, 2002); Alexandra Minna Stern, *Eugenic Nation: Faults and Frontiers of Better Breeding in Modern America* (Berkeley: University of California Press, 2005); Lorena García, "'Now Why Do You Want to Know About That?': Heteronormativity, Sexism, and Racism in the Sexual (Mis)Education of Latina Youth," *Gender and Society* 23, no. 4 (2009): 520–41; Salvador Vidal-Ortiz, "'The Puerto Rican Way Is More Tolerant': Constructions and Uses of 'Homophobia' among *Santería* Practioners across Ethno-Racial and National Identification," *Sexualities* 11, no. 4 (2008): 476–95.

4. *Pájaration* and Transculturation

1. Dennis Altman, "Global Gaze/Global Gays," *GLQ* 3, no. 4 (1997): 417–36.

2. Richard Parker, *Beneath the Equator: Cultures of Desire, Male Homosexuality, and Emerging Gay Communities in Brazil* (New York: Routledge, 1999), 225.

3. Ibid., 226.

4. Spanglish describes a mix of Spanish and English. It can refer to constant code switching between English and Spanish or to specific terms that incorporate English- and Spanish-language elements.

5. For a discussion of the concept of Latino cultural citizenship, see Rina Benmayor and William V. Flores, *Latino Cultural Citizenship: Claiming Identity, Space, and Rights* (Boston: Beacon, 1997).

6. Alejandro Portes and Alex Stepick, *City on the Edge: The Transforma-tion of Miami* (Berkeley: University of California Press, 1993), 161, citing Frederic Tasker, "Anti-Bilingualism Approved in Dade County," *Miami Herald,* November 5, 1980. This English Only legislation actually repealed an ordinance passed in 1973 by the county board, the Bilingual-Bicultural ordinance, which "designated Spanish as the county's second official language and called for the establishment of a Department of Bilingual and Bicultural Affairs, the translation of county documents into Spanish, and increased efforts to recruit Latinos to county jobs" (García, *Havana USA,* 114, 74).

7. Portes and Stepick, *City on the Edge,* 161.

8. Almaguer, "Chicano Men," 75–98. For literature on Mexico, see Joseph Carrier, *De los otros: Intimacy and Homosexuality among Mexican Men* (New York: Columbia University Press, 1995); Clark Louis Taylor, "El ambiente: Male Homosexual Social Life in Mexico City" (PhD diss., University of California, Berkeley, 1978); Héctor Carrillo, *The Night Is Young: Sexuality in Mexico in the Time of AIDS* (Chicago: University of Chicago Press, 2002). On Nicaragua, see Roger N. Lancaster, *Life Is Hard: Machismo, Danger, and the Intimacy of Power in Nicaragua* (Berkeley: University of California Press, 1992); Lancaster, "Subject Honor and Object Shame: The Construction of Male Homosexuality and Stigma in Nicaragua," *Ethnology* 27, no. 2 (1988): 371–90. On Brazil, see Parker, *Beneath the Equator*; Richard G. Parker, *Bodies, Pleasures, and Passions: Sexual Culture in Contemporary Brazil* (Boston: Beacon, 1991). On Cuba, see Young, *Gays under the Cuban Revolution*; Leiner, *Sexual Politics in Cuba*; Lumsden, *Machos, Maricones, and Gays.*

9. Fernando Ortiz, *Cuban Counterpoint: Tobacco and Sugar,* trans. Harriet de Onís (1940; repr. Durham, N.C.: Duke University Press, 1995), 97–103. For another discussion of transculturation in relation to Miami's ethnic cultures, see Alex Stepick and others, *This Land Is Our Land: Immigrants and Power in Miami* (Berkeley: University of California Press, 2003), 144–45.

10. The effects of non-Anglos on U.S.-based gay culture may be seen in exoticizing discourses of desire such as the eroticization of Latino masculinity in gay circles. Transculturation does not necessarily guarantee liberatory results.

11. For other analyses of linguistic innovations involving humor in Latino communities, see Jose Limón, "Carne, Carnales, and the Carnivalesque: Bakhtinian, Batos, Disorder, and Narrative Discourses," in *Situated Lives: Gender and Culture in Everyday Life,* ed. Louise Lamphere, Helena Ragoné, and Patricia Zavella (New York: Routledge, 1997), 62–82; Jose R. Reyna and María Herrera-Sobek, "Jokelore, Cultural Differences, and Linguistic Dexterity: The Construction of Mexican Immigrant Chicano Humor," in *Culture across Borders: Mexican Immigration and Popular Culture,* ed. David R. Maciel and Maria Herrera-Sobek (Tucson: University of Arizona Press, 1998), 203–25.

12. For a discussion of the use of the term *gay* in Latin America during the 1970s and 1980s, see Stephen O. Murray and Manuel G. Arboleda, "Stigma Relexification: 'Gay' in Latin America," in *Latin American Male Homosexualities,* ed. Stephen O. Murray (Albuquerque: University of New Mexico Press, 1995), 138–44.

13. This English-language translation provided by the editor of *Perra!* magazine (Eduardo Aparicio, interview with the author, January 21, 1999).

14. *Perra!* May 1995, 1.

15. During interviews conducted in Spanish, I tried to use a variety of English and Spanish versions of the concept of coming out. In this interview, I specifically asked, "¿Qué significa la expresión *coming out* para tí? ¿O 'salir del closet,' [o] 'declararse'?"

16. Decena, *Tacit Subjects,* 18, 19.

17. Early research on gay and lesbian people of color living in the United States employed an identity-conflict model. Identity-conflict models assume that gay and lesbian people of color must balance competing demands from their ethnic/ racial and sexual communities and that their ethnic/racial and sexual identities are, therefore, experienced as split or in conflict. Scholars such as Oliva M. Espín and James T. Sears have asked respondents to rank their sexual and racial/ethnic identities. In my research, I chose to take a step back and ask respondents whether they felt their identity was in conflict ("Do you feel you have to struggle to be both gay and Cuban?") (Espín, "Issues of Identity in the Psychology of Latina Lesbians," in *Lesbian Psychologies: Explorations and Challenges,* ed. Boston Lesbian Psychologies Collective [Urbana: University of Illinois, 1987], 35–55; Sears, "Black or Gay in a Southern Community: Jacob and the Bus Boycott," in *Growing Up Gay in the South: Race, Gender, and the Journeys of the Spirit* [New York: Haworth, 1990], 117–43). See also John L. Peterson, "Black Men and Their Same-Sex Desires and Behaviors," in *Gay Culture in America: Essays from the Field,* ed. Gilbert Herdt (Boston: Beacon, 1992), 147–64; Edward S. Morales, "HIV Infection and Hispanic Gay and Bisexual Men," *Hispanic Journal of Behavioral Sciences* 12, no. 2 (1990): 212–22.

18. I found some evidence of the reclamation of derogatory terms such as *maricón* and *pájaro* by Cuban American gay men. This reclamation could be a fourth linguistic practice. "Pájaration" can be seen as divesting *pájaro* of its negative power through humor. In a gay Latino club with Mariloly employing the term, the stigma-laden history of *pájaro* makes it funnier and inspires the crowd to heckle Mariloly. This, however, is a partial process, and the positive investment in these stigma-laden terms works only in particular settings.

19. I have purposely chosen to use the pronoun *himself.* The club where this performance was observed catered almost exclusively to men, and typically audiences were over 90 percent male.

20. *Mariposas en el andamio (Butterflies on the Scaffold)* (dir. Luis Felipe Bernaza and Margaret Gilpin; 1996).

5. Narratives of Nation and Sexual Identity

1. Flavio Risech, "Political and Cultural Cross-Dressing: Negotiating a Second Generation Cuban-American Identity," in *Bridges to Cuba, Puentes a Cuba,* ed. Ruth Behar (Ann Arbor: University of Michigan Press, 1995), 62. For another discussion of the publication *Zig Zag,* see García, *Havana USA,* 104.

2. Frances Negrón-Muntaner, "Feeling Pretty: *West Side Story* and Puerto Rican Identity Discourses," *Social Text* 18, no. 2 (2000): 83–106.

3. A *guayabera* is a type of button-down shirt commonly worn by Cuban men. Typically made of cotton or linen, the *guayabera* typically features painstaking rows of fine pleats and four front pockets.

4. Jose Esteban Muñoz, "No Es Fácil: Notes on the Negotiation of Cubanidad and Exilic Memory in Carmelita Tropicana's Milk of Amnesia," *Drama Review* 39, no. 3 (1995): 76.

5. Juan is technically a member of the 1.5 generation. He was born in Cuba but came to the United States at a young age. I group members of the 1.5 and second generation (U.S. born to Cuban-born parents) together, as they are most likely to have come of sexual age in the United States.

6. *Perra* is Spanish for a female dog. *Perrita* is the diminutive form of *perra*. *Madrinas* and *tías adoptivas* refer to godmothers and adoptive aunts, respectively.

7. Aparicio, "Editorial," *Perra!*, May 1997, 4. *Pajaritos* literally denotes small birds, but the term also connotes male homosexuals in Cuban Spanish.

8. Historically, *el malecón* is a place where both heterosexual and gay Cubans hang out and cruise. The term *guajiro* is used here to refer to someone who is not from the capital, Havana; more broadly, it might translate as hick or country bumpkin, implying both a person of rural origin and/or someone with little formal education.

9. Most "letters" Arocha answered were actually questions drafted by Aparicio in relation to the issue's theme.

10. Jorge Arocha, "Dime qué te pica," *Perra!*, April 1997, 5.

11. Inside, there is an article by the artist Ernesto Pujol critiquing patriarchy and the exaltation of a masculine ideal among native-born Cubans and Cuban exiles; an article by Lawrence La Fountain-Stokes about Carmelita Tropicana's performance of "Pingalito Betancourt" that pokes fun at the hypermasculine Cuban macho; and a review by Julie Mastrossimone of places of interest in for gays in Cuba.

12. Eduardo Aparicio, "Editorial," *Perra!*, April 1997, 4.

13. In 1997, County Commissioner Bruce Kaplan introduced the "Human Rights Ordinance," which would include sexual orientation in the county's anti-discrimination ordinance, making it illegal to discriminate against homosexuals in the areas of housing and employment (Karen A. Holness, "Defeat of Gay Rights Ordinance Seen as a Regressive Step by Dade," *Miami Herald,* June 26, 1997).

14. Don Finefrock, "Gay Rights Back on Table in Dade: Domestic-Partner Benefits Part of Commissioner's Proposal," *Miami Herald,* April 17, 1997.

15. Steve Rothaus, "1,000 Attend Gay Rally at Bayfront Park," *Miami Herald,* October 27, 1997.

16. Latinos were present in rallies both in support of and opposition to the ordinance, but this participation appeared to be divided along national lines. Whereas Cuban American gay men seemed actively to support the antidiscrimination ordinance, those struggling against gay rights appeared to include more recent arriv-

als from Central America who were affiliated with Christian organizations that aligned with the Christian Coalition to suppress homosexual rights. While the opposition outnumbered those in support at a rally I observed at the end of 1998, a Latino led the supporting contingent by chanting in both English and Spanish.

17. Ronnie Greene, "Gay Rights Measure Squeaks By," *Miami Herald,* November 6, 1998.

18. A majority of the voting commissioners were Latino. Jimmy Morales and Bruno A. Barreiro supported the ordinance. In addition, three African Americans (Betty Ferguson, Barbara Carey, and Dennis Moss) and two Anglos (Gwen Margolis and Katy Sorenson) also supported the ordinance, which had been introduced by Sorenson. Five Cuban Americans (Miguel Díaz de la Portilla, Javier D. Souto, Miriam Alonso, Natacha Seijas Milián, and Pedro Reboredo) and one African American (Dorrin D. Rolle) voted against the ordinance. Miami–Dade's Cuban American mayor, Alex Penelas, publicly backed the effort for gay rights, as did Cuban Spanish-language radio talk show host Tomas García-Fusté, who subsequently lost his time slot and was replaced by the antigay activist Reverend Oscar Agüero. That García-Fusté, a host in the world of conservative Cuban talk radio, would publicly support the ordinance on a show that had a likely audience of older Cuban Americans suggests the changing climate and the surprising intersection between gay rights and Cuban American politics. See Karen Branch, "Radio Host Replaced by Anti-Gay-Rights Minister," *Miami Herald,* January 6, 1999.

6. Families, Disclosure, and Visibility

1. D'Emilio, *Sexual Politics, Sexual Communities,* 11.

2. D'Emilio, *Sexual Politics, Sexual Communities;* Bérubé, *Coming Out under Fire.*

3. Cantú, *Sexuality of Migration,* 29; Lionel Cantú Jr., "A Place Called Home: A Queer Political Economy of Mexican Immigrant Men's Family Experiences," in *Queer Families, Queer Politics: Challenging Culture and the State,* ed. Mary Bernstein and Renate Reinman (New York: Columbia University Press, 2001), 115.

4. For more on immigrant sexuality, see Cantú, "Place Called Home," 112–36; Lionel Cantú Jr., "Entre Hombres/Between Men: Latino Masculinities and Homosexualities," in *Gay Masculinities,* ed. Peter M. Nardi (Thousand Oaks, Calif.: Sage, 2000), 224–46; Manalansan, *Global Divas;* Luibhéid and Cantú, *Queer Migrations;* Gloria González-López, *Erotic Journeys: Mexican Immigrants and Their Sex Lives* (Berkeley: University of California Press, 2005); Peña, "Latina/o Sexualities in Motion." See also Eithne Luibhéid, ed., "Queer/Migration," special issue, *GLQ* 14, nos. 2–3 (2008).

5. Cantú, *Sexuality of Migration,* 137.

6. Lisandro Pérez, "Immigrant Economic Adjustment and Family Organization: The Cuban Success Story Reexamined," *International Migration Review* 20, no. 73 (1986): 4–20; Pérez, "The Cuban Population in the United States: The Results of the 1980 U.S. Census of Population," *Cuban Studies* 15, no. 2 (1985): 1–18.

7. For early studies of gay and lesbian people of color and coming-out processes, see Connie S. Chan, "Issues of Sexual Identities in an Ethnic Minority: The Case of Chinese American Lesbian, Gay Male, and Bisexual People," in *Lesbian, Gay, and Bisexual Identities over the Lifespan: Psychological Perspectives,* ed. Anthony R. D'Augelli and Charlotte J. Patterson (New York: Oxford University Press, 1995), 87–101; Espín, "Issues of Identity," 35–55; Beverly Greene, "Ethnic-Minority Lesbians and Gay Men: Mental Health and Treatment Issues," *Journal of Consulting and Clinical Psychology* 62 (1994): 243–51; Edward S. Morales, "HIV Infection and Hispanic Gay and Bisexual Men," *Hispanic Journal of Behavioral Sciences* 12, no. 2 (1990): 212–22; Hilda A. Hidalgo and E. H. Christenson, "The Puerto Rican Lesbian and the Puerto Rican Community," *Journal of Homosexuality* 2 (1976–77): 109–21.

8. Weston, *Families We Choose* (New York: Columbia University Press, 1991), 56.

9. Carrington, *No Place Like Home: Relationships and Family Life among Lesbians and Gay Men* (Chicago: University of Chicago Press, 1999), 138–39.

10. Ibid., 139.

11. Frank Browning, *The Culture of Desire: Paradox and Perversity in Gay Lives Today* (New York: Crown, 1993), 144.

12. Ibid., 143.

13. Stephen P. Kurtz, "Butterflies under Cover: Cuban and Puerto Rican Gay Masculinities in Miami," *Journal of Men's Studies* 7, no. 3 (1999): 11.

14. For more on masculinity and masculine appearance, see chapter 7.

15. Weston, *Families We Choose,* 68.

16. Ibid., 50.

17. Carlos Ulises Decena also found a similar use of "amigo" among the Dominican immigrants ("Tacit Subjects," *GLQ* 14, nos. 2–3 [2008]: 342–43).

18. Fabiola Santiago, "The Poetry of Healing," *Miami Herald,* February 20, 1997.

19. Díaz, *Latino Gay Men and HIV,* 89.

20. Ibid., 96.

21. Ibid., 90.

22. Ibid.

23. Dennis Altman, *The Homosexualization of America* (Boston: Beacon, 1982), 128; Díaz, *Latino Gay Men and HIV,* 102.

24. Díaz, *Latino Gay Men and HIV,* 102.

25. Carrillo, *Night Is Young,* 132.

26. Ibid., 147, 149.

27. Decena, "Tacit Subjects," 340.

28. Decena, *Tacit Subjects,* 42.

29. Díaz, *Latino Gay Men and HIV,* 92, quoting G. Marín and B. V. Marín, *Research with Hispanic Populations* (Newbury Park, Calif.: Sage, 1991), 13.

30. Díaz, *Latino Gay Men and HIV,* 94.

31. Cantú, "Place Called Home," 112–36; Cantú, "Entre Hombres/Between Men," 226–29.

7. *Locas, Papis,* and Muscle Queens

1. Almaguer, "Chicano Men: A Cartography of Homosexual Identity and Behavior," *differences* 3, no. 2 (1991): 75–98.

2. Leiner, *Sexual Politics in Cuba,* 22.

3. Annick Prieur, *Mema's House, Mexico City: On Transvestites, Queens, and Machos* (Chicago: University of Chicago Press, 1998).

4. Lumsden, *Machos, Maricones, and Gays,* 133.

5. Prieur, *Mema's House.*

6. It is interesting that Miguel uses this reference to birds and feathers in the context of a completely English-language passage. The term *pájaro* is widely used in Spanish to refer to homosexual men, but I know of no such usage in English in Miami or in any other U.S. setting. However, the reference to feathers in this context is clearly understood by anyone familiar with the particular vernaculars of Miami. For another example of gay men of Caribbean descent using metaphors of *pájaro* and *plumas,* see Decena, *Tacit Subjects,* 169.

7. For example, see Carrillo, *Night Is Young;* Salvador Vidal-Ortiz et al., "Revisiting *Activos* and *Pasivos:* Toward New Cartographies of Latino/Latin American Male Same-Sex Desire," in Asencio, *Latina/o Sexualities,* 253–73.

8. Kurtz, "Butterflies under Cover," 13.

9. Charles Ramírez Berg, *Latino Images in Film: Stereotypes, Subversion, and Resistance* (Austin: University of Texas Press, 2002), 76.

10. Gutmann, *The Meanings of Macho: Being a Man in Mexico City* (Berkeley: University of California Press, 1996), 24.

11. Ibid., 24–26.

12. Maxine Baca Zinn, "Chicano Men and Masculinity," in Kimmel and Messner, *Men's Lives,* 67.

13. Cantú, "Entre Hombres/Between Men"; Alfredo Mirandé, *Hombres y machos: Masculinity and Latino Culture* (Boulder, Colo.: Westview, 1997).

14. Christopher Ortiz, "Hot and Spicy: Representations of Chicano/Latino Men in Gay Pornography," *Jump Cut,* no. 39 (1994): 83–90. Ortiz discusses two categories of gay pornography, videos that feature Latino men with black men and videos that feature Latino men with Latino men. White men appear briefly and in peripheral roles in the videos he discusses. Ortiz's analysis centers on representations of Chicano men, with an emphasis on the U.S. West Coast.

15. Ibid., 84.

16. Ibid., 85–88.

17. Ibid., 85–86.

18. Ibid., 87.

19. Both Ortiz and Richard Fung note the importance of the intended audience

of gay porn that represents men of color. Both analyze videos directed by Latino and Asian American men that invoke racist stereotypes and implied white gay male spectators. Ortiz remarks that whom a video is directed to is more important than who it is directed by. See also Fung, "Looking for My Penis: The Eroticized Asian in Gay Video Porn," in *Asian American Sexualities: Dimensions of the Gay and Lesbian Experience,* ed. Russell Leong (New York: Routledge, 1996), 181–98.

20. Gordon, *Ghostly Matters,* 4–5.

21. Michelangelo Signorile, *Life Outside: The Signorile Report on Gay Men* (New York: Harper Collins, 1997), xviii.

22. Russell Westhaver, "'Coming Out of Your Skin': Circuit Parties, Pleasure, and the Subject," *Sexualities* 8, no. 3 (2005): 352–53.

23. Ibid., 347–74; Russell Westhaver, "Flaunting and Empowerment: Thinking about Circuit Parties, the Body, and Power," *Journal of Contemporary Ethnography* 35, no. 6 (2006): 611–44; Ted B. Kissell, "Size Matters," *Miami New Times,* August 13–19, 1998.

24. Martin P. Levine also refers to the circuit in his discussion of the clone subculture. Like the circuit parties of the 1990s and 2000s, the circuit of the 1970s was highly associated with masculine gay clone culture and recreational drug use. As Levine describes, though, the 1970s circuit referred to places for social and erotic encounters for gay men within a particular city. In his description, circuit seems to refer to a network of places that catered to clone culture. A distinguishing feature of circuit parties of the 1990s is the way in which they were marketed to and attracted men from a range of geographic areas to one particular destination for a set of weekend activities (Levine, *Gay Macho: The Life and Death of the Homosexual Clone,* ed. Michael S. Kimmel [New York: New York University Press, 1998], 49–53).

25. Signorile, *Life Outside*; Eric Rofes, *Dry Bones Breathe: Gay Men Creating Post-AIDS Identities and Cultures* (New York: Haworth, 1998).

26. Eugene J. Patron and David W. Forrest, "SoBe: The Making of a Gay Community," *Gay and Lesbian Review Worldwide* 7, no. 2 (2000): 28–29.

27. Patron and Forrest, "SoBe," 28–29. Kissell has commented on the medical and cosmetic use of steroids by gay men in Miami and the relationship of this kind of steroid to circuit party culture (Kissell, "Size Matters," 25–32).

28. Glenn Albin, "To Live and Die in South Beach," *Out,* May 1995, 77.

8. ¡*Oye Loca!*

1. Throughout her career, Julie has used several variations of her name, including Julie Mastrozzimone, Julie Mastrossimone, and Julie Mastrozzimone D'Perugina.

2. For more on the significance of La Lupe, see Frances R. Aparicio, "La Lupe, La India, and Celia: Toward a Feminist Genealogy of Salsa Music," in *Situating Salsa: Global Markets and Local Meaning in Latin Popular Music,* ed. Lise Waxer (New York: Routledge, 2002), 135–60; José Quiroga, "Boleros, Divas, and

Identity Models," in *Cuba, the Elusive Nation: Interpretations of National Identity,* ed. Damián J. Fernández and Madeline Cámara Betancourt (Gainesville: University Press of Florida, 2000), 119–20; Muñoz, *Disidentifications*; Juan A. Moreno-Velázquez, *Desmistificación de una diva: La verdad sobre La Lupe* (San Juan, Puerto Rico: Grupo Editorial Norma, 2003); *La Lupe: Queen of Latin Soul,* documentary, directed by Ela Troyano, screened as part of *Independent Lens,* PBS, June 5, 2007.

3. Elinor Burkett, "The Price," *Miami Herald,* April 1, 1990.

4. There is no simple or direct translation to the term *arrepentido/a* that captures its Cuban cultural connotations. Literally, the term denotes the condition of being repentant or remorseful, but its connotation is closer to poser or wannabe. One critical difference is that English-language terms like *poser* point to the identity you *want to be* that you are *not,* whereas the term *arrepentido* points to that identity you *are* that you *do not want to be.* I argue that Mastrozzimone's *balsera–cubana arrepentida* exchange works primarily to correct a (feigned) claim to superiority. For a different approach to the term *cubana arrepentida,* see Olga Lorenzo, "Nostalgia, Shame, and the Transplanted Cuban: '*La cubana arrepentida,'*" *Portal: Journal of Multidisciplinary International Studies* 2, no. 1 (2005): 1–25.

5. Located on Calle Ocho, or Southwest Eighth Street in Miami, the Teatro Bellas Artes "usually [features] light comedies and translations of successful foreign plays" that cater to a predominantly older audience. Weekly at midnight, the theater becomes home to Midnight Follies, a long-standing drag queen revue. The audience here is still predominantly heterosexual and includes a small group of older Cuban women who regularly attend to support the show. For more on Cuban American Theater, see Lillian Manzor, "Cuban/Latino Theater Archive," University of Miami Cuban Heritage Collection, http://scholar.library.miami.edu/archivoteatral/review/viewVenue.php?venue_ID=174 (accessed June 22, 2011).

6. Reiterating Cuban American and Latino communities' interest in drag, one of the organizers of a female impersonator pageant indicated to the reporter José Cassola that the size of Miami's Hispanic population was one reason he chose to move the pageant from Atlanta to Miami in the late 1990s ("See Them Strut Their Stuff at Female Impersonators Pageant," *Miami Herald Neighbors,* March 20, 1997).

7. For audio of the song "Sanitario," see Mariloly, Myspace, www.myspace.com/eghttpwwwmyspacemariloly/music/songs?filter=featured (accessed June 21, 2011).

8. Although I discuss only one example here, I observed Mariloly deliver this type of joke several times. One respondent also remembered her telling a joke that equated a boatful of Haitians to a split-open papaya.

9. Marytrini, "El Blog de Marytrini," www.marytrini.net (accessed June 21, 2011).

10. *La Flor de Hialeah* was an original scripted show produced by América TeVé in 2007 in South Florida for a South Florida viewing audience. The nightly

half-hour show offers a hybrid format, combining elements of *telenovela* and situation comedy. *La Flor de Hialeah* features a mostly Cuban cast set in the Hialeah building that houses both the eponymous bar/restaurant and the home its owner, Chino Chao, shares with his family. Marytrini plays the role of Ninón, a transgender female dancer who presents herself and is accepted as a cisgender woman. Various story lines center on Ninón's fear that someone from her past will appear and reveal her transgender identity and her attempts to save money for sex-reassignment surgery.

Conclusion

1. Williams, *Marxism and Literature*.

INDEX

actos de repudio (acts of repudiation), 28–31
Adora, 147, 157–61, 167
Alfaro, Xiomara, 158–59
Almaguer, Tomás, xx, 80–82, 135–36. *See also* Latin American sex/gender system
antidiscrimination ordinances: Human Rights Ordinance in 1997, 113–16, 214n13, 214–15n16, 215n18; in 1977, 11–24, 197–98n43
antisocial, 28–29, 187n1
Aparicio, Eduardo, xxviii–xxix, 96–100, 108–15, 126–27, 146–49, 158, 179, 189n15. *See also* Coalición CUBA; *Perra! La Revista*
Arenas, Reinaldo, 9, 30–31, 67, 100

Baca Zinn, Maxine, 144
Basker, Robert, 11, 13, 20–21, 198n51
Bérubé, Allan, xvii, 119, 122–23
Beyond the Sea. See Más allá del mar
biolegal families. *See* families of origin
Brake, Bob, 11, 198n45
Brown, Warren, 47, 50–53, 69–70, 207n72
Bryant, Anita, 1, 11–18, 22–23, 178,

198n45, 198n60. *See also* Save Our Children Inc.

Campbell, Jack, 11, 13, 18, 21, 198n51
Canaday, Margot, 57
Cantú, Lionel, Jr., xxi, 119, 130
Carrillo, Héctor, 129
Carrington, Christopher, 120–21
Castro, Fidel, ix–x, xxii, 2–3, 27–29, 114, 166–67, 169, 193n3, 196–97n35. *See also* Cuban state
Castro, Raúl, 95–96, 196–97n35
Castro Espín, Mariela, 196–97n35
Centro Nacional de Educación Sexual (CENESEX), 196–97n35
chusma, 161, 163–64
circuit parties, 135, 151–53, 218n24
ciudad de las carpas, La, 64–67, 209n11
Class A medical exclusions, 34
clone, 150–51, 218n24
Club Miami, 17
Coalición CUBA (Cubans United for a Better Ambiente), 96–104, 114
coming out, 10–12, 87–89, 120, 123–26, 129–31, 137, 178–80, 213n15
Committees for the Defense of the Revolution (CDR), 30

Pérez, Lisandro, 120, 123
Pérez-Rey, Lisandro. *See Más allá del mar* (Pérez-Rey)
perra (expression), 87, 89, 93, 109, 214n6
Perra! La Revista, xxviii, 87, 108–15, 146–49, 163, 214n11
pornography, 145–46, 217n14, 217–18n19
Portes, Alejandro, 70–72, 210n23
precriminality, 5, 195n16
Public Health Service (PHS), 34, 37, 204–5n31

queer of color critique, 75–76

race, 57, 119; in Cuba, xxiv–xxv; in drag, 167–76; among Mariel entrants, 38; in Miami, xxi–xxvi, 97–98, 102–3, 150–54, 180–81. *See also papi*; queer of color critique
Ramos, Ovidio Heriberto "Herbie," 18–19
"Report on Status of Cuban Refugees at Fort McCoy, Wisconsin," 45–46, 48–49, 206n54
Risech, Flavio. *See Zig Zag*
Rockway, Alan, 14, 198n51
Roth, Robert, 18, 21
Ruiz, Ramón. *See* Muni, Alexias Ramón

Salas, Luis, 6
Save Our Children Inc., 11–18, 22–23, 113, 198n45, 198n47
Schwartz, Rachel M. *See* "Report on Status of Cuban Refugees at Fort McCoy, Wisconsin"
Sears, James T., 18–19, 21
Shack, Ruth, 11
"Siboney." *See* Lecuona, Ernesto
Sophia Devine. *See* Divas del Jacuzzi, Las

South Beach, xvii–xx, 73, 74–75, 96–97, 133–35, 150–54, 158–59, 166, 178, 189n19
structure of feeling, xix, 100–101, 181

Teatro de Bellas Artes. *See* Midnight Follies
Tent City, 61–69. *See also ciudad de las carpas, La*
Teresita "La Caliente." *See* Divas del Jacuzzi, Las
Toboso-Alfonso, Fidel, 202n7
transculturation, 78, 82–83, 92–94, 212n10
2-C classification. *See* Federal Correctional Institutions

Unidades Militares para el Aumento de Producción (UMAPs), 4, 10, 73, 110, 194n10
Universal Fellowship of Metropolitan Community Churches (MCC), 53–54, 198n51, 208n94
U.S. immigration policy, 32–58
U.S. Refugee Act of 1980, 33–34, 203n19, 203n20, 204n28

Villaverde, Miñuca. *See ciudad de las carpas, La*
voluntary agencies (VOLAGs), 37–39, 46–48, 52–54

Washington Post. See Brown, Warren
Weston, Kath, 120, 122–24
Williams, Raymond, xix, xxix, 181

Young, Allen, 49, 194n9, 194n11

Zig Zag, 95, 109

SUSANA PEÑA is director of the School of Cultural and Critical Studies and associate professor of ethnic studies at Bowling Green State University.